Henry Calderwood

On Teaching

Its Ends and Means

Henry Calderwood

On Teaching
Its Ends and Means

ISBN/EAN: 9783337167905

Printed in Europe, USA, Canada, Australia, Japan

Cover: Foto ©Paul-Georg Meister /pixelio.de

More available books at **www.hansebooks.com**

ON TEACHING:

ITS ENDS AND MEANS.

BY

HENRY CALDERWOOD, LL.D., F.R.S.E.

PROFESSOR OF MORAL PHILOSOPHY IN THE UNIVERSITY OF EDINBURGH,
AND CHAIRMAN OF THE FIRST SCHOOL BOARD FOR EDINBURGH.

London:

MACMILLAN & CO.

1885.

TO

THE MEMBERS OF THE FIRST SCHOOL BOARD

FOR THE CITY OF EDINBURGH,

THIS VOLUME IS RESPECTFULLY DEDICATED

BY ITS CHAIRMAN,

THE AUTHOR.

a 2

PREFACE TO THIRD EDITION.

THIS little book was originally designed mainly for professional teachers. Having had, however, repeated references made to it by parents concerned for the education of their children, I have attempted in the present edition to include the more important aspects of Home Training, specially as these are related to school work. I trust the chapter here added may extend the usefulness of the book by rendering some aid to parents, and at the same time drawing closer the bonds of friendship between Teachers and Parents.

H. C.

August 29, 1881.

PREFACE.

THIS little volume is published with the view of aiding young teachers in their work. It is designed to indicate what I think are usually regarded as the true ends of teaching, and to give such hints as to methods suitable for attaining these ends, as may prove suggestive to those who are in daily practice. If these brief discussions direct observation upon important points in procedure, and give form to reflection upon the occurrences of the School-room, they will have gained their primary design.

If this slight contribution to the cause of Education afford besides some encouragement to the Head Masters of our Primary Schools in their efforts to promote the higher branches of common instruction, and to aim at the higher results of teaching, I shall have additional satisfaction, as I am well aware that it is the desire of the Head Masters to guide their Assistant Teachers and Pupil Teachers in striving after an ideal much above what the Code prescribes and promises to reward.

Only one thing more I venture to name as an end which may be in some measure gained by a publication of this kind. I have often had occasion to remark the desire of parents to reach some clear conviction as to the best methods for forming the character of their children. I am not without hope that the hints here offered to Teachers may to some extent meet the requirements of a still wider circle. Should this be the case, I shall be specially thankful on account of the importance to be attached to a sound home-training as the true support of school-training.

As one who has spent a large portion of his life in professional teaching, and has been engaged in all forms of it, I would express the hope that under the new order of things inaugurated by the Education Act, we may see an advance in our whole system of education, specially the attainment of a uniform and graduated plan, under which National Schools, and those Schools maintained by private enterprise, or under public trust, may work well together, and in which primary instruction for the neglected may have as its accompaniment higher education for all.

H. C.

EDINBURGH, 17*th November* 1874.

CONTENTS.

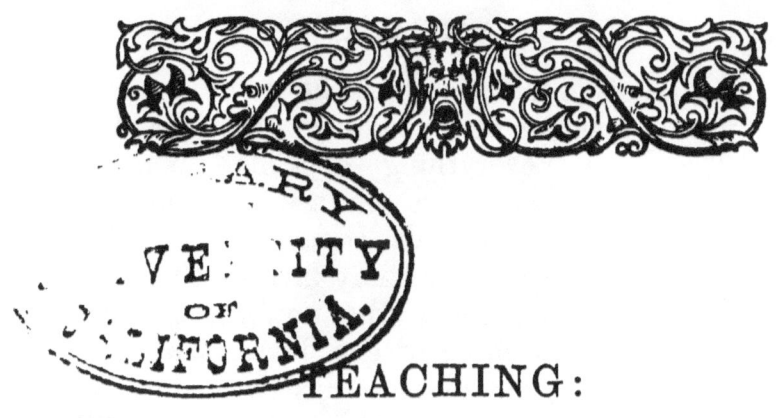

TEACHING:

ITS ENDS AND MEANS.

INTRODUCTION.

EVERY one recognises that a person can teach only what he knows. This is at once so clear and so important, that there is some risk of the opinion becoming general that teaching is merely the communication of so much knowledge. The progress of education in a country does not lessen the danger of general approval being given to such a view, but rather increases it. In organizing a National System of Education, and providing guarantees for its efficiency, we are inevitably tempted to narrow the sphere of education to the limits within which our tests are available. The examination test is far from being a complete test of educational results. Yet it is upon this we are constrained mainly to rely when we would take measures to secure a high standard of teaching. Consequently, from the earliest

A

stages of preparation for the profession, the young teacher has abundant inducement to think that everything depends upon the amount of knowledge he acquires, and the amount he afterwards communicates. The course of preparatory study favours this view. The fixed curriculum, the uniform examinations, the standards of excellence, the certificates of first, second, and third class, intended to indicate professional rank—all of them quite essential, every one will allow—tend to encourage the conviction that education is concerned only with knowledge. The certificated teacher has the requisite amount of instruction, and is by inference a competent instructor. He has attained what is essential for professional engagement.

Teachers need to guard themselves against this narrowing of their professional aims, and dwarfing of their own intellectual and moral nature. Many and weighty are the considerations which should lead members of the profession to support each other in maintaining a higher ideal of professional life. Happily many of our teachers are alive to the danger, and anxious to guard against it.

Even if the end of teaching be restricted to the communication of knowledge, it is plain that the possession of so much information is not the only requirement for instructing others. Knowledge of grammar, geography, history, and modern languages does not constitute any one a professional educator. While yet on the benches of the students' class-room, the candidates for office are constantly led to distinguish between knowledge and teaching power. They find a difference among instructors. It is not always the man who knows most who proves himself the best instructor. The beginner in teaching needs to carry with him the recollection of this difference. When he passes from the students' bench to the position of command on the floor of the class-room, he obtains fresh evidence every day that much more is wanted there, than is implied in drawing upon his stores of information. The test of practice brings out what written examinations had not previously discovered, but had rather obscured. New demands come with the practical work of teaching. He must be his own teacher in the art of teaching, while he is engaged in the practice. Even by his failures, as well as by such success as he is able to command at first, he must learn to rise to higher success. To perceive the need for this is the truest beginning.

The learning to which I refer is something very different from the continued study of books. Such study will secure a fuller knowledge and a higher culture, but the learning which is even more needful for the teacher is to be gathered by practice in teaching under carefully maintained self-observation. He who would succeed as a teacher must be a censor over his own practice. He must be thoroughly interested and observant as to his own success. As Dr. Arnold admirably said, when inquiring about a master, " I prefer activity of mind and an interest in his work to high scholarship, for the one may be acquired far more easily than the other." [1]

Further, however, it must be considered that the communication of information is not the sole end of teaching. A simple test may satisfy any one that a higher task has been by common consent assigned to the teacher. If the pupils of any school are rude, reckless, and riotous, the school management bears some considerable amount of blame. The common verdict in such a case is quite decided. Public opinion expects more than knowledge as the result of school attendance. The more this matter is considered the more obvious it will become that the expectation is just. I do not say that the teacher is always fairly judged in this relation, nor do I say that the expectations of parents are always reasonable. Home training is the earliest training, and all teachers are in some degree dependent on what that training has been. Deficiency here shows itself quickly at school. It is unreasonable to expect that school training can altogether make up for neglect or mismanagement at home. No doubt the school must somehow or other protect itself from the evil consequences which flow in upon it because of a break-down in home rule. In such cases, however, a burden is thrown upon the teacher which he should not in fairness have had to bear. Accepting, however, his responsibilities, encumbered with all the disadvantages

---

[1] *Life and Correspondence of Thomas Arnold, D.D.*, by Rev. A. P. Stanley, D.D., vol. i. p. 92.

which may gather around him, the teacher undertakes to exercise supervision over the deportment and conduct of the pupils.

The combination of such supervision with instruction is the greatest service the teacher can render to families and to the State. In the humblest sphere the teacher may claim this great work as his own. In a National System of education, proper training of the children becomes an important end. Modern civilisation wisely rejects the Platonic idea, that children should be more the children of the State than of their parents. The unity of national life is found to be most secure in the recognition of the sacredness of family life. At the same time, however, we can see the loftiness of aim and motive which made Socrates and Plato seek the good of the State, in the goodness of her citizens. In this we reach the root-idea, made grandly conspicuous by the Christian system, that goodness of character is the end of life. The teacher, then, seeks a grand result when he labours to contribute towards the formation of good character in the young, helping them to fight bravely against temptation, and to persevere in the way of rectitude through all difficulties.

The National Compulsory System of education, now fortunately secured for Scotland, suggests another point. The State has charged itself with enforcing the primary education of all the children in the land. This it has done, expressly with the view of meeting an admitted difficulty of vast magnitude, perplexing

to statesmen, philanthropists, and all students
of the social problems of our age. Compulsory
primary education is avowedly adopted as the
best instrument for attempting to cope with
the alarming increase of dissoluteness and vice.
There is no statesman—no thinker of any type
—who believes that good reading and counting
and writing will exercise a spell stronger than
the lures to profligacy. What the nation is
looking for is a sound moral training, along
with instruction, and by means of all the
accompaniments naturally attendant on the
instructor's work.[1] If the nation is disap-
pointed in this, it loses the higher of the results it looked for when setting in motion a
complicated and expensive machinery. It has
given the whole teaching profession a higher
status—an immense gain in itself—but, by the
same act, it has imposed a more extended and
more visible responsibility upon the profession.
The success of school training is to be tested
by the moral condition of the nation in after
years. The nation desires not merely that the
memory of the children be well stored, but that
the intellect be developed, and habits formed
which may remain as capital to draw from
when the work of life must be done. The
great difficulty of our modern civilisation, bred

---

[1] The German view of this matter is well put in these
words : "Primary instruction shall have for its aim to
develop the faculties of the soul, the reason, the senses,
and the bodily strength." Quoted in M. Victor Cousin's
Report on the State of Public Instruction in Prussia,
Miss Austin's translation, p. 55.

of our keen competitions, clash of interests, crowding together of multitudes of people, and consequent craving for excitement, is a waning morality. It meets us in all the narrow lanes of our cities—lanes which we Scotch naturally describe as " closes." In these piles of building, vice rather than poverty spreads out the signs of human wretchedness. In these shelters of misery multitudes of children have all that they can call a " home." The attractions of home—priceless to us—are altogether unknown to them. From their earliest days they have a hard and hardening life. Their chances of comfort and respectability are few. What the nation desires is, that skilful and kindly teaching extend to them the chance which they should otherwise altogether miss. Mainly for the sake of these children has our national compulsory system of education sprung into being. The primary education of the humbler classes in other spheres was comparatively well attended to, though that also will share in the gain coming with more popular and responsible management of our school system. But now special arrangements have been made that the little sufferers from parental neglect and profligacy have education provided for them. It is benevolently designed, and wisely projected in the interests of the children, and of all classes in the community. All concerned in the matter, parents who are alive to the interests of their children, members of our School Boards, who will care for those who are not cared for by their

natural guardians, teachers of our public
schools, with all members of the profession,
and the public generally, must desire to see
education in the truest and widest sense provided in our primary schools. Ultimately
success must depend upon intelligent and
hearty co-operation of School Boards and
Teachers. With this view it is needful that we
recognise that training, as well as instruction,
is to be aimed at. The task of training those
children who are not only altogether neglected
at home, but sadly ill-used, will no doubt be a
difficult one. It is not, however, an unreasonable task which is assigned to the teacher in
this case, but so far as its nature is concerned,
the common task of all school teaching, and
one for which the teacher is in every way
competent.

Some may object that this assigns more to
the teacher than belongs to him. On the contrary, success in the ordinary course of teaching implies all this. Truthfulness, honesty,
and self-denial are as needful in the discipline
of the school as in the regulation of the affairs
of life. They must be secured by the preference of the children themselves, if the teacher
is not to be daily hampered with the need for
enforcing right action by an exercise of authority in particular cases. Each successive day
of school life must tend to develop the virtues
of moral character among all the children, if
teaching is to proceed with success. If good
conduct is extorted only under force of authority, or even by a form of bribery, the work is

poorly done. Right actions must be admired by the children themselves, and be done by them as occasion requires, because of their recognised goodness, else there is an unnecessary and wasteful strain upon the educational machinery. All educational appliances work at a disadvantage when the effort of the teacher is not supported by a basis of character in the scholars. Hence a great deal is done in the earliest stages of education if a large amount of time is bestowed upon training the children in habits of self-government. Ingenuity may be exercised in discovering the most agreeable and varied methods of attempting this, but the thing itself must be done. The earlier it is begun the easier is the task; the more thoroughly it is done in the opening years of school life, the more rapid the progress in after years. But at no time in an educational course can the teacher wisely surrender all regard to the influence he is exercising upon the character of his pupils. In maturer years, when learning for its own sake may be expected from those who present themselves for instruction, we may reasonably expect that foundation-work is not to be done in morals, any more than in instruction, but even then no teacher can do his utmost for his pupils unless it is made obvious to them that he reckons on character, and deals with them on the assumption of its possession.

If all this be admitted, it must be clear that weight of moral character is essential for high success in teaching. The teacher can exercise influence over the scholars only according to what is in himself. He cannot lift them higher than he is himself, or induce them to attempt to reach an eminence which he is not himself striving to attain. Far above every other consideration, as a pledge of success in professional work, is the possession of high moral character.

CHAPTER I.

SELF-GOVERNMENT.

SELF-CONTROL is the first requisite for success in teaching. The work of governing even the youngest children requires government of one's-self. A man must have his powers under command, if others are to have the full benefit of his guidance. This rule holds in all spheres. It is essential for a high standard of success in any profession. Only in this way can the physician give his patient the full benefit of his knowledge and skill. On this condition alone can a man sway an audience with any share of that power which belongs to the orator. On no other condition can a teacher in reality become master over his scholars. Self-command is essential even for teaching a single child, much more when a person must govern, in order to teach, large numbers of children.

Another phase of this rule is seen when things are looked at from the children's point of view. The youngest children are quick in observation. They readily discover what degree of control is maintained by those over them. Guided by their own observations, they quietly submit to be governed only in so far as they recognise the elements of governing power in their superiors. Fond of liberty, prone to catch at a passing opportunity for diversion, children are quick in taking advantage of any deficiency in the power of command, any laxity in the exercise of control, or want of observation. These characteristics are so uniform that they cannot be overlooked. He who would succeed as a teacher must recognise them,—must enjoy their comical side, and not merely be disturbed by the test to which they subject himself,—but must utilize them so as to make them contribute towards government. The restlessness of children is inevitable,—their fondness for fun is delightfully helpful in saving school work from prosaic monotony. In harmony with these admissions, they must be governed. He who would control them easily and wisely must keep himself in harmony with the children, which certainly implies that he keep himself in good humour, and shun irritation.

School government must be a reign of justice. It must be recognised as such by the pupils, and honoured by them accordingly. For this self-control in the teacher is the one essential. Deficiency in self-command will speedily unsettle the very foundations of discipline. It will lead to frequent examples of injustice in the use of authority, which more than anything else risks the discipline of the school. Resentment, which naturally arises under consciousness of injustice, is roused in the hearts of the scholars. No obstacle to school-management could be more serious. The sense of right is opposed to existing authority, which is as perilous for the School as for the State. It is easy to conceive how detrimental to school-order this must be. Every one who has had anything to do with teaching understands it. Some of the pupils are swayed by a feeling of irritation against their teacher,— signs appear of a disposition to make game of the lessons,—the teacher becomes restless,—in an excited manner he challenges first one, then another; he threatens to do a good deal more than he carries out, and at last he is hurried into an angry castigation of some of his pupils without complete certainty of his position. His cane has been rattling mercilessly on the table, disturbing the nerves of everybody within hearing, but now it comes down upon the pupils in a style so unguarded that every one of them feels he needs to look out for his safety. Not unfrequently at such times scholars are punished, not for any fault of their own, but simply on account of the want of self-command in their teacher. The recollection of my own blundering in this way makes it easy to describe the scene; and the painfulness of the recollection greatly strengthens the desire I feel to contribute in some degree to the help of those who have to pass through the ordeal connected with the attainment of self-control. A teacher cannot hope altogether to maintain the calmness which implies an absence of all nervous excitement, but he must seek that calm which is gained in the absence of anger, and which admits of clear outlook and reflection.

Here, however, as in most things, a certain amount of painfulness must be expected in acquiring experience. The beginner must look for this, and, aided by the anticipation, bear quietly without dragging the children into a share of his uneasiness. To be without established habits of government, and yet be under the necessity of regulating the conduct and instruction of a troop of children, is a position of acknowledged difficulty. Every one admits this, and therefore complete success in school-management at the outset is not to be expected. Teaching would be altogether an exception to ordinary rule, if practice did not favour improvement. The teacher has experience to acquire, and it must be gathered in the school-room. In order to acquire it as rapidly as possible, a teacher needs observation and tact to apply his resources to the ends he has in view. No study of books, however valuable they be, and however helpful their suggestions, can suffice. No degree of reflection on the discussions submitted to review, important as such reflection is for gaining benefit from the experience of others, can meet the demands of the teacher's life. He must make a beginning for himself—must face his own difficulties (probably thinking that nearly the worst specimens of juvenile humanity have fallen into his hands),—must proceed through the midst of mingled failures and successes,—must note his blunders, and learn from them, as well as accept gladly the encouragement found in success. Only by slow degrees can dexterity in professional duty be attained. The real tests of advance are found in the measure in which intelligence and not feeling,—justice and not temper,—kindness and not mere force, have determined the management of classes. Upon all these things a teacher must carefully adjudicate, not as the scholars judge, by their own comfort or misery, but deciding how far the practice has been in conformity with the ideal which he keeps before his mind. In proportion as that ideal is lofty, and his purpose resolute, will be the freshness of interest with which he daily returns to work. He must throw off the burdensome sense of past failures; he must save his pupils from a painful inheritance from previous irritations, and seek by new efforts some conquest over temper and feeling, with freer use of his own intellect and conscience.

For success here, it is necessary to recognise the conditions which are unfavourable, but inevitable, and which must therefore be accepted. The bustle of the school is no doubt the reverse of favourable to a quiet spirit, but it is unavoidable. There are circumstances in which it would be a marvel if a man were anything but calm; the circumstances of the teacher are such as to make calmness specially difficult, and yet his duties make it essential. It is natural to wish for quiet when a difficult thing is to be done, but the teacher cannot have it. He may as well ask that difficulties be changed into simplicities. Hearing one read, and at the same time observing scores of others around, he must have an eye open for every movement, an ear for every sound, and yet he must carry forward without allowance for obstruction the real work of the school.

Further, it must be expected that the teacher's work will vary in difficulty according to the sphere which he occupies. The teacher cannot get pupils " made to order " in any case. But, granting that diversity of disposition is to be expected among pupils in all schools, the task of teaching becomes increasingly arduous according to the increase of numbers and deficiency of home-training. The degree of self-command which may be ample for the management of a class of thirty boys who have been long accustomed to the discipline of school life, may be utterly unequal to the task of governing a mixed school of two or three hundred children. Wider range of observation is required,—far greater tact in adaptation to the greater variety of demands, and withal there is a greater waste of brain and nerve energy, directly tending to increased irritability. A lower range of attainment may suffice for the teacher of a primary school than for the teacher of the highest classes in an advanced school ; but the teacher of the primary school will find a heavier demand made upon breadth of moral power and upon organizing and administrative ability than falls upon the teachers of the higher subjects of instruction. In fact, it must be recognised by our School Boards, and should be considered by teachers in judging of personal adaptation to various forms of work, that pre-eminent ability of one type is wanted for the government of our larger primary schools, and pre-eminent ability of another type for those who are to guide studies in classics, mathematics, and the higher literature. Pre-eminence in either field must carry with it a high remuneration. In the primary school, payment must be not only for what a man knows, but in addition for power of government, without which no eminence in attainment can suffice.

Returning now to what is common to all teachers, I would remark that speciality of disposition in a few of the pupils is likely to make a special demand on the self-control attained by the teacher. Specialities increase difficulties. This is apparent in the relation between school-management and self-government. All children cannot be governed on exactly the same model; the more peculiar the child in bent and emotional nature, the more consideration he requires from the teacher. If such consideration is to be given, and recognised specialities are not to be swallowed up in the mass, an additional strain is put on self-command. Your peculiar children are certain to discover their peculiarities at the most inconvenient times. When any such

B

turn comes, it must not be got over in a rough
and ready way. Nothing has worth here
which is not the result of thought. Hurry
may do grievous hurt. Skill in teaching may
be largely increased by the need for occasional
consideration of the most judicious, discriminating treatment of difficult cases. More careful
reflection is required for the proper management of a fiery spirit than can ever be needful
in the training of a gentle nature. There is
more test of a teacher's power in the attempt
to govern a stubborn child, and to help him in
honest efforts to govern himself, than in long
superintendence of the amiable. Whatever
the variety of disposition presented, the first
requisite for success in dealing with it is self-
command. This is only partially established if
it be equal to nothing more than the government of the more pliable class of pupils. A
teacher should accept a specially difficult case,
as a valuable test of his progress in professional
skill. Successfully managed, it not only
strains but strengthens a teacher's power.
Every child in the school reaps the advantage
of such a victory; submission to discipline is
more effectually established, and fresh influence
is gathered for future advantage to all. There
is thus a sense in which the bad cases are the
best cases, as I really believe that the most
troublesome of boys may turn out the best of
men. As a physician will concentrate his
interest on a critical illness, and feel a peculiar
joy in bringing his patient through ; as counsel
intrusted with the duty of placing a compli-

cated claim before the Court will set himself to master its details, and marshal the weightiest arguments; as a minister of religion will feel his mind attracted towards one assailed with doubts, striving to bring light in upon the darkness; so will the true teacher feel deep interest in seeking to prove the instructor and guide of one who resents and resists every form of control. A passionate child, whose anger rises on the slightest offence from a neighbour; a boy who will stand unmoved while repeating a series of falsehoods to screen himself from suspicion; a pupil who will greedily snatch at a passing opportunity for cheating a companion, will be the object of concern to a teacher, and often engage his private reflection. Corporal punishment does not afford the direct line to success; a teacher's task is not so simple as this would imply. There is no specific for the cure of all diseases, and there is no single method for correcting all the faults of children. Faults are not merely to be put down, but the dispositions from which they originate are to be rooted out and supplanted. Skill more than force is wanted for this; reflection more than flogging, which might be done by a machine—by "a thrashing-mill," as an ingenious school-fellow named a teacher given to the rough and ready use of the strap. Leather may be a useful commodity, but it is not a substitute for thought. Punishment may awaken fear, and fear may help reflection; but everything depends upon the justice of the punishment, and its adaptation to the case. Fear may suppress a threatened outbreak of anger, but it is insufficient to overcome the irritable disposition, as the teacher may see by a glance into the playground. Terror may drive back a falsehood from the tongue, but it may also afford a motive for the practice of deceit. The boy who will not cheat when there is risk of detection, may cheat with alacrity when advantage is certain. A reign of terror may thus encourage cowardice and cunning. For success in training others there is no easier method than the arduous task of self-government, reflection, and carefully devised experiments illustrating how those who are younger may become better.

When self-government has been attained in some considerable measure, the young teacher has the one grand essential for success in school-practice. Command of a school then becomes an easier thing, making allowance always for such occasional perplexities as are incident to all forms of effort. Children, recognising the power of command as a reality existing in the midst of them, never think of experimenting on the probability of a break-down. This occasions the difference recognised in a school when a stranger steps into command, and when the teacher is present who has established himself in the confidence of the pupils. In the latter case the children know that they have a strong hand over them, and they experience the comfort of settled government. Without self-command in the teacher, no amount of attainment will suffice to gain the respect and submission of the children. At the early stages of school life there is small reverence for learning. I shall never forget the warning on this subject which stands out before me from my recollections of school days. Our teacher was a gentleman of large attainments, and vast energy of character, with immense muscular power, but, unfortunately for himself and us, an irritable temper. He was in no wise restrained by the new-fangled notions adverse to corporal punishment. If sternness of manner and severity of chastisement could have deterred boys from disturbing a master, he should have dwelt in perfect peace. Instead of this, his life and ours were subjected to constant worry. The scourging went on hotly each day, and the disorder roared around in the grandest style. He was fond of a good implement, which would swing well round his shoulders, and come firmly down upon ours. This he found in a strap, which he applied with the buckle-end, after the strap had been drawn through the buckle. Soon after the school had been opened for the day, the din began to rise ; his eyes wandered about excitedly, his fingers twitched nervously around the belt ; speedily some poor unfortunate was observed committing a trivial offence, for which in ordinary circumstances a word of rebuke would have been ample punishment, but the teacher was incapable of resting with moderate measures ; this youth's fault gave occasion for the inevitable outbreak ; the " strapping" process began, and soon became general, to the mingled consternation and delight of most of us, who dreaded a " whack," but exulted in a " row." Government in such circumstances became hopeless. Worst of all, the teacher was often at fault in the distribution of his merciless strokes. The love of fair play awoke sympathy for the innocent sufferer, and enmity against the teacher. Once a book was thrown at the master by some one more daring than the rest. In his fury the teacher rushed upon one of the pupils and belaboured him. Unfortunately, he had selected the wrong boy. Things reached their climax. The actual transgressor stepped out on the floor, his face glowing with indignation, while he shouted : " Why do you strike him ? He did nothing. I threw the book." The scene of application was changed. The strap now flew round the proper shoulders, but a fight ensued, in which the teacher had the worst of it morally, if not physically. Teaching in such circumstances was hopeless, and the attempt soon came to an end. The teacher abandoned the profession, entered upon a business life, and afterwards rose to eminence in it. Self-command, if it be only made a primary consideration with the teacher, will save from perplexities unimagined by those who have not witnessed scenes of disorder at school. Nowhere can a man be more thoroughly tormented in our day than in the school-room, if he lack power of command.

There are few spheres in which one can have a more important field of usefulness, with interest to himself, and ample encouragement, if only he understand how to command others. For this the very first requisite undoubtedly is, that he be able thoroughly to command himself.

CHAPTER II.

SCHOOL DISCIPLINE.

FROM self-control we pass naturally to the management of the scholars. With the teacher, self-command is a means to a recognised end. He governs himself in order that he may the better govern others. We are here concerned with the practical aspects of school government. Such government exists for the two ends of instructing and training the children. All school arrangements must point towards these two results.

For successful government there must be harmony with the nature of the children. Regard must be had to their intelligence, and also to the motive forces which both quicken their intellectual life and sway their conduct. Bad motives will also be found playing their pernicious part, and suitable methods must be adopted to check their play. All this is involved in the maintenance of a healthy school discipline. The task is not an easy one, any more than the work of self-control. But the performance of it is an essential condition for successful teaching. The patience and discrimination requisite must be cultivated by all who aim at an honourable place in the profession.

And here it is to be observed that school government must proceed not only in the midst of lesson-learning, but while the lessons receive the chief attention. This secondary position, so far as arrangement and outward appearance go, must not be overlooked as that which belongs to the essential matter of government. The teacher is at all times engaged instructing, as if that were his only work, but he is covertly and by necessity governing all the while. It is in every way better for himself and for all the scholars if this latter exercise do not become very conspicuous. It best serves its end when it is quite secondary on the field of observation. Teaching does not exist for the sake of discipline, but discipline for the sake of teaching. Like the instrumental accompaniment to a song, it attends upon the teaching, supporting it throughout. This subordinate position is thoroughly compatible with efficiency ; for discipline is not to be secured by complicated methods such as might largely engross the attention of the teacher. Government with the least possible manifestation of care and effort is that which is most easily established. Once established, it accomplishes its object with the silent consent of all concerned.

The chief interest at this point gathers

around the question, What are the best methods for securing discipline? The teacher must have it clearly and finally settled in his own mind what are the conditions on which he can hope to sway a company of children. Such sway can be obtained only by taking account of what the children naturally look for in a superior, in order that they may respect and trust him. They want to see quietly and consistently the evidence not only of superior knowledge, but also of practical wisdom and of warm genuine sympathy. No one among them could tell in so many words what they wish to find in their teacher, but these are the things they are all alike feeling after. The teacher, then, must look at the scholars, teach them in every subject, and control them in their procedure, under constant recognition of the facts that they are amenable to reason and to good feeling, and are all anxious to live in the good opinion of their teacher. By these considerations he must be ruled, if he is to find it a reasonably easy task to keep order among a host of children.

It may not be unnecessary, however, to suggest here that a teacher needs to guard himself against the tendency to expect the impossible. He aims at the most complete order and quiet compatible with work, but he does not expect absolute stillness. Children are by nature restless, and that restlessness is to be allowed for. It is natural, and cannot be regarded as a breach of order without injustice, which must result in cruelty to the children, and must imperil discipline itself. The natural restlessness of youth must be considered, and school arrangements adapted to it. If there is a constant supply of fresh air, without exposing the children to currents, and if during winter a sufficient degree of warmth is at the same time maintained, the physical conditions are so far complied with under which children can be expected to conduct themselves as if they were comfortable. But still further in the same direction, it is a great aid to discipline if there be from time to time change of posture, as well as variation in the subject of study to suit the capacity of sustained attention in the pupils. It is useless to theorize on such matters. The observation of the teacher must decide upon the times and forms of variation desirable. What we need to be delivered from in such matters is a system of routine, blindly ordaining that all school life be crushed within cast-iron frameworks. A tramp through the school-room to a good march, played on the piano or harmonium, would at once change the feelings of scholars growing weary with work, and would secure order with greatly less toil to the teacher.[1] Regard to the physical conditions on which attention can be secured is

[1] Fröbel's Kindergarten system for interesting and training very young children deserves study. Fröbel was the worthy disciple of Pestalozzi. His method is presented in accessible form in a lecture by Joseph Payne, Professor of the Science and Art of Education in the College of Preceptors, London—*Fröbel and the Kindergarten System.* H. S. King and Co., London.

constantly required in teaching, but it is only preparatory to the more important intellectual and moral conditions.

Discipline is subjection to the teacher's authority, in accordance with the order which has been prescribed for educational ends. It must be all-pervading in the work of the school, but not always asserting itself. Silent as the air around them, it must provide for the healthy development of the children for whose life-wants it is adapted. What is wanted is the sense of subjection on the part of the pupils, with as little as possible of the assertion of authority by the teacher.

A variety of methods for swaying the action of his scholars lies open to the teacher. He must decide, on clear grounds, to what degree he may employ any of these, and to which preference should be given. Order must be maintained, and to this end obedience must, if needful, be enforced. The pressing question is, how best to secure the desired result. By looks, by words of encouragement, or by words of warning and reproof, and by appropriate punishment for breach of order, he may act upon the determination of the scholars. The teacher who would establish discipline on a sure basis must decide what is the most potent form of influence, and which ought, therefore, to be the prevailing form in use from day to day. I incline to think this may be decided clearly and finally. The use of the Eye is the basis of power; only after that in point of influence comes the use of the Voice, or of recognised signs, which may save the need for utterance; and only as a last resort, by all means to be avoided until dire necessity has arisen, Punishment.

The power of the Eye is the primary source of the teacher's influence. Only let the pupils feel that the eye of the teacher runs swifter to the mark than words fly to the ear, and his power will be felt. The conduct which is to be regulated must be observed. To the extent to which this is possible, everything done in the school must be under the eye of the teacher. To forget this, or to become indifferent to the need for it, is a serious mistake. As a pre-requisite, it is of consequence to have the scholars so placed that observation is easy. Any arrangement of seats which makes it difficult, involves a wilful surrender of a large part of a teacher's power, and at the same time of the children's benefit. The eye is much more the expression of all that the teacher is than the best-chosen words can be. The scholars can understand it more quickly than they can understand words, and there is nothing for which the eye is more available than the expression of satisfaction or dissatisfaction with what is seen. The eye is hardly misinterpreted by one who observes its play. In addition, it is the most quick and most silent of messengers. There is no quicker telegraph for the school-room, and it is practically free from risk of error in communication. Without the slightest interruption to school work, the eye conveys more encouragement, warning, and rebuke than there could be time to utter. To leave all this uncommunicated would be an unspeakable loss of influence. Through the eye an unexpressed, but clearly recognised, understanding is gradually established between master and pupil, which greatly aids school management. Connected with this form of control there is all the advantage of comparative secrecy in the midst of public procedure. It serves all the ends of a cipher in telegraphic communication ; and in school life private influence upon a single mind is of vast consequence. The teacher is constantly occupied in public exercises, yet more than most men he needs opportunity for communicating hints of purely personal application, which are best conveyed when they reach the person concerned without knowledge of those around. This holds specially of those timely warnings which are to check the beginning of wrong-doing. To utter every warning to a child in the hearing of all his companions would be to blunt the edge of the warning itself. In many cases the calling of general attention to what is being done would throw the mind of the offender into an attitude of defence, altogether unfavourable. A warning conveyed by a look gives the pupil all the advantage of profiting by it without injury to self-respect. Encouragement thus conveyed gives a great additional impulse, carrying a consciousness of a certain advance in the good opinion of the teacher, without the fact giving rise to pride, as it might otherwise do. On these grounds, it can be maintained that the eye is the vehicle of the quickest, widest, kindest, and most stimulating influence which a teacher can employ. If children while within school only be conscious that the eye of the teacher runs everywhere, they become insensibly convinced of his power, and yield to it without a thought of opposition.

Next in order of influence is the teacher's Voice. For mere purposes of discipline it cannot be so frequently in use as the eye. It must be more commonly appropriated to the work of general instruction. When used to promote discipline, the voice should convey the same lesson to all the scholars. In this way the teacher's voice should be a training power for the whole school. But words to be wisely used in this way must be sparingly used. There is not a greater mistake in this relation than to suppose that abundance of speaking is the measure of its power. Needless speaking is an offence against good government, as in the scholar it would be a breach of discipline. In every case it should be generally felt that there was real occasion for speaking. Besides, it must be remembered that even appropriate counsel may be overdone by frequency of repetition. Warnings lose their force if they are incessantly reiterated, and this unfortunate result is more rapid if they are invariably shouted at the pitch of the voice. As has been well said, "Nothing more impairs authority than a too frequent or indiscreet use of it. If thunder itself were to be continual, it would excite no

more terror than the noise of a mill." Incessant fault-finding involves a rapid evapora-
tion of moral influence. None of us likes to
be continually lectured, and children as naturally and reasonably dislike it as their seniors
do. A very little observation will suffice to
convince any teacher that similar warnings
closely repeated become a positive disturbance
to the whole school.

Last in the order of consideration—last, and
least to be resorted to in practice—is Punishment of offences. I do not exclude punishment from consideration, nor do I see how it
is to be excluded from practice while the
teacher fulfils the functions of his office. All
government must be supported by the sanction
of punishment for wilful violation of its authority. While, however, this is to be admitted,
it is to be hoped that the schools of our country
are for ever freed from the reproach of an irra-
tional and cruel resort to corporal punishment
for the most trivial offences. I do not deny
that the old *régime* could point in self-vindica-
tion to good results secured by its rough appliances. I do not deny that there are many—I
myself among the number—who look back on
the share of suffering experienced under well-
directed use of " the tawse " with acknowledgment of its value. But the records which can
be given of scholastic punishment in years not
far past are undoubtedly anything but honourable to our educational skill and study of
human nature. When the instruments for chas-
tising the scholars were in constant use, their

very commonness made them insufficient, and
tempted the teacher to a baneful inventiveness
of new and more humiliating forms of punishment. So it was that forms of punishment
utterly disgraceful came to be resorted to. I
can tell of a hapless boy who had the misfortune to be seized on the occasion of a general
outbreak, who was ordered (on a summer day)
to thrust his head up the chimney, and stand
in the grate. To add to the ignominy, his
companions, who had been participators in the
offence, many of them ringleaders in it, were
invited by the teacher to laugh at the victim
stuck up " in durance vile," and to meet with
a derisive shout his reappearance among them
with blackened face. One cannot think of the
infliction of such penalties, or of the moral consequences of their endurance, without a shudder.
So must one condemn all violent castigation.
No teacher can vindicate a blow with the fist
or the edge of his book. If by any chance he
be tempted to lift his foot, his feelings of concern should be such as effectually to guard
against the recurrence of such an action.
Kicking does not belong to the accomplish-
ments in school practice. However good the
teaching was under the flogging *régime*, and
every one who knows anything of the history
of our country knows it was careful and
thorough, the infliction of punishment was
often strangely separated from reflection and
justice. Even though such cases as that
described were only of occasional occurrence,
it is beyond doubt that the continual resort to

" the tawse" led many teachers to chastise their pupils more as the expression of their own irritation with the condition of things under their government than as a reasonable penalty for the offence of the sufferer. The frequency of chastisement became a temptation to the teacher. As little can it be doubted that it tended to harden, not to elevate, the scholars. I can recall in the experience of my own school life the miserable days spent under a teacher who seemed at times to lose all control of himself as he struck out wildly on all sides. The result soon appeared in signs of general insubordination, as in another case to which I have already referred. The consequence of this state of things was a chronic suspicion in the mind of the teacher that evil designs were being harboured. This suspicion gained such power over him that I have known him stand behind the door, "tawse" in hand, to get a speedy and favourable opportunity for venting his rage upon some one suspected of plotting mischief. The *ruse* could not be successfully repeated. The scholars became suspicious in turn. A precautionary peep through the chink of the door preceded entrance to the room. When a dark form was detected obscuring the light, the door was pushed well back, and a sudden leap was made into the room, which baffled the master, was the source of great delight to those already in their places, and gave the victim a fair chance for facing round and eluding the strap as it flew wildly about. Things soon came to a height there. A council of war was held, plotting treason against the reigning authority. It was decided that "the tawse"—instrument of offence to us all—should be disposed of. On a fitting opportunity the strap was seized and concealed. At the end of the day it was triumphantly carried out of the school. How to dispose of it was a temporary difficulty. An empty cab passing along the street afforded a suitable receptacle. Cabby, unconscious of the part he was playing, peaceably carried it away. When he overhauled his carriage on "the stand" that afternoon, it was an unusual piece of property which was added to the articles "found"—one not likely to be inquired after that evening. The loss of "the tawse" was matter of bewilderment for some days, and when at length a new strap appeared in untarnished drab, without a single crack, it was kept under lock and key, where, to the great relief of master and pupils, it was less handy for offensive purposes than was the old strap, as it lay conspicuous on the desk.

Such a description may suffice to indicate the grounds on which it is to be deeply regretted that corporal punishment was so frequent and so severe in the past. I grant, however, that power of punishment must belong to the teacher. There is a theory adverse to all corporal punishment, which is popular in our day, and advocated by those whose experience and judgment entitle their opinion to great weight. I must however confess myself unable to acquiesce in that theory. Its advocates have the advantage of decided support from the States in the American Union, which have reached the highest position in educational arrangements. Thus the Department of Public Instruction for the City of New York instructs its teachers that they "should never resort to violent means, as pushing, pulling, or shaking the children, in order to obtain their attention." The reason given is this : " All such practices constitute a kind of corporal punishment, and are not only wrong in themselves, but specially prohibited by the Board."[1] The Directory for the City of Baltimore, Maryland, is not so decidedly adverse to corporal punishment, though it indicates the same aversion to it which appears in the New York Manual. There is but one sentence under the head of Discipline, and it is this : " The schools shall be governed, as far as possible, without corporal punishment; and when such punishment shall be necessary, it shall in no case be inflicted by an Assistant, except when in charge of the school in the absence of the Principal." Turning from America to Prussia, we find the same spirit pervading that part of German legislation bearing on this subject. In the General Law of 1819 on the organization of Public Instruction in Prussia,[2] which was minutely analysed by M. Victor Cousin in

[1] A Manual of Discipline and Instruction for the Use of the Teachers of the Primary and Grammar Schools. New York, 1873. This is a Manual of great value in many ways.

[2] Entwurf eines allgemeinen Gesetzes über die Verfassung des Schulwesens im preussischen Staate.

his Report to the French Government (1831) on the state of Public Instruction in Prussia, there is a distinct deliverance on punishments. It is in these words : "No kind of punishment which has a tendency to weaken the sentiment of honour, shall, on any pretence, be inflicted : corporal punishments, in case they be necessary, shall be devoid of cruelty, and on no account injurious either to modesty or to health."[1] These extracts may suffice to show the resolute and long-standing aversion to frequent corporal punishment which is shared by all who have pondered the educational perplexities surrounding this subject. And they may be taken by young teachers who are conscious of considerable anxiety as to maintaining their authority over children, as evidence that mature reflection and long experience combine to prove that school discipline is dependent not so much on the physical force at the command of the teacher, as upon the intellectual and moral forces at work within the school. That there are offences which are best dealt with by chastisement I still think ; but such punishment, if at times needful, should be a last resort in extreme cases. As pupils advance in years, and gain in self-control, such punishment should be discontinued. Settled convictions on this subject seem to me essential for the teacher. There is no department of action within the school where there is more need to shut off the

[1] Report on the State of Public Instruction in Prussia, by M. Victor Cousin. Translated by Sarah Austin, 1834.

chance of acting upon momentary impulse. A sound practical test of general results may be put in the following form : School-government is most efficient where punishment is least frequent. Laxity of discipline may indeed square with this test for a short time, but not for many weeks, for there is nothing more cruel than the frequent punishment which is the inevitable result of unreasonable laxity ; hence the children themselves grow sick of good-natured pithlessness, which lands every-body in misery, and invariably prefer a de-cided uniform government, for the really strong government does not rest mainly on a power to punish. To a conscientious teacher, that is, a teacher seeking nothing but efficiency in school-work, the use of punishment must ever be an occasion of personal pain.

The question as to fit modes of punishment is a much more difficult one than many parents seem to realize. It is easier for parents to criticise the management of their children in school than to lay down practical regulations. I am not able to see that punishments which have in many cases taken the place of corporal punishment are really improvements. If I had my boyhood days back again, I should rather have my fingers tingle under the strap than be subjected to the milder penalties of the present day. From an educationist's point of view, I question their wisdom. Take, for example, the infliction of *pœnas*, whether for ill-prepared lessons or for breaches of discip-line. After having myself tried this form of penalty, and watched the effects, I felt constrained to abandon it. Punishment in any form must be irksome, but to require a considerable part of the day's lesson to be written out by a little offender, is a form of penalty attended by many disadvantages. At first sight it may appear that this plan really harmonizes with educational ends, as it may be supposed the writing of the lesson will impress it better upon the memory. If this be put to the test by the teacher, I think he will find that the result is not as expected. Besides, the writing of the *pœna* is thrown upon the time set apart for preparation of the lessons for the following day. This must be plain, except to those who would assign a "nine-hours" working-day to children as well as to grown men. If it be said that the intention of the penalty is to shorten the time for play, and lengthen the time for work, I reply, this settles the badness of the method. There is no worse plan for bringing a child into the physical and mental condition for learning than that of cutting in upon the play hours. An unexpected break in the work may quicken the mind, but an addition to the regulation time is unfavourable to mental action. Take the *pœna*, then, as an additional demand upon the time set apart for lesson-learning, and what is the result? This additional task hangs like a weight on the spirits of the learner, and the process of learning is retarded accordingly. If all the lessons for the following day are badly prepared, the *pœna* affords the explanation ; by its weight lesson-learning was reduced to drudgery. The sense of this spreads into the next day, and works further mischief. If, in view of the impossibility of managing well all that must be got through, the pupil write out as hurriedly and carelessly as he can, the educational benefit is lost, and educational injury is being done. Many of the same objections apply to the plan of keeping a child in the school after the others have got free. Greatly better in its effect upon the scholar (and greatly better for the teacher) than half-an-hour of solitary confine-·ment, would be five minutes spent in kindly private remonstrance in cases of serious offence. I have seen the most beneficial results from this form of dealing in the most perplexing cases.

There is room for considerable diversity of opinion as to the best forms of punishment. Granting, however, that punishment of some kind may at times be needful, the success of its use depends largely on the spirit in which it is inflicted. If it is to impress the offender aright, and at the same time exert a wholesome influence upon the other scholars, it must be plain that it has been inflicted solely because of the serious nature of the offence committed. The fault must be obviously a source of grief to the teacher, and the infliction of the punishment a painful necessity.[1]

[1] The whole question of punishment is ably discussed in *Education and School*, by the Rev. E. Thring, M.A., Head Master of Uppingham School. Macmillan and Co., 1864. See p. 221.

What I venture to plead is, that punishment should not be a common element in school government. It should be a last and painful resort, when an offence of unusual gravity has been committed. It must stand out as the public testimony that neither falsehood, nor dishonesty, nor cruelty, nor any form of immorality, can be allowed to break in upon the order which has been established for the good of all, and which must be maintained at all hazards.

. The inquiry may here be pressed, How is punishment to be restricted to cases so special as those now indicated? Some suggestions may be offered by way of reply. More trivial offences should be seen without being publicly noticed. When a pupil is obviously striving to do well, it may often be judicious even to avoid showing him that his fault has been recognised. At other times—and these the most frequent—it may be well to let the child see by a look that the fault has been observed, though not publicly condemned. This course of procedure is often of great value. A look may be found to carry rebuke enough. Excess of punishing is most readily avoided by a full use of the minor or most silent methods of expressing displeasure.

Further, it must be remembered that children often incur displeasure by being allowed to step across the boundaries of reserve and self-restraint. All 'the surroundings encourage them to take the step, and then by necessity, though unjustly nevertheless, the teacher is

forced to drive them back to the ground beyond which they should not have been allowed
to trespass. Kindle enthusiasm, and keep it
alive. Under these conditions the pupils do
not so easily yield to temptation. Use carefully the natural desire of the scholars to stand
well in the opinion of their master. With this
view, make them feel as often as possible the
encouraging influence of a favourable judgment
of their efforts. Encouragement in well-doing
is one of the most powerful checks on evil-
doing. Experiencing the pleasure of approval,
they will strive more earnestly to excel, and
will shun public reproach, as they would bitter
disappointment or a heavy loss.

One thing deserving of careful consideration
is the importance of bringing the habit of
obedience very early into play. [If children are
accustomed from their very earliest school experience to move together in accordance with
fixed signals, the work of discipline is greatly
simplified. Simultaneous movements—as in
rising, taking seats again, or marching—always
contribute to the result in a way very pleasing
to those who are being so trained.] An admirable example of this kind of training is seen
in the marching of the pupils in some of the
American schools as they enter the hall for
opening exercises. The folding desks adopted
by the London School Board have been well
utilized to serve the ends of training. Each
desk accommodates two. The desks are set
in rows, with a passage running down between
the ends of the desks, and not behind, as com-

monly. The front part of the desk, on which
the arm rests when writing, folds back to
facilitate egress. The boy going from the
right of one desk meets the boy coming from
the left of another desk. To avoid confusion,
each boy who moves by the right takes front
rank; each one moving by the left takes rear
rank. This understood, movements are sig-
nalled by the figures 1, 2, 3. When the
teacher says 1, that is "Fold desks;" 2,
"Stand;" 3, "Move into the passage." The
movements are executed as promptly as the
figures are named.] [Any such form of drill is
an aid to discipline, training the scholars to
instantaneous obedience.] Children take delight in the rapid execution of such movements.
Musical accompaniment for guiding a march
increases the pleasure obtained from the exercise. When changing classes—gathering or
dismissing the pupils—time is not mis-spent,
which is given up to secure a steady march in
or out. This aid to discipline is largely adopted
in Germany and in America. [The most successful example of an entrance march I have yet
witnessed was executed by the boys of the
juvenile division in Thirteenth Street School,
New York. A few minutes before nine o'clock
the Rector was seated alone on the platform of
the large hall situated on the third or upper
floor of the building. [I joined him as he sat
there. Exactly at nine, a boy stepped in and
touched a series of bell-pulls ranged along the
wall behind the platform. A teacher then sat
down before the piano in front of the platform,

and struck up a march. Five entrance doors
provided for different lines of approach. By
each of these a line of boys began to enter
single file, the boys being so closely together
as to touch one another, or nearly so. With
military precision, and a specially firm beat of
the left foot, the march proceeded until the
lines were interlacing, and some were defiling
by the front of the benches. In little more
than four minutes, one thousand boys had
taken their places, and the hall was crowded.
At the request of the Rector, I read a portion
of Scripture ; thereafter the boys repeated
aloud the Lord's Prayer ; two public recita-
tions were given, the one an original essay,
the other a poetical passage. The counter-
march began to a different tune, and in a short
time the hall was left with three small classes
stationed in different parts of the wide area.

An example of a similar kind, but considerably more varied, and therefore more extended
in its effect, I witnessed in one of the large
school-rooms of Berlin. A single class was put
through a round of exercise, which varied from
slow march to smart running. First, the children were started in slow time, and put through
a series of evolutions ; then the pace was advanced to quick step ; and at length the speed
was brought to the " double," the children
moving in single line, not upon a straight
course, but curving in a graceful wave-like
movement. When the running pace had been
started, time was suddenly changed from the
most rapid to half or quarter, and responded

to instantly all along the line. The direction, as well as the time of their movements, was constantly varied, thereby greatly increasing the demand upon the attention and agility of the pupils. It was a class of girls which I saw put through this exercise, and they enjoyed it exceedingly. The natural fondness for active exercise was not only gratified, but the exercise served the double purpose of relaxation and training. By such exercises habitual and hearty obedience is greatly promoted.

Very particularly must it be kept in view by the teacher that quietness in governing is most naturally allied with good discipline. A loud voice, reiterating commands in an authoritative tone, is often considered favourable to submission among the scholars. It is not really so. A quiet way of issuing orders is favourable to quietness of disposition among the scholars. It conveys a double impression—that obedience is expected, and that there is a large reserve force at command, if the teacher should have occasion to put it to use. The demand for silence, shouted out at the pitch of the voice, preceded by a sharp crack of the cane upon the desk, is out of harmony with the thing desired. A sudden shout may check the noise for half a minute, as a gust of wind sweeps the falling water off the direct line of descent; but when the gust is over the water falls as before. Quietness in ruling is the sure sign of conscious and acknowledged power. This suggestion may be taken from experience in all departments. Look, for example, at the command of a huge

Atlantic steamer, with over a thousand persons on board. The captain on the bridge amidships hardly utters a word except in conversational tone to a subordinate officer, who sends on the message from one to another. Far removed from the steersmen, the commander simply points the finger of the dial-plate upon the course, a corresponding change takes place upon the dial within sight of the steersmen, and the order is executed without the crowds on deck knowing that an order has been given. Only on an occasional emergency is an order so conveyed as to be overheard on deck. This is the model type of true government. The school-room may well illustrate this secret of power. Teachers will find it in every way an advantage to spare their voice, making the fact of control much more frequently felt than the sound of orders is heard.

CHAPTER III.

INSTRUCTION.

I DO not here touch the question concerning the relative value of the several subjects of study. My purpose does not lead me to treat of a subject which has given occasion for quite enough controversy. I wish rather to direct thought on the best modes of giving instruction in any subject. I am here concerned only with the essential conditions of successful teaching.

Whatever the age and attainment of the pupils under charge, the first requisite for communicating instruction is to gain and keep their attention. Teaching, to be successful, must therefore be adapted to win attention. At the earlier stages of school life this is the one pressing requirement. Somehow, attention must be made possible even to the most restless little ones, to whom the first restraints of school life are irksome. Accustomed to have every new object attract their interest just as long as they recognised anything attractive in it—permitted to change from one engagement to another as caprice dictated —they must be made familiar with restriction. They must begin to be regulated by the will of another. Taking this as self-evident, we are prone to say that they *must* do so, whether they will or not. This is one of our superficial current phrases which cover over many points needing careful consideration. Attention is not to be secured by mere exercise of authority. Authority has a great deal to do through the whole course of school life, but we cannot "command" attention, as we say, by merely demanding that it be given. A radical mistake is made if a teacher lean on his authority in the school as the guarantee for attention by the scholars. He must consider the requirements of the undisciplined mind, and adapt himself to them. Children attend to what interests them. This must determine the kind of assistance to be given them in acquiring habits of attention. To help them in this is an obvious part of a teacher's work. It devolves upon him to put his instructions in such a way as to awaken interest in the subject taught. This duty, indeed, falls on every one who attempts to instruct others. The literary man, the special pleader, the lecturer, the orator, must all of them bestow much thought on the laws which determine the mind's interest in any subject set before it. The master of a school in this respect shares a task which is common to all who essay to teach others. In this appears the true place and power of the profession. Still more important does the work of the schoolmaster appear when it is considered that he lays the foundation for all later and more advanced teaching. He initiates into the process of learning, which is to be continued in all after-life. The educator of youth does not merely communicate so much instruction from year to year; he develops the receptive and acquisitive tendencies of mind, which are afterwards to play their part in the intellectual activity of the nation. He trains the intelligence of those who are afterwards to be the teachers of others, as well as of those who are only to be interested inquirers after truth.

In his efforts to maintain attention, the teacher is aided by the natural curiosity of his pupils, though it is equally true that he is tried by their natural restlessness. Curiosity is to be utilized as the corrective of restlessness. To awaken expectation—to keep it alive, and even to add to its strength by that which it feeds upon—is to succeed in teaching. Here arise several considerations deserving notice from the schoolmaster. Children are most susceptible of what comes through the senses. It is therefore a great point gained when the eyes as well as the ears of the pupils can be kept in exercise during the lesson. To reach the mind by double avenues at the same moment is to increase the chance of success. The value of sight as an agency of instruction is generally recognised. However true it may be in any case that hearing may suffice to convey the whole truth, there is in every one a natural disposition to resort, nevertheless, to sight as a favourite auxiliary. Every one is conscious of the desire to see a speaker while listening to his statements. Every experienced speaker is aware that he sacrifices much of his power if he does not speak to the eye as well as to the ear. We all know how strong is the desire to watch the performances of the several members of an orchestra while we listen to the piece which they are rendering. In all probability we should more accurately realize the composer's design if we completely closed our eyes and simply listened, but the fascination of sight is too strong for most of us to make it easy to content ourselves with the feast of sound. This keenness of interest in what is seen is experienced by boys and girls perhaps even more intensely than it is by their seniors. Hence the value of the black-board in all departments of teaching, up to the very highest; hence also the value of object-lessons for beginners ; hence the greater interest commonly felt in observational and experimental science than in abstract thought. Every schoolmaster needs to give great weight to this consideration. Children universally desire to see their teacher while he guides the class-work. This desire continues powerful as long as the teacher continues to interest the children by what he says. As long as he succeeds in this respect, the eyes are bright, and fixed on the common centre of attraction. So soon as his teaching becomes slow, monotonous, and wanting in intellectual energy, the eyes lose their lustre, and begin to wander off from the common centre. Thus it becomes obvious that the teacher must himself be thoroughly interested in order to interest his scholars. If school-work is only a monotonous routine to him, it cannot be anything better to them. We cannot so reverse the natural relation of things as to make the pupils responsible for the intellectual life of the school. Children may, indeed, at times find or create interest for themselves, but that is as likely to be away from the subject of instruction as in it. The lesson may in some cases carry sufficient interest in itself. More commonly the opposite will be the case, and then it depends upon what the teacher makes the lesson appear, whether the scholars are attentive or listless.

One thing, however, must never be forgotten. There are limits to the possible continuance of interest in any one subject. Neither teacher nor scholar is to blame if interest by and by begin to flag. What is greatly wanted for successful instruction is change of subject as often as the necessities of the pupils seem to require. A timely break in the order of lessons may be of great consequence for continued mental activity. I venture to think that Time-Tables, however important in themselves, should never be so rigidly adhered to as to prevent variation. Many disadvantages would be experienced if there were needless deviation from the fixed order of study. But a lesson may be specially difficult, and that must imply that it is more irksome for the scholars. In such a case it is a practical mistake to insist that the children must be kept on the strain quite as long as when the work is comparatively simple. "The Code" can hardly be expected to do anything less than attach supreme importance to the "Time-Table." But to measure school-work for all days of the year by the yard-measure, or by the clock, is to deny to intelligence its fit place in the school-room. It is of far more consequence for ultimate results that the teacher should observe and judge for himself as to the wisest distribution of the several parts of work for a day, than that all our schools come under regulation-drill, which would turn any slight deviation from the Time-Table into a serious offence. By all means let us be saved from blind "rule of thumb." It is to be hoped that our national schools will not become circumscribed by rule in such a manner as to deter our teachers from exercising their own sagacity as to minor deviations which a regard to efficient teaching may suggest.

Considerable diversity of arrangement should appear in the adaptation of lessons to the capacity of children, in accordance with their age and advancement. Powers of observation are those first in exercise, and these chiefly must be called into play in the case of beginners. Those who devote themselves to infant-school teaching need a speciality of teaching gift. Vivacity of manner, aptness of descriptive power, play of imagination, facility

in passing lightly and rapidly from one theme
to others somewhat analogous, with strong
delight in the simple unrestrained ways of
little children, are the qualifications which
specially point out the teacher suited in a
marked degree for training those who are only
in the earliest stages of school life. Pictorial
illustrations and object-lessons must supply
attraction to the youngest scholars. The
earliest demands upon memory should for
the most part involve little more than involuntary recollection. It is enough at such a time
if facts are recalled because the picture illustrating them is attractive, or the story connected with them interesting, or the tune
pleasing to which the verses of a hymn or song
are sung.

There are some who object to have lessons
made easy in this way. They dislike adventi-
tious attractions. They regard this deliberate
selection of the easiest and most attractive
methods of instruction for beginners as a
method wanting in the sternness of the olden
times. I quite sympathize in the aversion to
having all things made easy and agreeable, as
if children were to be screened from difficulty
and hardship. But the realities of school life
are such that there is little need for fearing
that children grow up strangers to labour and
trial. There is certainly reason enough for
attempting to lessen the difficulties and smooth
the path of progress. The testimony of Dr.
Carpenter on such a subject will be readily
accepted as deserving of attention. He says:

" Those ' strong-minded ' teachers who object to
these modes of ' making things pleasant,' as an
unworthy and undesirable ' weakness,' are ignorant that in this stage of the child-mind, the
Will—that is, the power of *self*-control—is
weak ; and that the primary object of Education is to encourage and strengthen, not to
repress, that power.   Great mistakes are often
made by Parents and Teachers, who, being
ignorant of this fundamental fact of child-
nature, treat as *wilfulness* what is in reality just
the contrary of Will-fullness ; being the direct
result of the *want* of Volitional control over the
automatic activity of the Brain.   To punish a
child for the want of obedience which it *has
not the power* to render, is to inflict an injury
which may almost be said to be irreparable." [1]

Passing from involuntary observation and
recollection, children must make a beginning
with voluntary concentration of attention.
This brings us to the regular *tasks*, appropri-
ately so named.   The effort of preparation
always constitutes a task, and in the early
periods of school life a peculiarly wearisome
one.   Scholars must early begin the work of
self-directed effort, success in which must
regulate their progress, and determine their
influence through subsequent life.   The greatest
importance attaches to the judgment which a
teacher forms of the best methods for helping
scholars to make the needful effort.   This is
the turning-point where it is decided what is

[1] *Principles of Mental Physiology*, by Dr. W. B. Carpenter, p. 134.   H. S. King & Co., London.

to be the type of a teacher's success. That it
is part of the teacher's work to render help in
this matter will not, I think, be doubted. In
order to make the help genuine, however, the
aim must be to encourage the scholars to work
for themselves. A teacher succeeds in this in
proportion as he awakens an enthusiasm for
acquisition, and guides and satisfies it when
awakened. The object must be to stimulate
inquiry, and then to render help in such a way
as to encourage it, not to forestall the experience of delight the mind has in discovering for
itself what can. be known. There must be
among the scholars not only a thirst for knowledge, but a sense of power in the self-direction
of their faculties. This involves a distinct use
of voluntary observation and reasoning, not
mere exercise of memory. No doubt all children must commit to memory a good many
things they do not rightly understand.
Such storing of the memory belongs less or
more to all study. There is force here in what
has been said by Mr. Thring : "It must be
borne in mind that with the young memory
is strong, and logical perception weak. All
teaching should start on this undoubted fact.
It sounds very fascinating to talk about *understanding everything, learning everything thoroughly,*
and all those broad phrases which plump down
on a difficulty and hide it. Put in practice,
they are about on a par with exhorting a boy
to mind he does not go into the water till he
can swim."[1] To begin on the supposition that

[1] *Education and School,* p. 196.

everything is to be explained, would indeed be a serious aggravation of a teacher's difficulties. Still it is true, as Professor Hart, of Princeton, New Jersey, U.S., has well said : "This is the true mental order : Knowledge first, and then Memory. Get knowledge, then keep it."[1] The teacher must early begin the work of explaining. His success as a teacher will depend largely on how he does this. Merely to keep on repeating formal explanations is not enough. What is to be sought is skill in suggesting points of thought, in questioning so as to lead the understanding on the way, and in placing the subject of study in a variety of lights and relations which may interest different minds. All these will be gained by breaking up the lesson with clearness into its component parts, touching upon the relations of the parts, and suggesting associations chiefly of the nature of similarity, which may at once help memory and stimulate thought.

From this sketch of what is to be aimed at, will appear what I understand to be the teacher's true function. It is to *teach*, and not merely to *hear lessons recited*, and be a *censor* of failures and a *marker* of results. Above everything else, he is to teach. Whatever else he does is to be subsidiary to this, and to contribute to its efficiency. In their own place, hearing and censuring and marking may all contribute to his end; but a teacher comes down from his true elevation, and lowers the

[1] *In the School-room : Chapters in the Philosophy of Education.* Philadelphia : Eldredge and Brother.

ideal of his professional work, if he content himself with these alone. He becomes a drudge, and the work of the school will be drudgery to the scholars. He becomes a task-master, and the scholars will soon cease to regard him in any other light. But the man who wishes to teach, and not merely to hear lessons, must put himself in living sympathy with the learners, must detect their difficulties, and by his own superior knowledge supply the helps which contribute to the activity and interest of the mind. The real Teacher is not only something higher than a task-master, but something greatly higher than an Examiner. The true teacher may feel the examiner's work quite irksome. Leave him the luxury of teaching, and he may be quite willing to hand over to others the work of examination or inspection. Such a teacher will be ready enough to be judged by results; nevertheless, he has the satisfaction of knowing that he has produced results which the machinery of examination cannot gauge. The radical distinction between teaching and examining touches very closely on all that concerns success in professional work. If a teacher allow himself in thought and in fact to take the attitude of simply judging of the extent of preparation made by the scholars on the previous evening, he deliberately sacrifices all that is grandest in a teacher's life.

How, then, can the teacher be more than a simple hearer of lessons? How can he help the scholars in the work of learning? Before

attempting an answer, there are some precautionary considerations which need to be
present to the teacher's mind.

The children are not to be over-tasked.
Quantity is not the test of success. Undue
amount may peril the whole results. It is
in every sense better to err on the side of too
short lessons than on the side of great length.
There is in our day a vicious appetite for
quantity, which leads to pernicious results.
If a child must face an array of lessons which
threatens to turn the whole evening, as well as
the day, into a period of work, there is a dis-
heartening sense of oppression which is very
unfavourable to progress. Some children have,
indeed, an avidity for learning, which gives
them no sense of oppression in such circumstances; but it would be greatly better for
themselves and for their parents, and for the
nation too, if there could be awakened in them,
and regularly gratified, some avidity for play.
As a general rule, it may be taken as beyond
dispute that, for educational results, it is undesirable that the whole evening be set apart
to lesson-learning. Responsibility for home
arrangements devolves on the parents or guardians of the children; but the responsibility of
adjusting the task to the recognised capacity
and advancement of the scholars rests on their
teacher. Many of the perplexities and trials
which fall upon both teachers and scholars are
the result of want of due consideration as to
the amount of work assigned. If in the hurry
of closing up for the day, a teacher, without

much consideration, specify work more extended than ordinary, the result will be a night of gloom for the scholars, and thereafter a day of perplexity for himself. In such circumstances, the vexations of teaching are self-made troubles.

It must further be remembered that if pupils become addicted to partial preparation, and grow familiar with wriggling through the day's work in haphazard fashion, they are so far demoralized. Their standard of school requirement is lowered. Preparation is less a matter of concern to them than it should be. Such a result is to be guarded against as earnestly as a break-down in discipline. On the same grounds, it is to be desired that parents should cease from regarding a school as really efficient simply because a great quantity of work is pressed through. The test of efficiency is not found in the amount of work done, but in the thoroughness with which the work attempted has been performed.

For Teachers in our Primary Schools it is specially important to consider the amount of home-preparation which may reasonably be expected. It seems to me altogether unlikely that satisfactory advance can be made in the work of education through means of these schools, unless school-work be largely planned upon the admission that only slight home-preparation can be expected. A large proportion of the children are so situated at home that preparation of lessons must be very slight, and often completely neglected. It seems unwise to shun this admission; we must suit ourselves to the existing state of matters. Teaching must proceed largely on the assumption that the scholars are practically commencing the learning of the lesson when their teacher begins class-work. I do not incline so to view a teacher's work as to regard this position of affairs as occasion for special condolence. On the contrary, I favour the opinion, that in all cases it would be well if the classes in which primary instruction is communicated were conducted on the avowal that comparatively little is expected in the form of home-preparation. Even if lesson-learning were entirely restricted to school hours for the first two or three years of school life, I think we should gain and not lose in educational results. In the interests of health and physical development it is to be desired that the brain should not be subjected to continuous work for more than a few hours of each day. As far as possible, we should guard against the excitement of class-work flowing in upon the homes of the children, and even upon their sleeping hours. At present we have too much experience of uneasy restlessness of brain among young children. In the interests of the teachers of our primary schools, burdened as they are with the extra strain of maintaining the attention of large numbers of very young children, I would wish to see a saving of strength in teaching. Escape from the irritation experienced on account of the discovery of inadequate preparation would be a considerable help in this respect. There would be less fretting for a teacher (and it is fretting which most quickly exhausts the strength), by deliberately undertaking the work of teaching the lesson from the foundation. There would also be a higher training in the real work of teaching. Mere lesson-hearing is a comparatively slight and commonplace exercise; but to lead the young mind into the knowledge to be understood and remembered is an exercise in every way worthy of large knowledge and much skill.

To the main question : How is the teacher to lend help to the pupils in the learning of their lessons ? The most important part of the reply is, that all hearing of lessons should be designedly managed in such a way as to contribute towards a better learning of these lessons. The best prepared child has still much to learn from the lesson; many of the children are likely to have the greater part to learn; but still more importance attaches to the consideration that the work of learning will proceed with increasing alacrity in proportion as the intelligence of the children is called into exercise. All efficient teaching must, indeed, afford a model of the best methods of learning. What all pupils require in a teacher is the suggestiveness which brings the understanding to the aid of the memory. He must contribute for their help the appliances which superior intelligence and experience in the work of instruction suggest for facilitating acquirement.

First in importance for this end is the use

of ANALYSIS.   If learners are shown the true
methods for reducing difficult combinations to
their elements, many difficulties are taken out
of the way.   Mastery of the remaining difficulties will then prove a help for subsequent
effort.   This work of analysis is greatly simplified in later stages, if progress in elementary instruction has been by advancement on
a careful system from the simplest elements of
language to the more complex combinations.
Intelligence is the avenue to memory. A passage may be accurately and rapidly read or
recited, and yet not in any proper sense learned.
The contribution to the real education of the
child is comparatively small, unless the understanding is called into exercise.   In education
what may be described as a "local" or "verbal"
memory is of slight influence in comparison
with an intelligent or rationalizing memory.
Association by reference to locality or verbal
sequence is a temporary coherence, which
generally breaks up when the occasion for it
is gone.   But if facts are contemplated, and
truths are understood, memory keeps what it
receives, and intelligence begins to utilize what
it has gathered.   It is therefore of the utmost
importance that analysis become a familiar
instrument in all educational work.   The
ordinary round of school duty gives constant
opportunity for its use.   In spelling, for
example, to break up a word into its component
parts is to bring the understanding into play,
affording memory the aid it requires for accurately retaining and recalling that word.

This is the only really efficient protection
against bad spelling. So it is, most plainly,
with reading. Accurate reading of a passage
which is not fully understood is simply impossible. Daily familiarity with the analysis
of a few of the longest sentences in the lesson
is the simplest and surest method for attaining
just appreciation of punctuation, intonation,
and emphasis. Again, acquiring the grammar
of any language is certain to be drudgery if
assigned merely to " word-memory," with the
help of as much patience as a child can command. The same task will have sources of
pleasure connected with it if memory has
called to its service even an occasional play of
intelligence. The teaching of grammar is
indeed a fair test of teaching power. Its requirements fully illustrate the value of analysis.
Of all the forms of misery connected with
school life, there is nothing more vexatious
than the sight of a child entangled in the intricacies of grammar, with nothing but the dis-
agreeable remembrance of tiresome tasks, and
nothing in store but increased bewilderment,
in absence of intelligent appreciation of what
had gone before. In view of the fact that in
multitudes of cases parents can render no help
to their children in such studies, there is
urgent need for constant use of analysis, however slow the progress may be. Sure understanding, however slow it be, is progress ;
rapidity with uncertainty is progress of the
delusive sort, the semblance without the reality.
There is no great wisdom in a rapid dash into

a tangled, thorny thicket, two miles deep. A few minutes spent in seeking a pathway may save hours of laborious and useless struggle. To make grammar something else than a bewildering thicket is the teacher's part. It is, indeed, more than the most careful teacher can hope for, that none of his scholars shall have a task of bewilderment. But the aim of the teacher must be to secure that the great majority in each class advance clearly together in the understanding of what is being taught. It certainly is not enough that the sharpest children make head-way, while the majority get into confusion. Such a result is failure, however well the upper marks appear when the test comes.

The use of the eye to aid the understanding is of great importance in all analysis. For this reason the *black-board* presents an invaluable auxiliary. Its use may seem to consume time ; in reality it greatly saves time. What is made visible will be understood much more rapidly than what is merely explained in words. A word of several syllables written out on the board in separate parts will much more easily be made familiar than if it be only looked at as printed in the ordinary lesson. Familiarity with the analysis of words will soon be gained in this way, rendering continued use of the board unnecessary, and setting it free for use at some other point of difficulty. There is no need to continue illustrations when writing mainly for those who are professional teachers. The value of the black-board is not likely to be overlooked. The more a teacher can avail himself of all the avenues to the mind, the more efficient his teaching must become.

Next to analysis as an instrument of instruction comes skilful COMBINATION. When pupils are encouraged to make for themselves fresh combinations of things already known, additional progress is certain. Variety of exercise in this way is as attractive to children as many of their games. If, when such exercises are given, the rivalry involved in taking places were discontinued, and all extraneous excitement avoided, the play of intelligence would bring an ample reward. I plead for discontinuance of rivalry in such exercises, because, while it stimulates some, in other cases it hinders and even stops the action of intelligence. If any teacher doubt this, he may subject a class to experiment by watching the faces of the pupils, and next asking from the child who has been corrected an explanation of the reason for the correction. Hurry in such things is an injury, and so is all commingling of antagonistic motives. All fear hinders intellectual action, and the fear of wounded ambition offers no exception to the rule. The fear of being punished is more seriously detrimental than any form of fear which can be stirred. It is essentially antagonistic to the action of intelligence. Let mind have free play. There is hardly a better exercise for a class than that of allowing a scholar to write out on the black-board the tense of a verb, or any other portion of grammar; requiring the others to offer correc-

E

tions of what has been written; interlining the corrections as suggested; and then inquiring into their warrant. Ritter, the celebrated geographer of Germany, pointed to the value of skilful combination in the suggestion he made as to teaching geography. He proposed the combination of history and geography. He recommended that an outline map should be drawn, the mountains traced, and the courses of the rivers; and that localities should be marked in connexion with events of historic importance, or with information concerning the products of the soil or of manufacture. The suggestion is a valuable example of the type of combinations which must greatly facilitate education and deepen its interest. The learning of geography is of comparatively little value if it be nothing more than lists of names in moderate doses, with the understanding that they belong to England or to France. But if a teacher roughly sketch an outline map upon the board, and bid one after another of the pupils fill in a part of it, and then unroll the printed map, the impression upon all will be greatly deepened. History would undoubtedly gain greatly in interest if outstanding events were associated with map-drawing. The Germans have advanced beyond most nations in teaching geography. Government instructions may lie behind this, and perhaps even military reasons may lie at the back of these instructions, but there can be little doubt of the fact. During the Franco-Prussian war it was said the German soldiers knew the geography of France

better than the French themselves. Special
education for the army is, however, provided
in Germany to an extent as yet unknown in
any other country. The German soldier is not
left merely to become familiar with drill; he
has regular school training, as well as military
exercise. But the school children are unusually
well instructed in geography, with minute
topographical information. When resident in
Berlin, I had the opportunity of putting a
variety of questions to a smart boy of thirteen
years of age—a favourable example of the
school, I should think—and found that he had
a degree of topographical knowledge rarely
possessed by those who have not travelled in a
country. The boy could describe the whole
aspect of the country around Edinburgh as not
one-third of the boys of Edinburgh could have
done. It may be, however, that the influence
of Ritter in Berlin had something to do with
proficiency of geographical instruction in that
city. I have referred more particularly to
grammar and geography here, for they afford
the most obvious illustrations of the value of
suggested combinations. The general principle
to be applied in all departments of instruction
is this—Education is invariably promoted by
the gathering of suitable associations around
the subject of study.

As auxiliary to these methods of instruction
I venture to place A FREE AND FRIENDLY
MANNER OF COMMUNICATION BETWEEN TEACHER
AND SCHOLARS. This greatly stimulates the
interest and enthusiasm of the pupils. There

is, indeed, a familiarity which is destructive of discipline, and quite unfavourable to application on the part of the scholar. This is so clearly recognised in the profession, that there is hardly need for precaution against misunderstanding. The communication here referred to is that which has purely educational ends in view. What I point to is far removed from everything which would favour undue familiarity. It even presupposes the impossibility of it. Anything which interferes with the simple relation of teacher and taught is a hindrance. What is to be commended is freedom of communication exclusively for purposes of instruction, and connected with the matter in hand, as the sole attraction for the time. It is a freedom which, instead of being unfavourable to discipline, must tend to establish it. What is mainly to be desired is free communication of difficulties from the scholar to the teacher, as there should be full instruction from the teacher to the scholar. There is an exercise of authority by a teacher which utterly ignores and frowns upon any tendency to direct inquiries to him. He will question in order to ascertain what the scholars have learned; but they must not question him, in order to learn what they have failed to understand. Everything is made to depend upon the thoroughness of the teaching at every stage; and this again depends upon the teacher's own reflection, without any sure discovery of his pupils' need. To every teacher such a method is inadequate, because insecure. The most

experienced teacher will allow that he needs to
be helped to the discovery of his pupils'
difficulties. But if a teacher cultivate a dis-
tant reserve he cannot have the help which
only the scholars can give. The instruction
must roll on. If the scholars catch all they
need, so far well; if they fail to understand all
that is expressed, there is no help for it. If
such a system be preferred under the apprehension that anything else would weaken
discipline, there is either a consciousness of
weakness in the teacher, or else a want of
thorough reflection on the necessary conditions
of school discipline. If a scholar may not
freely inquire during some suitable opportunity
afforded for the purpose, but must depend
entirely upon catching the full meaning of all
that has been said, the relation between teacher
and scholar is constrained and unhealthy.
There is quite enough disadvantage connected
with the incessant change of places, making it
a pupil's interest to conceal his ignorance,
without anything else being allowed to increase
that disadvantage. I do not undervalue competition among the children in the same class,
nor do I think we can wisely dispense with
the stimulating power it involves; but it is an
obvious misfortune that, where all goes by
expressed knowledge, a premium is put on
concealment of ignorance, which is apt to
establish concealment as a settled article in
the policy of school life. In view of this
danger, I am increasingly impressed with
the need for opportunities for free com-

munication at times when the confession of
ignorance may be specially encouraged. The
spirit of inquiry, so valuable in all departments of education, could be greatly stimulated
in this way. In the school, as everywhere else,
we want to escape *routine*.[1] Neither teacher
nor scholar should feel that the procedure each
day is simply a repetition of the procedure of
the preceding day. A sense of monotony is to
be dreaded as one should the nightmare. If
scholars are shy to speak out, as under our
system they are apt to be, deliberate attempts
should be made to draw them out, and ascertain what they still need to learn. It is quite
essential to success that it should be somehow
ascertained how much the children have got
only by rote without understanding, how much
they have misunderstood, and what they have
never thought about which should have engaged
their attention. There is nothing which more
impresses one in visiting the public schools of
the United States of America than the unrestrained freedom with which the pupil makes
an appeal to the teacher, in the assurance of
that appeal being encouraged and met as far
as possible in the circumstances. This feature
struck me as a general characteristic in all the

[1] Dr. Noah Porter, President of Yale College, Con-
necticut, U.S., in a series of articles in *The College Courant*
of Yale, writes upon "special defects in the operation of
modern schools." He signalizes these two : "The spirit of
formalism and routine which has grown up in our modern
schools," and "the tendency to stimulate to excess the
spontaneous or verbal memory." We may take warning
from American experience.

schools I visited, from the primary to the normal schools. The pupils regard this as a natural feature of school life. I remember on one occasion entering the class-room of a teacher of physiology in one of the normal schools when he had just finished the lecture for the day. He was saying to the members of his class, "I shall examine on this lecture to-morrow; just let me see if your notes are accurate." One pupil at once asked what had been said as to the average weight of the human skull. The answer was immediately given. Another question followed, and another, until all were satisfied, after which the few closing minutes of the hour were spent in supplementing the lecture with such remarks as the questions seemed to suggest. This is only an example of what is common in American schools. I must express my admiration of this characteristic. I am averse to "cut and dry theories" as to the best possible ways of teaching. I would have each teacher observe and reflect for himself; but by all means save us from routine. A teacher needs knowledge of human nature, and he needs freedom of action to avail himself, without reserve, of all the varied resources fitted to awaken attention and stimulate mental activity.

CHAPTER IV.

FORMATION OF CHARACTER.

IN the previous chapter attention has been directed exclusively to the development of the intellectual powers. I proceed now to speak of the regulation of the emotional nature, —the government of all the springs of action. This brings into view the teacher's part in aiding his pupils to use intelligence for the guidance of their conduct. I have already indicated the grounds on which I conceive that this department of oversight and training belongs to the teacher. He is an instructor in the widest sense. To him is intrusted the development of the whole nature, in so far as that is found to be needful for school discipline, and possible through means of it. The two departments, instruction and training, are indeed quite distinct, and admit of separate treatment. But both ends must be sought in the midst of the same school exercises. From the one point of view, the teacher seeks to make his scholars observant, reflective, well-informed, and prompt in the use of their faculties. From the other he seeks to make them upright, generous, and brave. The relative importance of these two ends will be at once recognised. As meanness of disposition is worse than slowness of intellect; as selfishness is worse than defective memory; as cowardice is worse than ignorance,—special importance is to be attached to the department of moral training. The teacher cannot, indeed, raise such training to the position of primary importance, since all the school arrangements are made expressly for instruction in the ordinary branches of knowledge. But there is no need for this, since moral training is gained not so much by formal inculcation of duty as by practice in well-doing throughout the common engagements of life. If, however, moral training do not expressly engage the attention of the scholars as a subject of study, it is to be continually the subject of consideration with the teacher. It makes no difference whether it be grammar, or geography, or history which is being taught, the formation of character goes on with equal facility. So generally is this recognised in the profession, that Mr. Currie has set this down as his first statement in his valuable work on Education :—" Education comprises all the influences which go to form the character."[1]

On the other hand, it is not to be forgotten that it is much easier to instruct than to train. The conditions under which these two pro-

[1] *Principles and Practice of Common School Education.*

ceed differ greatly. If a man be himself instructed, and if he only explain things with a
fair amount of interest, he is sure of success in
communicating information; but character is
not formed thus. ⟨You may state and enforce
moral law with the greatest clearness, without
securing conformity to it. What is wanted is
not explaining so much as warning and
encouraging. Thus it happens that, while we
may instruct in the mass, in the work of
training we need much more carefully to distinguish individuals. ⟩

For success in training, the first requisite
is intelligent sympathy with the children in the
difficulties they experience while attempting to
control their conduct. Before a true and influential sympathy is possible, the teacher
must observe peculiarities of disposition. It
will thus appear how essential it is to dis-
criminate carefully, in order to make a satisfactory beginning. At the same time the
general truth must be recognised and applied
for the guidance of our procedure, that a child's
ruling dispositions are as truly inherited as his
intellectual powers or his bodily constitution.
This will not be disputed, and therefore I do not
insist upon it; but the consideration must
have a directly practical bearing upon school
government. If it be not uniformly recognised
and acted upon, justice cannot be done to the
children, nor can sagacity have proper exercise
in dealing with them. One child is naturally
irritable, another is naturally amiable. The
one is not to be blamed, nor is the other to be

praised, for what he has inherited. If under sudden provocation the one shows a sensitiveness which the other does not discover, no marvel. The result is exactly that to be expected from the different natures of the two. What is of chief interest to the educationist is, that the irritable child can gain the mastery over the ruling tendency of his nature, and can be helped in striving for the victory. But it is unjust to punish a child because he has inherited an irritable disposition. In many cases it is no less so to punish him because that disposition has suddenly started into activity under provocation. One child is naturally timid, another naturally rash. It is unreasonable to blame the children, or to do anything but consider what are the special difficulties of each, and how best each can be helped in overcoming these. The one has inherited a highly sensitive nervous constitution, which is readily excited by the slightest changes, and which throws in upon the mind the agitation originating in the organism. To punish such a child for his timidity, or mock him on account of it, is a grievous practical blunder, which indicates want of knowledge and reflection as to the necessary conditions of moral training. If a teacher is not to run the risk of inflicting life-long injury upon one intrusted to his care, he must have some clearly defined plan in harmony with the known laws of mind, suitable for allaying fear and promoting courage. Another child is naturally impulsive. The former thinks and shrinks. This child does not shrink, because he does not take time to think; he is unconscious of the restraints arising from a nervously sensitive organism. He is not readily checked by rising fears; his misfortune is that he has not enough of fear. He is like the youth in the fairy tale, who had never learned to " shiver and shake," consequently, he has an unenviable facility in knocking his head against posts, which could easily be shunned. We must take this child as he is, and, understanding his difficulty, deal with him in such a manner as to promote thoughtfulness and caution, by all means avoiding anything which would tempt him to extremes.

To draw the distinction between *nature* and *character* is essential for an educationist. Every child has in his nature certain dispositions to be vanquished. These cannot go to form any part in a good character. I do not here go into ethical distinctions, which are not required for my present purpose. The fact to which I am pointing is clearly recognised, and must have attention. It goes far to explain the difficulty of the teacher's task, and to account for the perplexity often experienced in deciding upon the wisest mode of treatment. It is much more difficult to carry through a wise repression than to promote healthy development of a natural power. The process is a delicate one, requiring careful discrimation as to circumstances. It is here that the largest demand falls upon the sagacity of parents and teachers. To draft a code of rules sufficient to regulate procedure in all cases is simply impossible.

Something is done, however, towards regulation of our procedure in this perplexing department if we mark with exactness THE LIMITS OF A TEACHER'S POWER IN TRAINING. He cannot form the character, but can only aid the pupil in efforts to form his own character. This consideration is of vital importance in the determination of method. Character implies established habits of self-government. Its formation is thus essentially a personal matter. Whatever be its type, it is the result of habits voluntarily cherished. So long as the predominant natural dispositions sway the conduct unchecked, moral character is unformed. The beginning of its formation can be traced from the time that there are signs of voluntary restriction and regulation of these dispositions. Whenever a degree of self-control appears, it indicates the sway of intelligence. Character, whether good or bad, is in no case the result of involuntary tendency. Its formation in a good and healthy type is a most delicate process, needing to be continued through many years. Nothing is more likely to injure, by retarding, or it may even be perverting, the process, than efforts after coercion. Will-power must regulate the course of conduct, and the only safe stimulants of the action of will are intelligence within, and the encouragement of intelligent sympathy from superiors who have already won respect.

On the other hand, it must be remembered that children are greatly hindered or aided in the formation of a good character by the influ-

ence of those around them. If their seniors
make light of moral distinctions, they will do
so too. If their companions are selfish, and
unchecked in that tendency, they too will
begin to give way to the same hideous disposition. There is in human nature enough
of the desire for self-gratification, and a sufficient sense of the irksomeness of self-restraint,
to favour ready yielding to the easier way of
life. But self-denial is the necessary condition
of self-government. The effort it involves,
and the pain connected with that effort, try us
most at the commencement. But both the
effort and the pain will be considerably lessened
if seniors give encouragement and companions
share the difficulties. In this way, all the
order and discipline of the school should support the virtues and promote their growth.[1]

This, however, is still but a part of what a
teacher can do towards the formation of a
sound moral character in the pupils. The
discipline maintained in school provides favourable circumstances in the midst of which good
intentions can be carried out. But favourable
circumstances do not in themselves afford all
that is requisite. Dismiss the best disciplined
class, and observe the moral characteristics of
the children when they are free to act according to inclination. It will be found that there
is considerable diversity among them, and that
some very readily inflict wrong upon their
companions. Discipline is the product of

---

[1] Dr. Donaldson has well said that the teacher's function
is "to make good citizens."--*Lects. on Education,* p. 30.
So also, Mr. Laurie, in *Primary Education,* p. 5.

authority. Character does not grow by mere
force of authority. There is even peril to
character in the constant strain of authority,
which demands unquestioning submission on
pain of punishment. Obedience in such a
case is often reluctantly rendered, and reluc-
tant submission is apt to be unfavourable to
character. A rooted aversion to restraint is
then cherished, which carries in it serious fore-
bodings of evil. A child must be taught to
walk alone, else a reckless career may follow
escape from the hated restraint. The most
perfect form of drill cannot establish moral
character ; the best educational machinery is
unequal to the task. Circumstances, even the
most favourable, cannot produce the character
which must itself be superior to circumstances.
Character must grow from within, in accordance with the invariable laws of mind.

To render aid in the formation of character,
a teacher must INDIVIDUALIZE. One hundred
children may be instructed in the same branch
of knowledge at once, but development of
character cannot proceed in this way. The
prevailing dispositions and tendencies of each
scholar must be ascertained. Ignorant of these,
a teacher can do little which will render really
effective help. A physician might as well
write prescriptions at random, and distribute
them in order, as he made the round of his
patients. Knowledge of each pupil is the
essential requisite for real training. It may
be objected that professional duty leaves a
teacher no leisure for this ; but one who has

made it a practice to observe character, as every teacher must have done in order to be successful, needs no special time for the necessary observation. He cannot help observing. He only requires the routine and bustle of school life to afford the opportunities he needs. A private talk with each pupil, when constrained, and quite on his guard, will be of little worth for purposes of observation. You must see children excited by rivalry—tried by the irritating conduct of fellow-scholars—subjected to unexpected disappointment—and roused by the exercise of the playground—in order to ascertain what are the characteristics of each one, and what a teacher should most strive to do for each. In such scenes observation is inevitable, and a child is never allowed to feel as if he were watched. Everything is " above-board," and comes under observation in natural course. The teacher soon knows who are irritable and who are of a stubborn disposition; who are rash and who shrinking; who are inclined to conceal their purposes, and practise cunning; and who are prone to be domineering. Seeing these things, a teacher sees his work. He recognises that a common discipline, touching all alike, is not equal to the demand. Help appropriate in form, and well timed, he must endeavour to give. Scarcely noticed by the school generally, hardly remarked upon by the child more immediately concerned, a look of encouragement or rebuke will make a child conscious of success or failure. A mere glance of

the eye may not reckon for much in the log-
book of the school, but it has left its impress
on the sensitive surface of a young heart. A
word of rebuke dropped softly at the fitting
moment into that ear alone for which it is
meant may be enough to start a resolution of
improvement upon which a teacher may continue to operate from day to day. Such a
word may live long in the memory. I remember now, as if it had been yesterday, the look
and word of a venerated preceptor,[1] who had
detected a case of oppression of a fellow-
scholar, "There was one boy in the group I
did not expect to see consenting to such conduct." The look and word were for me, and
how the lesson went home may be judged by
the vividness of the present recollection.

Formation of character is begun in each case
only when the pupil is induced to begin the
work of self-control. A child must see that
this is his own business, and a work for all
times. He must be awakened to the sense of
that power which is power over self. He must
have aroused to activity those motive forces
which impel the mind to the work of self-control as one of living interest. He must taste
the joy as well as feel the difficulty of self-
government. Only thus can the building up
of character proceed. For a teacher, then,
there is no other way possible than that of
helping the scholar to help himself in what
must be his own work. If we fail to induce the
pupil to take to this in earnest, we fail in the

[1] Dr. Boyd, of the Edinburgh High School.

F

first condition of success. From the very centre of the being must come the determination of the forces which are to be allowed to sway the conduct. Who can overcome selfishness but the person who feels it? How can generosity be planted in the mind except by personal admiration of it, and personal exercise? The best that can be done from without is to show what should be done, and to give encouragement towards the doing of it; but the doing must proceed from within. Let us not spoil the whole by attempting too much; there is enough to engage observation, exercise patience, and occupy the thought of the teacher in what is really within his power. The hardest part is that which the child himself must do. The sooner his attention is directed upon it, and he begins the struggle with evil dispositions, so much the easier the task will be, and the more certain will be the result.

SELF-CONTROL BEGINS WITH REFLECTIVE-NESS. It has its sure commencement in thought as to right and wrong in human conduct. But this thought, to be of any real value in character-building, must be concerned more with the inward dispositions than with the outward forms of conduct. It is in the suggesting and encouraging of such thought that a teacher can give to a pupil the full benefit of his superior intelligence, and greater calmness of observation. But some consideration needs to be given to the lines of thought which it is of real consequence to suggest. A child needs no lecturing in proof of the position that falsehood is wrong, unless his thinking on the subject has been already perverted by pernicious home-training. There is nothing a child more resents than being deliberately deceived. In like manner it is not needful, under ordinary conditions, to convince a child that stealing is wrong; with a child trained from the earliest days to steal it is otherwise. Every child is, however, quick enough at crying out against the theft of his own property. No one, however unfortunately placed in respect of parental influence, is ignorant of the fact that kindness is right. He has recognised that, a long while before he came to school. What a child needs is, not so much help to know what the right is, as help to do it, especially when circumstances tempt to the opposite.[1] A child needs help to turn his attention on the rising disposition, which, if allowed to gain strength, will tempt to evil-doing. A child is prone to allow attention to be absorbed with what is external, and scarcely turns attention on the feeling which is swelling in the breast. He needs frequent help in beginning reflective exercise. Reflectiveness in the proper sense comes as one of the later attainments, and needs not a little effort for its cultivation. A teacher's help in this matter is

[1] I fully agree with much that Mr. Jolly, H. M. Inspector of Schools, has said in his admirable Report for 1872, as to providing for moral education, only I think formal instruction on this subject is best given in connexion with some occasion for its application.

invaluable ; it is at hand when most needed. It comes just when the strain begins. The teacher knows that if the attention be decidedly turned on the rising disposition, the first requisite is gained for the building up of moral character. He must, therefore, aim at a discriminating, prompt, and sympathetic help, such as may be conveyed in a look, a word, or some understood signal. At such a time it is that something can be done to turn a child upon the work of self-mastery. The help to which I here point is the most delicate and vital part of the work requisite for the true development of a human being. Skill in such work is an enviable attainment.

If in these few sentences an accurate representation has been given of the conditions under which character is formed, it is clear that a teacher's power for good depends upon the degree in which he secures the respect and affection of his pupils. Without these a teacher is powerless in this matter. The respect of the children will be secured by the evidence of self-control and moral worth in himself. A quiet, dignified deportment, which constantly conveys the impression of a large reserve power, commands the confidence of all the pupils. A burdened, care-worn look, restlessness of disposition, irritability of temper, with an irritating style of government, are all apt to convey to the children the impression of weakness, which may be slighted. For commanding affection, there is nothing more potent than a genuine sympathy, and if this take such forms

as indicate distinct recognition of personal difficulties, affection for a teacher may grow to enthusiasm. There is immense importance in this.
Unawakened affection is a treasure of influence
undiscovered. When school-work is reduced
to routine—daily begun, continued, and ended
in a cold mechanical way—it becomes a soul-
less thing, potent in drill, but pithless in
morals, and fruitless in respect of all the
highest results of tuition. Tested by the
" Code," it may command a most favourable
report. As the record stands on the " log-
book," it may wear the appearance of order
and efficiency; but tested as to moral training, even by a moderate standard, its general
result must be unsatisfactory. A glance at the
army will illustrate my meaning. The drill-
sergeant can produce in a given time certain
patent and valuable results ; but under his drill
moral results are rare, and hardly contemplated.
A perfect drill and a low morality are quite
compatible. And so it may be in the school,
if there do not stand before the mind of the
teacher a lofty ideal of training, to fall beneath
which would be humiliating failure. Even a
teacher who keeps well up to time—is ready
for every ringing of the bell—and goes through
his work with exactness of method, will never
rise to high power if he come to his task with
lack of interest in it, and with no strong out-
flow of sympathy towards the scholars, and if he
break off from it as one weary with chiselling
all day at a hard stone. If there is no interest
for the teacher beyond exact spelling, good

reading, accurate reciting, prompt reckoning of accounts, and well-rounded turns on a copy-book, his ideal is that of the drill-sergeant, not that of a discriminating, experienced instructor, capable of unfolding all the best qualities of mind. If a teacher has no sympathy with the shifting interests, the flowing mirthfulness, the strong, though idle, fears, the passing anxieties, the perplexing puzzles, and the sore disappoint-ments of childhood—if to him these are all alike childish, and beneath consideration—he is out of sympathy with the real life-work of the teacher of youth. Better that such an one betake himself to what he regards as more manly work, and leave to others the delicate and difficult task of bringing a cultured man-hood and a refined womanhood out of feeble, undeveloped childhood. If a loud voice, a stamping foot, a strong cane, a heavy strap, books, maps, pens, and paper, exhaust his materials for educating, he can never reach a high place in the profession. Its leading men work on a higher level, with finer tools. We have heard of "half-timers" among the scholars. Such a teacher would be in another and worse sense a "half-timer" even under a full "time-table." If, besides formal appliances, a teacher has a living interest in the whole experience of his pupils, he can lend his aid to them in the work of self-government as well as in that of acquiring knowledge. If there be for him a fascination in the work of guiding the slowly opening mind—if there be a pleasure in lighten-ing childhood's burden—if it be something akin

to the return of the joyousness of his own boyhood to look on the unchecked mirth of his
pupils—he can help them, sway them, check
them, and stir in their hearts the higher motive
forces of human life, as he could not otherwise
do.   A clear stream of warm sympathy must
flow from the teacher to the scholars if real
progress is to be made in the formation of
character during the early years of school life.
Thus only can difficulties be surmounted, sufficient motive awakened, and an attractive glow
of golden sunshine sent over the pathway of
arduous duty.

In aiding the formation of character in the
young, the first aspect of the teacher's work is
that of REPRESSION.   This is a more difficult
and trying work than the encouragement of
good.   But evil tendencies must be checked,
in order that the nobler dispositions may have
room to grow.   If the check is to be wisely
and successfully put on, much more is wanted
than that the check itself be a strong and
severe one.   Fortunately, the most powerful
form of restraint is a form of encouragement
to the person restrained.   Taking for granted
that evil inclinations must be mastered, and
demanding this of the children themselves, the
teacher gains the strongest position when he is
neither the lawgiver nor the imperious authority requiring its fulfilment, but is the friendly
counsellor, suggesting the best means of gaining
the victory.   A suitable hint dropped in the
ear, showing that the difficulty has been seen
and measured, and that the teacher will be a

sharer in the joy of success, will stir new
resolution, and change some part of a naturally
irksome task to attractiveness.   There is great
need that we keep in view the painfulness of
the experience involved in conflict with powerful tendencies in the nature.   To appreciate
the difficulty of the task any child has on hand
carries one a great way towards proving a real
helper.   But the painfulness of the work must
in nowise give exemption from it.   Such painfulness is part of the necessary experience of true
development.   To favour a child escaping from
the determination and suffering connected with
self-denial is no kindness, but the worst form
of cruelty.   There is but one way for mankind
securing a clear escape from this painfulness, that
is, to face the effort which occasions the pain,
until by facility of effort the pain itself gradually
diminishes, until the pleasure of pure and lofty
motive is felt greatly to outweigh the uneasiness.   Neither parent nor teacher can wisely
screen children from the bitter ordeal which
self-denial entails.   " A spoilt child " has been
spoiled by encouragement in self-indulgence,
which at each turn has been allowed under
name of " kindness," and which has prevented
reflection where it might have arisen, and a
struggle for self-mastery which might have
been attempted.   It is a weak and altogether
pernicious type of sympathy which inclines a
teacher or guardian to save a child from the
pain of conflict with his own evil tendencies.
This is " blind sympathy," one of the worst
illustrations out of a considerable variety which

give force to the adage that "love is blind."
Wisdom is the true guide of love, for there is
no more glaring practical mistake than the
notion that the law of love is all we need to
make our life noble. The love which shelters
from the pain of self-denial is soon blind even
to the faults which spring from the want of re-
straining power. There is therefore great need
to guard against love degenerating to softness.
Even tender years must not be allowed to
plead for self-indulgence. In kindness, the
teacher must remember that the sooner the
work of self-restraint begins the easier it
proves. But when this work is bravely faced,
let us give all the sympathetic aid in our
power, always remembering that the work
itself must be the child's own. Real sympathy
helps the youth in his battle with evil within.
And a heavy demand there ever must be for such
sympathy, while selfishness must be crushed,
anger must be restrained, and wrongs must
be endured without retaliation. The task may
be harder for some than for others, but in
every case it must be carried through. A
clear recognition of all that this requires is of
greatest value to a teacher. Happy are the
children placed under the care of teachers who
see the moral requirements of their case, and
take pleasure in individualizing. The victory
is half won if a child has a strong helper in
his instructor. However young the child be,
he feels and appreciates the help ; for here it
is worth observing that children clearly dis-
criminate between the different forms and

effects of what their seniors often classify
under the single name " kindness." They
have a sensitiveness of nature, rather emotional
than intellectual, which distinguishes between
the affection which tends to feebleness, and
the affection which both makes sacrifices and
demands that they be made. Children have
one kind of affection for the good-natured,
easy-going master, whom they would describe
as a "jolly fellow," who winks at a great deal
that should be checked, and yields almost
anything that is clamoured for. They have a
different and deeper regard for the guide who
looks both before and behind, and will neither
himself yield, nor allow those for whom he is
responsible to yield anything that concerns
right conduct. It is a perilous mistake if we
dissociate love from law, and yield to a tenderness which lowers the standard of personal
goodness, and lessens the task of self-government. There is only one thing worse, that is,
the discovery of a softness of nature which
encourages children to resort to fawning and
cajolery, in the hope of gaining what has been
formerly denied them. Such weakness of
government is positively demoralizing. It
both trains and rewards cunning, a vice which
is the ruin of all moral character. Instead of
laying the foundations of a good character, the
superior, whether parent or teacher, is undermining the foundation on which alone he can
build with success. Transparent honesty is
essential for sound building, and if a child is to
be guided and encouraged as he ought, he must

be led very early in life to yield conformity to moral laws, which are as unchangeable and unvariable as physical laws.

The repression of wrong-doing introduces us to some of the most perplexing educational problems. Upon these I am not disposed to theorize down to minute details. In no other way is it possible to govern, and at the same time help by governing, than by the exercise of practical sagacity, which grasps the whole aspects of each case, and decides upon it by reference to moral law, and a full understanding of the nature of the child concerned. There are moral offences which must call down upon them condemnation tó be felt by the whole school. I do not return here to the question of suitable punishments. But it must be clear that falsehood, cruelty, and dishonesty cannot go unpunished. The necessities of discipline, even if no higher ground were taken, demand that they be effectually checked. The sense of the wrongness of such conduct must be borne in upon the mind. It is not enough that the scholars account them as hazardous, because certain to entail punishment if detected. The shrinking from physical pain is so great, that the risk of having to endure it is apt to be the first consideration with a child. This is one of the peculiar disadvantages of corporal punishment. The risk of this is so great that it becomes matter of special importance that the moral aspect of the offence be impressed upon the mind of the offender. Mere punishment may be quickly administered, but the child may be nothing the better; he may even be the worse. What is needed is to make him reflect until he sees for himself the wrongness of the act. He must perceive that it is impossible to approve the act,—that he would have resented it exceedingly had it been done to himself,—that the utmost disaster would be the result of its frequent commission. The time taken up in this way is well spent. Thus the teacher is doing his part to lay solidly the great stones for a sure foundation.

Keeping in view the exceeding sensitiveness to impression discovered by the mind, it is well to economize influence by doing the utmost possible with the least instrumentality. It is a mistake to suppose that we are most effective when most severe. There is a fineness of sensibility over the spirit which vanishes at the first threatening of severity. Rough handling will in an instant spoil the surface on which you wish to impress an accurate transcript of moral law. An economy of material is compatible with the best results. "James!" or "Jessie!" uttered in a tone of surprise, will in many cases make a deep and lasting impression upon the mind of one seen transgressing. And in general the teacher has gained a great deal if in a few clear, calm statements, he set forth the essential evil of an act such as falsehood, and find the pupils overawed by a consciousness of the impossibility of anything but condemnation being applied to such a deed. A few weighty words, slowly and quietly uttered in the midst of general stillness, are in their practical effect worth far more than hours of the loudest storming.

Beyond such general dealing comes the great perplexity of school life. How shall we deal with those who are wilful, stubborn, and defiant? It is a question hard to answer. There are some who object entirely to corporal punishment. As already indicated, I am not able to agree with this view. Alternatives are hard to find, though it is most desirable to avail ourselves of all that seem to promise efficiency. Expulsion from the school I regard as an extreme measure, to be shunned up to the verge of endurance. Unless in the case of unruly pupils at an advanced age for school life (such as are not unfrequently to be found in evening schools), expulsion from the school can hardly be looked at as an available course. It is escape from a difficulty, not mastery of it. It is a practical admission of failure, which, if possible, should never be made in face of a school. Instead of increasing the moral influence of a teacher, it detracts from it. Let kindly treatment, as occasion offers, calm and sympathetic remonstrance in private, assurances of patience, and promises of help, be all accumulated around the offender. Let everything be done which tenderest sympathy can suggest rather than that the offender be banished from the school, and turned over as a pest upon the hands of some unsuspecting brother in the profession. There is a very graphic account of the conflict with a stubborn and wild youth which deserves perusal, given in one of the

books of Dr. Eggleston,[1] descriptive of school
life in the midst of the rude settlers in the Far
West of America. Very touching is the story,
naturally recalled here, which is told by Dr.
Guthrie in his own pathetic style : " A soldier,
whose regiment lay in a garrison town in England, was about to be brought before his commanding officer for some offence. He was an
old offender, and had been often punished.
' Here he is again,' said the officer, on his name
being mentioned ; 'everything—flogging, dis-
grace, imprisonment—has been tried with him.'
Whereupon the sergeant stepped forward, and
apologizing for the liberty he took, said, ' There
is one thing that has never been done with him,
sir.' 'What is that ?' was the answer. 'Well,
sir,' said the sergeant, ' he has never been forgiven.' ' Forgiven ! ' exclaimed the colonel, sur-
prised at the suggestion. He reflected for a
few minutes, ordered the culprit to be brought
in, and asked him what he had to say to the
charge ? ' Nothing, sir,' was his reply ; ' only I
am sorry for what I have done.' Turning a
kind and pitiful look on the man, who expected
nothing else than that his punishment would
be increased with the repetition of his offence,
the colonel addressed him, saying, ' Well, we
have resolved to forgive you ! ' The soldier
was struck dumb with astonishment ; the tears
started in his eyes, and he wept like a child.
He was humbled to the dust ; he thanked his
officer and retired—to be the old refractory,
incorrigible man ? No ; he was another man

---

[1] *The Hoosier Schoolmaster.* Routledge, London.

from that day forward. He who tells the story had him for years under his eye, and a better-conducted man never wore the Queen's colours."[1] Such a case, even though it be regarded as one in a hundred, is worth pondering. At the same time it needs to be remarked that it is the case of one hardened by punishment, and is a case of pardon which could not have been renewed if the experiment had proved unsuccessful. But there is in tenderness of dealing a power so great that a teacher may well venture at times upon an experiment with the view of ascertaining how wide a range of application may be allowed to it.

In carrying forward the work of moral training, some attention needs to be given to the moral RISKS CONNECTED WITH SCHOOL MANAGEMENT. There are such risks, against which it is an important duty to have the scholars kept on guard as far as possible. The rivalries of school life carry with them temptations to jealousy. The daily competition, the marking of places, the reckonings which are to determine the prizes, all excite the children in a way which is apt to break in upon the work of self-restraint. Eagerness for honour tempts either to seize at an advantage or to cherish enmity because such an advantage has been secured by another. The stimulus of competition has undoubtedly a high value; but this fact must not blind our eyes to the accompanying evils. The influence of numbers is great, and the

---

[1] *Speaking to the Heart,* p. 36.

rivalry of open competition quickens interest in the round of school work. To dispense with such stimulus seems hardly wise. And yet it cannot be matter for surprise that many teachers have been led seriously to question whether there is a real educational gain from these rivalries. It would be difficult to decide the dispute by careful comparison of the evidence for the opposing views. One consideration seems to me conclusive. Competition is an invariable attendant on human effort. There is no sphere of life which altogether escapes its influence. In the great majority of the spheres in which life is spent the results of rivalry are met at every turn. For this school training should prepare, as for one of the certainties of human life. To bear one's-self with calmness, fairness, and generosity in the midst of the rivalries of business is of the highest consequence both for personal interests and for the harmony of social life. It is, indeed, a great service which is rendered to the community if school training prepare for this. The teacher's thoughts must often revert to the subject, if the scholars are to be guarded against the perils, and guided to the attainment of the requisite power. Ambition, that "last infirmity of noble minds," may be turned to ignoble ends, and may change strength to weakness, nobleness to meanness.

Taking now a somewhat wider survey of the requirements of our national life, a teacher's attention would need to be turned to OUR PREVAILING NATIONAL VICES, and the best

means for fortifying the young against them.[1]
Early school life should do much to guard
against the rudeness and coarseness which turn
domestic life to bitterness, and prepare the way
for outbreaks of violence. A constant stream
of refining influence should flow through the
minds of the pupils. Everything favourable
in the reading-book, in history, or in the inci-
dents of the school-room, should be utilized
for this end. By all means at our command,
let us seek to refine and elevate. Our aim
must be to give a softened tinge to the
character, like the mellow bloom on the dark
rich clusters of the vine. Thus a higher life
is in some measure reached by a child, and he
wields a gentler influence, checking the asperi-
ties of life. In mixed schools, such as we have
in Scotland, there is ample opportunity for
training boys to cherish a respectful and
generous demeanour towards girls—a lesson
of high value in itself, and far-reaching in its
effects. Encouragement in right practice is
real training. While harshness to a companion

---

[1] Professor Hodgson (University of Edinburgh) presented
this in admirable form in his address at Norwich, as President of the Education Department of the Social Science
Association—Congress 1873. He at the same time forcibly
indicated the present state of public opinion on this subject. He says, "Everywhere around us we find coarseness
of manner, cruelty both to animals and to our fellows,
petty dishonesty, disregard of truth, wastefulness, evasion
of duty, infidelity to engagements, not to speak of graver
forms of wrong-doing; and WHO BELIEVES IN HIS HEART
THAT SCHOOL TRAINING COULD DO ANYTHING TO PREVENT
THEM ?"

G

is shown to be wrong in itself, the whole school should be made to feel that it is additionally offensive when a boy has been the aggressor and a girl the sufferer. And this impression needs to be conveyed in such a manner, that while the boys are conscious of restraint laid upon them, the girls may not be led to suppose that a law less strict applies to them, or that they are to be sheltered from the consequences of their own actions. A skilful hand must steady the balance. An outburst of rudeness on the part of a girl should be felt additionally odious, because of its utter incongruity with the native gentleness and modesty of the sex. A true teacher will do his utmost to deliver men from coarseness, and to preserve for women that gentleness which achieves higher results than brute force. When teaching aims at such ends as these, it takes to itself the guardianship of a lofty ideal. The effects will not appear when the inspection of the school takes place. Under our system of "payment by results," these effects will not have any record in the return of "grant" from the Education Department, and will not appear in the cash-book of the School Board. But, what is of infinitely more consequence to us all, they will, as living results, spread throughout society in after years, and tell upon succeeding generations.

If there be any one vice against which the teachers of our country should seek to warn the young, it is DRUNKENNESS. Our national reproach because of this one vice is a bitter one; our national loss and suffering appalling

to a degree not realized by those who do not
ponder the statistics of the subject. Our
national weal depends largely on our casting
off this loathsome evil. Intelligence and de-
bauchery cannot go long together, either in
personal or in national history. Drunkenness
is a vice at which school training should level
its heaviest blows. There are at present fearful odds against the teacher's hand here, more
particularly in the midst of the poverty-stricken
districts in our large cities, blighted by the
baneful influence of strong drink. But if the
teacher be observant as to opportunities, per-
sistent in his plan, hearty in his utterances,
and judicious in his avoidance of ridicule, he
can do much in fixing unseen convictions, and
may be aided, unconsciously to himself and to
the poor children, by the sad experience of
the misery and brutality which a drunken life
occasions. A steady moral influence quietly
returning, as opportunity offers, to impress upon
the mind the evils of drunkenness, and the
value of temperance as a root virtue, will help
largely towards the training of a race strong
in the self-control of a temperate life. The
waste of substance which drunkenness causes,
—the weakness and weariness of body,—the
debasement of mind,—the desolation of homes,
are such as to afford the teacher many links of
association making reference easy and natural.
There is enough in the thought of these things
to deliver childhood from the risk of making
mirth of the drunkard. There is enough to
favour one who desires to awaken loathing in

a young mind. But in all allusions to this subject there is need for great delicacy of feeling and tact. The teacher needs to remember into how many homes in our land the horrid vampire has entered, and how many young hearts are smarting under the wounds it has inflicted. The revelations which our School Boards in the great cities have had to contemplate during the brief period of their labours already passed, are painful beyond all utterance. They have discovered to us the enormity of the evil, and the urgent need that the children rescued by the "compulsory clause" be fortified against the fearful temptations to be met. Well may the teachers speak often about drunkenness, but in all that is said, we must deal tenderly with the sacred feelings of childhood, and make our teaching strengthen filial interest and devotion, where there is so much to strike at the roots of both, to the terrible aggravation of the evil.

The other and more pleasing aspect of the teacher's work in aiming at the formation of character is the ENCOURAGEMENT OF ALL GOOD DISPOSITIONS. The nourishment of the good is the surest way of repressing the evil. Thus, the growth of generosity is the decay of meanness; so it is all round. The life of the virtues is the death of the vices. Where there is sensitiveness as to the feelings of others, there is shrinking from rudeness. Generosity quickens the sense of shame at the rise of a selfish feeling. The love of truth will summon courage to its aid, rather than screen itself from suffering behind the mean shelter which a falsehood might afford. In this way it is apparent that a teacher can do much to prevent the outbreaks of evil by the judicious and hearty encouragement he gives to all examples of well-doing.

Here, then, our question is,—How can the teacher most effectively contribute towards the development of the noble qualities of moral character? The first and most constant form of help is that afforded by the spirit in which school discipline is maintained. If that illustrate throughout the play of good disposition, the children are unconsciously won to admiration and imitation of the same. It is not despotic government which is favourable to the growth of virtue, but the government of reason and sympathy—in other words, a government founded on moral excellence. If the children have any occasion to complain of injustice, some injury is done to their moral training. Let the atmosphere of justice and kindliness pervade the school-room, and the scholars will grow up in robustness of moral life. In speaking, however, of this pervading influence, it is not implied that a teacher may uniformly succeed in reaching his own ideal. This is not the condition upon which sound moral training can be maintained. Personal perfection is not by any means needful in order to success in training others. But those who are under a teacher's care must be satisfied that he has a noble ideal which he sincerely admires, and which he honestly strives to reach. Their confidence in this must not be shaken by his failures; it must even be strengthened by means of these. The suggestion may seem incongruous, but if it be reflected upon it will appear that we often judge even more confidently of a person's character by the manner in which he acts when conscious of having done wrong, than we do in observing the more ordinary examples of well-doing. This is peculiarly true as to the judgment which children form of their instructor. If he do a wrong, and be found denying it, or be seen resorting to shifts to conceal it, nothing is more quickly made the subject of remark. But if one who is constantly laying down the law, and reflecting upon them for failures, do himself acknowledge that he has fallen into mistake, or has done what he openly regrets, the children have great confidence in the sincerity of his counsels, because they believe in the reality of his own effort to do what he requires others to do. If an unintentional injustice has been done, let the error be freely, and if needful publicly, acknowledged, and let the error be rectified as far as possible. None of us professes to be perfect; it would be purest affectation to conduct a class on the assumption that we are. It does not lower the dignity of a teacher to own a fault on a fitting occasion. But the acknowledgment must be a proof of strong moral purpose,—not a painful admission of weakness and bewilderment. It must give evidence of the power of self-command,—not of the want of it.

Next in importance is the power of direct encouragement. If the teacher gain the affections of his scholars, and give regular evidence of his wish to stimulate them in well-doing, his influence over them will be great. They have a desire to stand well with their teacher, and if this desire be utilized it becomes easy to contribute daily towards the formation of a good character. In order to preserve this influence, however, it is needful to remember that praise as well as blame must be used sparingly. The child must know and feel that he has gained approval, but only at rare times should he hear himself praised before others. So delicate a process is that by which character is developed, that there is danger from frequent commendation, just as there is on the other side from frequent fault-finding. The dangers here are two—that of encouraging pride while encouraging well-doing, and that of tempting a child to suppose that there is something peculiarly meritorious in simply doing his duty. The former is the more conspicuous, and is certain to attract attention if it arise, and thereby suggest the need for counteractives. But the latter is one not so easily observed, and which goes much more quickly in the direction of undermining the character. The child must be made to recognise that if he has done well, he has only done what is naturally required of him, and what he must be required to do a hundred times a day with as much ease and fixedness of purpose as appear in his use of speech. In view of the danger thus indicated, it is desirable that a child more commonly *feel* that he has gained approval rather than *hear* the expression of it. It is with encouragement, as with so much besides,—it is most easily conveyed through the eye, and by this vehicle of communication there is least risk of error or injurious effects. A look is, indeed, fleeting, and cannot be long sustained; but there is an advantage in this for the purpose here contemplated. On the other hand, however fleeting, a look of encouragement is long remembered by a child. It is greatly more appreciated, and much better remembered than a geography lesson. In the case of those who are apt to be crushed with the sense of frequent failure, and are in danger of having feeling embittered, some words of encouragement will be greatly more influential than heavy punishment. Only, the occasion for commendation must come naturally. It must first be felt to have been deserved, else it blunts the finer feelings and hurts the character. Genuineness is essential everywhere. Merited commendation should however be readily given. "Honour to whom honour is due." To a child who finds it hard to do what is right, a single statement made privately that his efforts in this direction have been observed and appreciated, will spread out its influence over whole days. In all this we need to beware of allowing ourselves to be hampered by the fear of promoting the growth of pride. Observation and sagacity are required as to times and ways of expressing approval. We must guard ourselves against favouring a proud disposition ; but we must no less anxiously guard against the peril of fostering a mock humility. Certain things are to be blamed, let them be blamed undeviatingly : other things are to be praised, let us give them their due no less freely. If only mutual understanding be established between teacher and pupil, a most powerful impulse in the direction of moral improvement can be communicated from day to day. In the learning of lessons, in conflict with evil passions, and in all forms of well-doing, there is an immense difference between one discouraged and one who is warned and cheered by a friendly counsellor. The task for the scholar is in any case the same. But when encouraged he works with more ardour and expectation of success. He feels all about him the moral support of one older and more experienced, who is personally concerned in a result to be reached by slow stages, and which is so important as to colour the whole life.

The opening RELIGIOUS EXERCISES of each day, if properly conducted, must greatly aid the work of training. The ratepayers of the country have declared unmistakeably for religious teaching as the true support of moral training. Teachers who include moral training in their ideal of professional duty will be thankful for the decision. The " Conscience Clause " frees a teacher from irksome apprehensions as to interference with the religious convictions of those who have intrusted him with the delicate task of training their children. The teacher is assured that in these opening religious exercises he is starting the work of the day as the great bulk of the people wish him to do, while complete protection has been provided for exceptional cases. As a moral trainer, the teacher is immensely aided by opportunity for touching the deeper feelings of human nature. To lift the whole set of duties into the light of God's eye, and to associate childhood's efforts with the wealth of divine sympathy and help, is at once to raise life higher, and make effort easier and more gladsome. To link the moral sentiments with the religious feelings is to bring the strong forces of the human mind into play for support of arduous effort. I do not touch the underlying problems of religious conviction with which every thinker must concern himself. The teacher is as likely as any— more likely than most—to feel the interest of such problems. But, as a teacher, his work is practical, not speculative. He seeks a full culture for the children, within the limits which their slender capacities prescribe. The religious exercises with which the school is opened favour him greatly in his plan. Nothing can more contribute to thoughtful self-control than simplicity of devotional service, and familiarity with the touching scenes in the life of our Saviour. But here, as everywhere, reality is the test of efficiency. Formality in devotion and carelessness in reading Scripture destroy the value of the opening exercises, and turn them into a source of danger. The prayers and Scripture lessons do not carry their own meaning to the pupils. The manner, tone, and style of utterance adopted by the teacher constitute the vehicle of thought and feeling to the young mind. The familiar petitions of " the Lord's Prayer," for example, must become the living desires of the teacher, and find true emotional utterance, if the prayer is to become more than a decent form. Bible-reading by the teachers should be an example of good reading—that is, reading which conveys the apprehended thought to the listening ear. The affecting scenes in the life and death of our Lord Jesus Christ must have their pathos actually expressed if they are to exercise any moulding influence over the disposition and conduct of the pupils.

CHAPTER V.

CLOSING WORDS TO TEACHERS.

WHAT has been said as to the ends of teaching, and the means to be employed for attaining them, is enough to show that the duties devolving on a teacher are of no slight difficulty. But to a competent teacher the work never can be uninteresting. Those who wish an easy life would act wisely did they turn in some other direction than the school-room. Those who are willing to give thought, and patience, and strenuous effort to the work of life will find in the school-room a most attractive sphere of usefulness. Much is said of the routine of a teacher's life. It is a one-sided view which leads to the remark. In so far as the subjects to be taught are concerned, it is routine, but in no other sense. There is, indeed, endless variety in school life. The unfolding of youthful minds, with the varying phases of curiosity and carelessness, erroneous apprehension, and quick recognition of what is taught, presents an increasing source of attraction. The early attempts at self-government,

108

with their comical failures and more serious outbreaks, their flow of feeling, now playful, now serious, and again deepening into passion, make a teacher's life one of the most lively. If a dull feeling of sameness creep over our minds, there is something wrong with ourselves in our teaching. With the lofty end the teacher has in view, and the variety of nature presented in a considerable gathering of children, a teacher's work should never seem tame.

The grand ends of teaching are embraced in the two words *Instruction* and *Training.* Failing in these, or in either of them, the teacher fails to attain the end he has set himself to reach. A lower aim cannot be accepted without falling beneath the true professional level. No true teacher can make salary the end of effort. No matter in what profession a man may be, if pay is the one end for which he works he is self-degraded. We come very near the source of sound moral life in this matter. The discussions of ancient philosophers as to receiving payment for teaching show how much the dignity and power of the teacher were conceived to be dependent on superiority to the mercenary spirit. If these philosophers discussed the question, not only with eagerness, but even with undue keenness of feeling, this shows how important it seemed in their eyes. We can discuss the question now free from the feeling occasioned by the conduct of professed Sophists. We clearly see how honourable it is that a man should live by his profession; but we as clearly perceive that it is unworthy of a man to hold his profession exclusively for the living it affords. It is, however, well for us, and for all interests concerned, that pay is needed by all workers in the several spheres of human activity. This granted, it is clear the teacher's salary should be such as to give him a good position in society. If the general standard of income for teachers be low in any country, it indicates either want of spirit among the people, or want of reflection as to the real value of education. Our country is not without blame in this respect, but fortunately a remedy has been provided. The School Boards of the country. have shown their sense of the value of liberal remuneration for efficient service. High efficiency and high pay must go together. This is a lesson which by force of circumstances the School Boards are likely to press on each other's attention. On the other hand, it is of unspeakable importance that the teacher keep his own mind fixed on some end vastly higher than payment. There is a wide difference between making a livelihood by one's profession, and discharging professional duties for the sake of the livelihood. Toil and remuneration are naturally associated ; but money is a poor reward for life-long effort in any sphere. " A fair day's wage for a fair day's work " is a just maxim to be put to use by all. But the man who makes this maxim the sole test of contract degrades himself, whether he be employer or employed. On the one side, much depends upon what is meant by fair pay ; on the other, what is meant by fair

work. The rule so often repeated as the em-
bodiment of justice, can afford, as we daily
see, shelter for a very low ideal of life. As to
"fair work," much more is involved in it than
a time-measure can indicate, or than muscle-
force, or even brain-force, can supply. Routine
work implies a worker who is a drudge, and
who cannot comply with the maxim in any
righteous sense. To have an ideal of our work,
and to come as near to it as possible, should be
the great aim with us all. I have touched the
question of pay only because under the arrangements of our national system teachers seem to
be exposed to special temptations. "Payment by result" is only a special modification
of the maxim,—"A fair day's wage for a fair
day's work." It is equitable, and in the
management of a general scheme, inevitable.
But it leaves the highest things unacknow-
ledged, and is apt to turn attention from them.
It can be easily squared with a vulgarized type
of school management. It can take the finer
and nobler qualities of influence entirely out of
school life. It is a sound principle within its
own field of application, but applied beyond its
own appropriate and narrow sphere it becomes
actually pernicious. None but the teacher can
defend the nation from the evil consequences
of its own system of pecuniary rewards. To
work to the "Code" is needful, to work to no
higher standard is voluntary degradation. The
most favourable report of an inspector speaks
only to the former, and may by its expression
of approval cover with respectability a most

serious deficiency. The teacher must aim at satisfying the "Code," and doing a great deal more. Children must be taught to read, write, and count. This much the Education Department must require, and the attainment in each case can be exactly tested. But educated children must contribute a great deal more to national life than these attainments imply. Results in this higher sphere the Department has no means of testing. Development of character cannot be codified and measured by results. There are results of teaching which are unspeakably important, yet which will not bring a single shilling of addition to the school grant. But parents will appreciate what the inspector has to pass by unnamed. School Boards will estimate at a high rate what the Department cannot place in the schedule.

Work has its real reward in the end it seeks. Work which cannot be reckoned for in money payments has a better recompence. To make good citizens, as Plato was wont to argue, is better than to seek pleasure; or better still, as Christianity teaches the lesson, to aid others in attaining moral goodness in all its forms is a task worthy of the highest endowments. Here it is the teacher can render the greatest service. No nation can keep in the front rank except by education. For stability and influence the nation must look to parents and teachers, who are moulding the character of the rising generation. During the Franco-German war, the oft-repeated remark was that the schoolmaster had gained the German victories. The fact was clearly established. Germany had the best intelligence of the country in the ranks. Under our military system nothing akin to this can happen; but the roots of national influence go immensely deeper than the army, and stretch immensely wider. It is the morality underlying the intelligence which is the secret spring of vital energy in a people. The war test we do not wish to see applied; but if British teachers can quietly and steadily turn the forces of vice and crime, we shall have reason to rejoice more than the Germans did over the return of their victorious troops. Our worst foes are within our own borders. Our best friends are those within our own lines, who promote intelligence, self-control, and devotion to a noble life. Amongst these our teachers stand conspicuous. But it is never to be overlooked in our estimate of teaching that moral fruits are the best. If a teacher, year by year, present the great bulk of his scholars for examination, and succeed in passing over 90 per cent. of them in all departments, he may well be congratulated. But there is another aim higher still. It is to have his scholars so habituated to self-control, that they shall be prepared for wise direction of their own conduct when all the checks and helps of home and school are completely withdrawn. In such a case the after-life of the scholars will reflect honour on his labours as discovering, though at a great distance of time, the fruits of the discipline of school life. This is the highest result of educational effort. It is the full reward of anxious

H

thought and toil. In such a case the teacher sees his own better life reproduced in those who caught from him many of their early impulses towards a life of moral elevation.

CHAPTER VI.

HOME TRAINING.

EDUCATION cannot all be done at school. The discipline of the class-room does not fully meet educational requirements. Home must supply the influence reaching deepest, with most effective appreciation of individual peculiarities, both checking and encouraging, as these are required. Parents cannot rightly estimate home training without placing it high among the educational appliances at command.] They cannot give themselves to it without being soon convinced that the most important part of it is the work of encouragement. A power to check, and to go to the roots of motive in doing so, is needful; but its wise exercise requires sparing use. Encouragement should be the prevailing influence, streaming in upon the home, like the sunshine which brightens all things. Cloudy times should be rare. To lighten the discouragements of school, to aid the struggle for self-control, to keep the mind alive to the inducements to work, these are the results which wise home training can secure. Success in this requires much thought and effort. Parents cannot succeed, any more than teachers can, without self-discipline.

Prominent in the plan for early training should be maintenance of harmony between school work and home management. To call in the aid of professional teachers is at the same time to undertake the responsibility of fostering in our children respect for their teachers. But this is only the first and most general aspect of parental duty in this rela- . tion. Co-operation in a still wider sense is required. The arrangements of the home should to the utmost harmonise with the work of the school. The two agencies may readily conflict. For genuine educational success, they must be tributary to a common end. The home must help the school, in order that the latter may be reasonably required to contribute its full influence for the intellectual and moral development of the children.

This leads directly to the question of home preparation for school work, and this to the grand home grievance, the burden of lesson-learning. After the day has been spent at school, the evening is spent in learning what is to be the subject of examination on the day following. School gets the fresh hours, home the later hours, when the young people are wearied, and consequently more irritable, and less disposed to learn. The elements of parental (I fear mainly maternal) burden are thus inevitably accumulated, and the question comes to be, how to lessen the burden for parents by lessening it for the children. As already said, this lies first with the school, for teachers are not to be mere lesson-hearers, nor are they to be burden-makers. By them care must be daily directed on the amount of work which can be wisely imposed in view of the age and progress of the pupils. There is, however, an important share of responsibility resting on the home circle. Parents need to be specially guarded in their expectations as to the quantity of work to be overtaken at school. There is a reasonable amount to be expected; but educational results are not wisely judged by a standard of quantity, though parents are peculiarly prone to make this the rule. It is a rough-and-ready test, but not the most reliable, for every one sees that quantity may be imposed to the serious injury of instruction and training. The rule for parents must be to moderate expectations as to quantity. The true test of progress is not the number of pages overtaken in a book, nor the number of branches included in a course of instruction, but the interest, appreciation, and self-control of the pupils. Interest requires freshness of material; appreciation is possible only through action of intelligence; and self-control can be judged reasonably only by guarding against over-exaction. These things are to be pondered by parents as well as by teachers.

The government of the home must, however, deal in its own way with this burden of lesson-learning—a sore enough burden for most of the learners, to be lessened by all reasonable means.   Observation is best turned on a prudent mixture of play and work after school hours.   Fortunately, children for the most part readily find amusement for themselves if they are only set free.   But some degree of inventiveness may be required, specially to meet the case of children having no great inclination for active exercise.   Physical exercise of some kind, fresh air as much as possible, and general hilarity, are the grand requisites. Let the play hours be bright and free, with as few restrictions as possible.   This touches the easiest part of the business, but a part to be guarded with unwavering determination.   Still the question remains, What can be done when the body is weary, interest flagging, and the lessons only half finished?   Superintendence of the work must take note of the state of the learners.   A break of fifteen minutes, wisely used by judicious direction of interest in a new channel, may secure effective work for an hour thereafter, instead of weariness and fret.   Skill in relieving tedium is a valuable acquirement for those who superintend young learners.   At the same time it is needful that the learners have constantly in mind the fact that difficulties must be faced, cannot be escaped.

This subject introduces a speciality which should distinguish the Boarding-school, where the difficult combination of School and Home is undertaken.   A valuable part in our educational work is fulfilled by our Boarding-schools, which, however, encounter their own special difficulties. What they have to aim at is to provide home life, distinguishing in a marked way between the rigid discipline of school hours and the relaxation of home engagements, as well as the work of home preparations. Only the skilful disciplinarian can succeed well in this task, which requires self-command in an unusual degree. Relaxing of stern rule; ready allowance for individual preference; breezy, cheery humour that hurts nobody, but helps everybody; and true sympathy with all the difficulties to be met; these are the achievements of one who has the gift of genial home management, along with command in the classroom.

Reverting, however, to the work of parents in home training, it is needful to do all that can be done to secure thoroughness of preparation. The risks of careless preparation are great. If these are to be shunned, it is impossible to escape toil. And such toil is well expended at the early stages of school life, when the habits of children are being formed. Parental discrimination should provide for greater patience and more direct help, in cases where lessons are harder to learn. A mind naturally interested and absorbed may not need much supervision or interference; but a mind to which the occupation is unpleasant, and the process slow, needs guidance and suggestion. The method at once the most direct, and the most effective, is that the parent (or tutor) be as far as possible a learner of the lesson along with the pupil. Mere lesson-hearing may be as unsatisfactory in the home circle as in the schoolroom. It may be a bootless discovery of the ignorance already well known to the young scholar. The most effective supervision is that which attacks the task of learning at an earlier stage, aiding the memory by suggestion, and the understanding by suitable explanation, leading the child into the knowledge he has to acquire. This may seem quite an unreasonably laborious way of helping, but it may prove the least laborious, as it is certainly the most effective.

Beyond this question of lesson-learning, and apart from conjoint arrangements with school, there rises the wider aspect of home training. This brings into view the whole influence of parents in regulating the life of their children, so as to stimulate and develop their powers. Definiteness of plan, or intelligent preconception, is required here in all directions. In the matter of amusements, extremes are to be shunned. Restriction there must be, but a predominantly restrictive plan is unfavourable. It is undesirable that a child should be always encountering checks like a caged bird. On the other hand, regulation of amusement, so as to limit its forms, and the amount of time given to it, is essential. The training of children to regulate their own amusement, and to recognise fitting occasions for self-denial, is a large achievement. In the matter of general conduct, self-regulation in acknowledgment of the right, is the goal to be reached, and parental

influence is valuable in the proportion in which
it promotes this. Authority over a child there
must be, but bare authority is dangerous in
exercise; the limit for us being, that it gain
the assent of our intelligence, and be fitted to
secure the child's approval when calm and
unbiassed. To shift from the rule of inclination to that of intelligence is an arduous business, not soon over; but the effort must begin
early, under parental sway, and it is most
effectually aided when parental government is
sympathetic and reflective. A child's difficulties must be fairly measured, but a child's
desires must not rule. In view of the delicate
and difficult work to be done, with certainty
of not a little blundering on the part of parents,
as well as of children, much depends on the
general spirit and style of home life. A pervading moral and religious influence should
encompass everything in domestic life, as the
atmosphere surrounds the earth, the common
abode of mankind. All need an ultimate
appeal, an indubitable certainty, an unques-
tionable authority, and these we find in the
laws of right conduct, and the sway of God
ruling over all in righteousness and mercy.
Parents and children find a common level in
a common subjection to sovereign authority.
Parental control is safely exercised in habitual
acknowledgment of the highest authority.
Subjection to home government of this type
involves a sense of security and peacefulness,
for it implies, in the main, escape from the
fickle rule of shifting moods, or rising and

falling passion. Parents want some clearer rule than natural affection. It is a fallacy, however popular, to maintain that love will accomplish all. Love seeks the good of its object, but intelligence sees what that good is. Love should be encompassed by reverence, within which its own promptings must often be restrained, for even love itself cannot escape subjection to law; while an unregulated, or ill regulated affection may injure those it means to favour. The blending of intelligence and affection with reverence for the Most High, constitutes the true excellence of human nature, and provides for the wisest and most beneficent domestic rule. This will make parents the companions and friends of their children, attracting them by an unseen influence towards the qualities of character which will enable them to do their true part as men and women.

While a pervading parental influence is the grand instrumentality, the family table affords the best opportunity for advancing education in its most important sense. The family board is the meeting-place where converse is freest, formality is banished, all that concerns life comes up for consideration according to natural suggestion, and opportunities for training occur in the most valuable form. Here there is fellowship of spirit which is the grand prerequisite for educational power, unreserved utterance disclosing feelings and dispositions, as well as the suggestions from others which have impressed the mind, and, with these, opportunity for stirring thought and awaking impression, the more valuable that the conversational style is constantly maintained, while formality of direct teaching is avoided. The family table is the most powerful educational agency, when rightly used. If this observation be taken as a paradox, the fact will illustrate how prone we are to underestimate indirect influence, and to fall into the error of supposing that children learn only what they are formally taught. No teaching is so powerful with children as that which does not seem to be teaching. What is the influence of a companion narrating some exploit, or depicting some expected enjoyment! How large is the interest for young people in a debate on the fairness of a move in a game, or on some advantage made at the cost of another, or on the merits of a race or contest of any kind! And are not all the questions of morals being canvassed in this way, and materials being supplied for conversation? Let the day's interest flow freely around and over the family table; there is no better method for supplying educational opportunities. Let the things of greatest moment in the parents' lives be talked over as freely as things more immediately coming under the observation of the children. Let a higher life touch their life at points likely to awaken interest. At the family board, we must guard against limitation of range, for there are few things in which we are more seriously at fault than in the unexpressed opinion that matters of public concern cannot engage children. The sources of human interest include what is common to all, though the area varies in range. The wider area may therefore provide for the narrower. The family circle presents the strongest claim to the best influence of those at its head, as its gatherings afford the best opportunities for contributing to the enriching of thought and feeling. The children of a household should be favoured according to the range of observation, thought, and experience of their parents. If what has now been stated be true to reason, it is manifest that an immense educational gain is secured when all the children of a family meet regularly around the family board. There children are not hearing commands issued,—they are not being talked down to, as from an eminence,—each contributes a share to what is spoken, and is encouraged in doing so, while the blending influence of father and mother is most advantageously felt. There is more humour, quaintness of thought, play of fancy, odd suggestiveness, perplexed thought, and tremulous feeling in a family circle, than is ever known unless from the un-trammelled conversation of the table. To carry forward home training in its truest sense the children must be regularly with their parents at the table. Some may regard this as too troublesome, breaking in on needful quiet. Such a view involves a double mistake. Conversation in the family circle occasions little strain, and supplies the most quietly refreshing influences. Our household arrangements either surrender or preserve the most valuable of our educational appliances. A nursery table may be in some respects convenient, but, except for very young children, it involves a serious sacrifice of educational opportunity and power. It must be an unexpected result, if a nurse can do as much for the training of children as parents can do. So little is this likely to be the case, that there seems to be a clear educational gain in the history of families who cannot summon the aid of attendants, provided the parents themselves be more than attendants to their children. And in estimating training, it must be recognised that drill in manners has only a subordinate value in comparison with culture of the intellect and good dispositions. The influence of well-directed conversation can indeed hardly be overestimated. By this means, children gain acquaintance with great national occurrences; have their hearts stirred by examples of courage and self-sacrifice; are trained to genuine sympathy with others; begin to feel a personal concern in great efforts of practical benevolence, and specially in the grand enterprise of the Christian Church in seeking to evangelise the world. Every incident worth dwelling upon—every benevolent enterprise engaging the efforts of men—every event of national or international importance, becomes an aid in the work of education. Better that the conversation be at times over the heads of the children, than that table-talk should be reduced to commonplace.

A humorous story, well told; a touching incident, feelingly narrated; a public transaction,
carefully explained; a course of conduct deliberately canvassed; praise and censure distri-
buted with obvious deliberation and justice;
all have high educational value. Thus children
are helped to see the bright side of things; to
feel for others; to understand the intricacies
of social life; to decide on the right and wrong
in conduct. In observation of such results
parents are allowed the satisfaction of witness-
ing their success in the early training of their
children.

PRINTED BY T. AND A. CONSTABLE, PRINTERS TO HER MAJESTY,

AT THE EDINBURGH UNIVERSITY PRESS.

WORKS BY PROFESSOR CALDERWOOD.

I.

The Philosophy of the Infinite:

A Treatise on Man's Knowledge of the Infinite Being, in Answer to Sir William Hamilton and Dean Mansel. 8vo. Out of print. 7s. 6d.

"It is the most independent metaphysical essay we have read for a long time."
—*North British Review.*
"A book of great ability."—*British Quarterly Review.*

II.

Handbook of Moral Philosophy.

12mo.   Tenth Edition.   6s.

"It is, we feel convinced, the best handbook on the subject, intellectually and morally, and does infinite credit to its author."—*Standard.*

III.

On Teaching: Its Ends and Means.

12mo.   Fourth Edition, with Chapter on "Home Training." 2s. 6d.   A Book for Teachers and Parents.

"Eminently sensible and suggestive."—*Scotsman.*
"Here is a book which combines merits of the highest (and, alas! the rarest) order. . . . We have rarely met with anything on the subject of teaching which seemed to us to appeal so directly both to the teacher's head and heart, and give him so clear an insight into the true nature of his calling."—*Monthly Journal of Education.*

IV.

The Relations of Mind and Brain.

Second Edition, revised and enlarged, with an additional Chapter on Animal Intelligence.   8vo.   12s.

NOTICES OF FIRST EDITION.

"Professor Calderwood exhibits an extensive acquaintance with the facts of Cerebral Anatomy, Physiology, and Pathology worthy of any technical Neurologist."—*Nature.*
"Altogether his work is probably the best combination to be had at present in England of exposition and criticism on the subject of physiological psychology."
—*Academy.*
"Dr. Calderwood's is an able and excellent book."—*Spectator.*
"The subject is treated in a manner worthy of its importance."—*Brain.*

The Relations of Mind and Brain:—

NOTICES OF SECOND EDITION.

"Contains the suggestion of a principle which may prove to be capable of explaining much that is at present obscure in the relations between the mind and the body."—*The Scotsman.*

"Professor Calderwood's 'Relations of Mind and Brain' is one of the most cautious, and at the same time exhaustive treatises which we have on the subject." —*British Quarterly Review.*

"In the new chapter on Animal Intelligence, Dr. Calderwood does excellent service by bringing expressly into view the peculiarities of Sense-Endowment distinguishing the different classes of animals (ants, dogs, etc.) for which exceptional intelligence is claimed; and he is thus able to account for much in their action that is too readily regarded as mysterious."—*Mind.*

V.

The Parables of our Lord Interpreted in view of their Relations to each other.

12mo.   Second Edition.   6s.

"A book which must survive many others on the same subject."—*The London Quarterly Review.*

VI.

The Relations of Science and Religion:

A Statement of the Scientific Position.   Being the Morse Lecture for 1880.   12mo.   5s.

"It must be admitted that Professor Calderwood is a candid writer."—*Westminster Review.*

"Of great interest and value to the theological student."—*John Bull.*

"Marked both by ability and moderation in tone. . . . Dr. Calderwood's argument breathes throughout the true spirit in which science and religion should approach each other."—*Saturday Review.*

MACMILLAN & CO., LONDON.

Sept. 1891

A Catalogue

OF

Educational Books

PUBLISHED BY

Macmillan & Co.

BEDFORD STREET, STRAND, LONDON

CONTENTS

A

CLASSICS.

Elementary Classics; Classical Series; Classical Library, (1) Texts, (2) Translations; Grammar, Composition, and Philology; Antiquities, Ancient History, and Philosophy.

*ELEMENTARY CLASSICS.

18mo, Eighteenpence each.

The following contain Introductions, Notes, **and Vocabularies,** and in some cases **Exercises.**

ACCIDENCE, LATIN, AND EXERCISES ARRANGED FOR BEGINNERS.—By W. WELCH, M.A., and C. G. DUFFIELD, M.A.

AESCHYLUS.—PROMETHEUS VINCTUS. By Rev. H. M. STEPHENSON, M.A.

ARRIAN.—SELECTIONS. With Exercises. By Rev. JOHN BOND, M.A., and Rev. A. S. WALPOLE, M.A.

AULUS GELLIUS, STORIES FROM.—Adapted for Beginners. With Exercises. By Rev. G. H. NALL, M.A., Assistant Master at Westminster.

CÆSAR.—THE HELVETIAN WAR. Being Selections from Book I. of The Gallic War. Adapted for Beginners. With Exercises. By W. WELCH, M.A., and C. G. DUFFIELD, M.A.

THE INVASION OF BRITAIN. Being Selections from Books IV. and V. of The Gallic War. Adapted for Beginners. With Exercises. By W. WELCH, M.A., and C. G. DUFFIELD, M.A.

SCENES FROM BOOKS V. AND VI. By C. COLBECK, M.A.

THE GALLIC WAR. BOOK I. By Rev. A. S. WALPOLE, M.A.

BOOKS II. AND III. By the Rev. W. G. RUTHERFORD, M.A., LL.D.

BOOK IV. By CLEMENT BRYANS, M.A., Assistant Master at Dulwich College.

BOOK V. By C. COLBECK, M.A., Assistant Master at Harrow.

BOOK VI. By the same Editor.

BOOK VII. By Rev. J. BOND, M.A., and Rev. A. S. WALPOLE, M.A.

THE CIVIL WAR. BOOK I. By M. MONTGOMERY, M.A. [In the Press.

CICERO.—DE SENECTUTE. By E. S. SHUCKBURGH, M.A.

DE AMICITIA. By the same Editor.

STORIES OF ROMAN HISTORY. Adapted for Beginners. With Exercises. By Rev. G. E. JEANS, M.A., and A. V. JONES, M.A.

EURIPIDES.—ALCESTIS. By Rev. M. A. BAYFIELD, M.A.

MEDEA. By A. W. VERRALL, Litt.D., and Rev. M. A. BAYFIELD, M.A. [In the Press.

HECUBA. By Rev. J. BOND, M.A., and Rev. A. S. WALPOLE, M.A.

EUTROPIUS.—Adapted for Beginners. With Exercises. By W. WELCH, M.A., and C. G. DUFFIELD, M.A.

HERODOTUS. TALES FROM HERODOTUS. Atticised by G. S. FARNELL, M.A. [In the Press.

HOMER.—ILIAD. BOOK I. By Rev. J. BOND, M.A., and Rev. A. S. WALPOLE, M.A.

BOOK XVIII. By S. R. JAMES, M.A., Assistant Master at Eton.

ODYSSEY. BOOK I. By Rev. J. BOND, M.A., and Rev. A. S. WALPOLE, M.A.

HORACE.—ODES. BOOKS I.–IV. By T. E. PAGE, M.A., Assistant Master at the Charterhouse. Each 1s. 6d.

LIVY.—BOOK I. By H. M. STEPHENSON, M.A.

BOOK XXI. Adapted from Mr. Capes's Edition. By J. E. MELHUISH, M.A.

BOOK XXII. By the same.

THE HANNIBALIAN WAR. Being part of the XXI. and XXII. BOOKS OF LIVY adapted for Beginners. By G. C. MACAULAY, M.A.

THE SIEGE OF SYRACUSE. Being part of the XXIV. and XXV. BOOKS OF LIVY, adapted for Beginners. With Exercises. By G. RICHARDS, M.A., and Rev. A. S. WALPOLE, M.A.

LEGENDS OF ANCIENT ROME. Adapted for Beginners. With Exercises. By H. WILKINSON, M.A.

LUCIAN.—EXTRACTS FROM LUCIAN. With Exercises. By Rev. J. BOND, M.A., and Rev. A. S. WALPOLE, M.A.

NEPOS.—SELECTIONS ILLUSTRATIVE OF GREEK AND ROMAN HISTORY. With Exercises. By G. S. FARNELL, M.A.

OVID.—SELECTIONS. By E. S. SHUCKBURGH, M.A.

EASY SELECTIONS FROM OVID IN ELEGIAC VERSE. With Exercises. By H. WILKINSON, M.A.

STORIES FROM THE METAMORPHOSES. With Exercises. By Rev. J. BOND, M.A., and Rev. A. S. WALPOLE, M.A.

PHÆDRUS.—SELECT FABLES. Adapted for Beginners. With Exercises. By Rev. A. S. WALPOLE, M.A.

THUCYDIDES.—THE RISE OF THE ATHENIAN EMPIRE. BOOK I. CHS. 89–117 and 228–238. With Exercises. By F. H. COLSON, M.A.

VIRGIL.—SELECTIONS. By E. S. SHUCKBURGH, M.A.

BUCOLICS. By T. E. PAGE, M.A.

GEORGICS. BOOK I. By the same Editor.

BOOK II. By Rev. J. H. SKRINE, M.A.

ÆNEID. BOOK I. By Rev. A. S. WALPOLE, M.A.

BOOK II. By T. E. PAGE, M.A.

BOOK III. By the same Editor.

BOOK IV. By Rev. H. M. STEPHENSON, M.A.

BOOK V. By Rev. A. CALVERT, M.A.

BOOK VI. By T. E. PAGE, M.A.

BOOK VII. By Rev. A. CALVERT, M.A.

BOOK VIII. By the same Editor.

BOOK IX. By Rev. H. M. STEPHENSON, M.A.

BOOK X. By S. G. OWEN, M.A.

XENOPHON.—ANABASIS. Selections, adapted for Beginners. With Exercises. By W. WELCH, M.A., and C. G. DUFFIELD, M.A.

BOOK I. With Exercises. By E. A. WELLS, M.A.

BOOK I. By Rev. A. S. WALPOLE, M.A.

BOOK II. By the same Editor.

BOOK III. By Rev. G. H. NALL, M.A.

BOOK IV. By Rev. E. D. STONE, M.A.

SELECTIONS FROM BOOK IV. With Exercises. By the same Editor.

SELECTIONS FROM THE CYROPÆDIA. With Exercises. By A. H. COOKE, M.A., Fellow and Lecturer of King's College, Cambridge.

The following contain Introductions and Notes, **but no Vocabulary :—**

CICERO.—SELECT LETTERS. By Rev. G. E. JEANS, M.A.

HERODOTUS.—SELECTIONS FROM BOOKS VII. AND VIII. THE EXPEDITION OF XERXES. By A. H. COOKE, M.A.

HORACE.—SELECTIONS FROM THE SATIRES AND EPISTLES. By Rev. W. J. V. BAKER, M.A.

SELECT EPODES AND ARS POETICA. By H. A. DALTON, M.A., Assistant Master at Winchester.

PLATO.—EUTHYPHRO AND MENEXENUS. By C. E. GRAVES, M.A.

TERENCE.—SCENES FROM THE ANDRIA. By F. W. CORNISH, M.A., Assistant Master at Eton.

THE GREEK ELEGIAC POETS.—FROM CALLINUS TO CALLIMACHUS. Selected by Rev. HERBERT KYNASTON, D.D.

THUCYDIDES.—BOOK IV. CHS. 1-41. THE CAPTURE OF SPHACTERIA. By C. E. GRAVES, M.A.

CLASSICAL SERIES
FOR COLLEGES AND SCHOOLS.

Fcap. 8vo.

ÆSCHINES.—IN CTESIPHONTA. By Rev. T. GWATKIN, M.A., and E. S. SHUCKBURGH, M.A. 5s.

ÆSCHYLUS.—PERSÆ. By A. O. PRICKARD, M.A., Fellow and Tutor of New College, Oxford. With Map. 2s. 6d.

SEVEN AGAINST THEBES. SCHOOL EDITION. By A. W. VERRALL, Litt.D., Fellow of Trinity College, Cambridge, and M. A. BAYFIELD, M.A., Headmaster of Christ's College, Brecon. 2s. 6d.

ANDOCIDES.—DE MYSTERIIS. By W. J. HICKIE, M.A. 2s. 6d.

ATTIC ORATORS.—Selections from ANTIPHON, ANDOCIDES, LYSIAS, ISOCRATES, and ISAEUS. By R. C. JEBB, Litt.D., Regius Professor of Greek in the University of Cambridge. 5s.

*CÆSAR.—THE GALLIC WAR. By Rev. JOHN BOND, M.A., and Rev. A. S. WALPOLE, M.A. With Maps. 4s. 6d.

CATULLUS.—SELECT POEMS. Edited by F. P. SIMPSON, B.A. 3s. 6d. The Text of this Edition is carefully expurgated for School use.

*CICERO.—THE CATILINE ORATIONS. By A. S. WILKINS, Litt.D., Professor of Latin in the Owens College, Victoria University, Manchester. 2s. 6d.

PRO LEGE MANILIA. By Prof. A. S. WILKINS, Litt.D. 2s. 6d.

THE SECOND PHILIPPIC ORATION. By JOHN E. B. MAYOR, M.A., Professor of Latin in the University of Cambridge. 3s. 6d.

PRO ROSCIO AMERINO. By E. H. DONKIN, M.A. 2s. 6d.

PRO P. SESTIO. By Rev. H. A. HOLDEN, Litt.D. 3s. 6d.

SELECT LETTERS. Edited by R. Y. TYRRELL, M.A. [In the Press.

DEMOSTHENES.—DE CORONA. By B. DRAKE, M.A. 7th Edition, revised by E. S. SHUCKBURGH, M.A. 3s. 6d.

ADVERSUS LEPTINEM. By Rev. J. R. KING, M.A., Fellow and Tutor of Oriel College, Oxford. 2s. 6d.

THE FIRST PHILIPPIC. By Rev. T. GWATKIN, M.A. 2s. 6d.

IN MIDIAM. By Prof. A. S. WILKINS, Litt.D., and HERMAN HAGER, Ph.D., of the Owens College, Victoria University, Manchester. [In preparation.

EURIPIDES.—HIPPOLYTUS. By Rev. J. P. MAHAFFY, D.D., Fellow of Trinity College, and Professor of Ancient History in the University of Dublin, and J. B. BURY, M.A., Fellow of Trinity College, Dublin. 2s. 6d.

MEDEA. By A. W. VERRALL, Litt.D., Fellow of Trinity College, Cambridge. 2s. 6d.

IPHIGENIA IN TAURIS. By E. B. ENGLAND, M.A. 3s.

ION. By M. A. BAYFIELD, M.A., Headmaster of Christ's College, Brecon. 2s. 6d.

BACCHAE. By R. Y. TYRRELL, M.A., Regius Professor of Greek in the University of Dublin. [In preparation.

HERODOTUS.—BOOK III. By G. C. MACAULAY, M.A. 2s. 6d.

BOOK V. By J. STRACHAN, M.A., Professor of Greek in the Owens College, Victoria University, Manchester. [In preparation.

BOOK VI. By the same. 3s. 6d.

BOOK VII. By Mrs. A. F. BUTLER. 3s. 6d.

HESIOD.—THE WORKS AND DAYS. By W. T. LENDRUM, M.A., Assistant Master at Dulwich College. [In preparation.

HOMER.—ILIAD. BOOKS I., IX., XI., XVI.-XXIV. THE STORY OF ACHILLES. By the late J. H. Pratt, M.A., and Walter Leaf, Litt.D., Fellows of Trinity College, Cambridge. 5s.

ODYSSEY. BOOK IX. By Prof. John E. B. Mayor. 2s. 6d.

ODYSSEY. BOOKS XXI.-XXIV. THE TRIUMPH OF ODYSSEUS. By S. G. Hamilton, B.A., Fellow of Hertford College, Oxford. 2s. 6d.

HORACE.—*THE ODES. By T. E. Page, M.A., Assistant Master at the Charterhouse. 5s. (BOOKS I., II., III., and IV. separately, 2s. each.)

THE SATIRES. By Arthur Palmer, M.A., Professor of Latin in the University of Dublin. 5s.

THE EPISTLES AND ARS POETICA. By A. S. Wilkins, Litt.D., Professor of Latin in the Owens College, Victoria University, Manchester. 5s.

ISAEOS.—THE ORATIONS. By William Ridgeway, M.A., Professor of Greek in Queen's College, Cork. [In preparation.

JUVENAL.—*THIRTEEN SATIRES. By E. G. Hardy, M.A. 5s. The Text is carefully expurgated for School use.

SELECT SATIRES. By Prof. John E. B. Mayor. X. and XI. 3s. 6d. XII.-XVI. 4s. 6d.

LIVY.—*BOOKS II. and III. By Rev. H. M. Stephenson, M.A. 3s. 6d.

*BOOKS XXI. and XXII. By Rev. W. W. Capes, M.A. With Maps. 4s. 6d.

*BOOKS XXIII. and XXIV. By G. C. Macaulay, M.A. With Maps. 3s. 6d.

*THE LAST TWO KINGS OF MACEDON. EXTRACTS FROM THE FOURTH AND FIFTH DECADES OF LIVY. By F. H. Rawlins, M.A., Assistant Master at Eton. With Maps. 2s. 6d.

THE SUBJUGATION OF ITALY. SELECTIONS FROM THE FIRST DECADE. By G. E. Marindin, M.A. [In preparation.

LUCRETIUS.—BOOKS I.-III. By J. H. Warburton Lee, M.A., Assistant Master at Rossall. 3s. 6d.

LYSIAS.—SELECT ORATIONS. By E. S. Shuckburgh, M.A. 5s.

MARTIAL.—SELECT EPIGRAMS. By Rev. H. M. Stephenson, M.A. 5s.

*OVID.—FASTI. By G. H. Hallam, M.A., Assistant Master at Harrow. With Maps. 3s. 6d.

*HEROIDUM EPISTULÆ XIII. By E. S. Shuckburgh, M.A. 3s. 6d.

METAMORPHOSES. BOOKS I.-III. By C. Simmons, M.A. [In preparation.

BOOKS XIII. and XIV. By the same Editor. 3s. 6d.

PLATO.—LACHES. By M. T. Tatham, M.A. 2s. 6d.

THE REPUBLIC. BOOKS I.-V. By T. H. Warren, M.A., President of Magdalen College, Oxford. 5s.

PLAUTUS.—MILES GLORIOSUS. By R. Y. Tyrrell, M.A., Regius Professor of Greek in the University of Dublin. 2d Ed., revised. 3s. 6d.

AMPHITRUO. By Arthur Palmer, M.A., Professor of Latin in the University of Dublin. 3s. 6d.

CAPTIVI. By A. Rhys-Smith, M.A. [In the Press.

PLINY.—LETTERS. BOOKS I. and II. By J. Cowan, M.A., Assistant Master at the Manchester Grammar School. 3s.

LETTERS. BOOK III. By Prof. John E. B. Mayor. With Life of Pliny by G. H. Rendall, M.A. 3s. 6d.

PLUTARCH.—LIFE OF THEMISTOKLES. By Rev. H. A. Holden, Litt.D. 3s. 6d.

LIVES OF GALBA AND OTHO. By E. G. Hardy, M.A. 5s.

POLYBIUS.—THE HISTORY OF THE ACHÆAN LEAGUE AS CONTAINED IN THE REMAINS OF POLYBIUS. By W. W. Capes, M.A. 5s.

PROPERTIUS.—SELECT POEMS. By Prof. J. P. Postgate, Litt.D., Fellow of Trinity College, Cambridge. 2d Ed., revised. 5s.

SALLUST.—*CATILINA and JUGURTHA. By C. Merivale, D.D., Dean of Ely. 3s. 6d. Or separately, 2s. each.

*BELLUM CATULINÆ. By A. M. Cook, M.A., Assistant Master at St. Paul's School. 2s. 6d.

JUGURTHA. By the same Editor. [In preparation.

TACITUS.—THE ANNALS. BOOKS I. and II. By J. S. REID, Litt.D. [*In prep.*
THE ANNALS. BOOK VI. By A. J. CHURCH, M.A., and W. J. BRODRIBB, M.A. 2s.
THE HISTORIES. BOOKS I. and II. By A. D. GODLEY, M.A., Fellow of Magdalen College, Oxford. 3s. 6d. BOOKS III.-V. By the same. 3s. 6d.
AGRICOLA and GERMANIA. By A. J. CHURCH, M.A., and W. J. BRODRIBB, M.A. 3s. 6d. Or separately, 2s. each.
TERENCE.—HAUTON TIMORUMENOS. By E. S. SHUCKBURGH, M.A. 2s. 6d. With Translation. 3s. 6d.
PHORMIO. By Rev. JOHN BOND, M.A., and Rev. A. S. WALPOLE, M.A. 2s. 6d.
THUCYDIDES.—BOOK I. By C. BRYANS, M.A. [*In preparation.*
BOOK II. By E. C. MARCHANT, M.A., Assistant Master at St. Paul's. [*In the Press.*
BOOK III. By C. BRYANS, M.A. [*In preparation.*
BOOK IV. By C. E. GRAVES, M.A., Classical Lecturer at St. John's College, Cambridge. 3s. 6d.
BOOK V. By the same Editor. [*In the Press.*
BOOKS VI. AND VII. THE SICILIAN EXPEDITION. By Rev. PERCIVAL FROST, M.A. With Map. 3s. 6d.
BOOK VIII. By Prof. T. G. TUCKER, Litt.D. [*In the Press.*
TIBULLUS.—SELECT POEMS. By Prof. J. P. POSTGATE, Litt.D. [*In preparation.*
VIRGIL.—ÆNEID. BOOKS II. AND III. THE NARRATIVE OF ÆNEAS. By E. W. HOWSON, M.A., Assistant Master at Harrow. 2s.
XENOPHON.—*THE ANABASIS. BOOKS I.-IV. By Profs. W. W. GOODWIN and J. W. WHITE. Adapted to Goodwin's Greek Grammar. With Map. 3s. 6d.
HELLENICA. BOOKS I. AND II. By H. HAILSTONE, B.A. With Map. 2s. 6d.
CYROPÆDIA. BOOKS VII. AND VIII. By A. GOODWIN, M.A., Professor of Classics in University College, London. 2s. 6d.
MEMORABILIA SOCRATIS. By A. R. CLUER, B.A., Balliol College, Oxford. 5s.
HIERO. By Rev. H. A. HOLDEN, Litt.D., LL.D. 2s. 6d.
OECONOMICUS. By the same. With Lexicon. 5s.

CLASSICAL LIBRARY.

Texts, Edited with **Introductions and Notes**, for the use of Advanced Students ; **Commentaries and Translations.**

ÆSCHYLUS.—THE SUPPLICES. A Revised Text, with Translation. By T. G. TUCKER, Litt.D., Professor of Classical Philology in the University of Melbourne. 8vo. 10s. 6d.
THE SEVEN AGAINST THEBES. With Translation. By A. W. VERRALL, Litt.D., Fellow of Trinity College, Cambridge. 8vo. 7s. 6d.
AGAMEMNON. With Translation. By A. W. VERRALL, Litt.D. 8vo. 12s.
AGAMEMNON, CHOEPHORŒ, AND EUMENIDES. By A. O. PRICKARD, M.A., Fellow and Tutor of New College, Oxford. 8vo. [*In preparation.*
THE EUMENIDES. With Verse Translation. By BERNARD DRAKE, M.A. 8vo. 5s.
ANTONINUS, MARCUS AURELIUS.—BOOK IV. OF THE MEDITATIONS. With Translation. By HASTINGS CROSSLEY, M.A. 8vo. 6s.
ARISTOTLE.—THE METAPHYSICS. BOOK I. Translated by a Cambridge Graduate. 8vo. 5s.
THE POLITICS. By R. D. HICKS, M.A., Fellow of Trinity College, Cambridge. 8vo. [*In the Press.*
THE POLITICS. Translated by Rev. J. E. C. WELLDON, M.A., Headmaster of Harrow. Cr. 8vo. 10s. 6d.
THE RHETORIC. Translated by the same. Cr. 8vo. 7s. 6d.
AN INTRODUCTION TO ARISTOTLE'S RHETORIC. With Analysis, Notes, and Appendices. By E. M. COPE, Fellow and late Tutor of Trinity College, Cambridge. 8vo. 14s

THE ETHICS. Translated by Rev. J. E. C. WELLDON, M.A. Cr. 8vo. [*In prep.*
THE SOPHISTICI ELENCHI. With Translation. By E. POSTE, M.A., Fellow of Oriel College, Oxford. 8vo. 8s. 6d.
ON THE CONSTITUTION OF ATHENS. Edited by J. E. SANDYS, Litt.D.
ON THE CONSTITUTION OF ATHENS. Translated by E. POSTE, M.A. Cr. 8vo. 3s. 6d.
ON THE ART OF POETRY. A Lecture. By A. O. PRICKARD, M.A., Fellow and Tutor of New College, Oxford. Cr. 8vo. 3s. 6d.
ARISTOPHANES.—THE BIRDS. Translated into English Verse. By B. H. KENNEDY, D.D. Cr. 8vo. 6s. Help Notes to the Same, for the Use of Students. 1s. 6d.
ATTIC ORATORS.—FROM ANTIPHON TO ISAEOS. By R. C. JEBB, Litt.D., Regius Professor of Greek in the University of Cambridge. 2 vols. 8vo. 25s.
BABRIUS.—With Lexicon. By Rev. W. G. RUTHERFORD, M.A., LL.D., Head-master of Westminster. 8vo. 12s. 6d.
CICERO.—THE ACADEMICA. By J. S. REID, Litt.D., Fellow of Caius College, Cambridge. 8vo. 15s.
THE ACADEMICS. Translated by the same. 8vo. 5s. 6d.
SELECT LETTERS. After the Edition of ALBERT WATSON, M.A. Translated by G. E. JEANS, M.A., Fellow of Hertford College, Oxford. Cr. 8vo. 10s. 6d.
EURIPIDES.—MEDEA. Edited by A. W. VERRALL, Litt.D. 8vo. 7s. 6d.
IPHIGENEIA AT AULIS. Edited by E. B. ENGLAND, M.A. 8vo. 7s. 6d.
*INTRODUCTION TO THE STUDY OF EURIPIDES. By Professor J. P. MAHAFFY. Fcap. 8vo. 1s. 6d. (*Classical Writers.*)
HERODOTUS.—BOOKS I.-III. THE ANCIENT EMPIRES OF THE EAST. Edited by A. H. SAYCE, Deputy-Professor of Comparative Philology, Oxford. 8vo. 16s.
BOOKS IV.-IX. Edited by R. W. MACAN, M.A., Reader in Ancient History in the University of Oxford. 8vo. [*In preparation.*
THE HISTORY. Translated by G. C. MACAULAY, M.A. 2 vols. Cr. 8vo. 18s.
HOMER.—THE ILIAD. By WALTER LEAF, Litt.D. 8vo. Books I.-XII. 14s. Books XIII.-XXIV. 14s.
THE ILIAD. Translated into English Prose by ANDREW LANG, M.A., WALTER LEAF, Litt.D., and ERNEST MYERS, M.A. Cr. 8vo. 12s. 6d.
THE ODYSSEY. Done into English by S. H. BUTCHER, M.A., Professor of Greek in the University of Edinburgh, and ANDREW LANG, M.A. Cr. 8vo. 6s.
*INTRODUCTION TO THE STUDY OF HOMER. By the Right Hon. W. E. GLADSTONE. 18mo. 1s. (*Literature Primers.*)
HOMERIC DICTIONARY. Translated from the German of Dr. G. AUTENRIETII by R. P. KEEP, Ph.D. Illustrated. Cr. 8vo. 6s.
HORACE.—Translated by J. LONSDALE, M.A., and S. LEE, M.A. Gl. 8vo. 3s. 6d.
STUDIES, LITERARY AND HISTORICAL, IN THE ODES OF HORACE. By A. W. VERRALL, Litt.D. 8vo. 8s. 6d.
JUVENAL.—THIRTEEN SATIRES OF JUVENAL. By JOHN E. B. MAYOR, M.A., Professor of Latin in the University of Cambridge. Cr. 8vo. 2 vols. 10s. 6d. each. Vol. I. 10s. 6d. Vol. II. 10s. 6d.
THIRTEEN SATIRES. Translated by ALEX. LEEPER, M.A., LL.D., Warden of Trinity College, Melbourne. Cr. 8vo. 3s. 6d.
KTESIAS.—THE FRAGMENTS OF THE PERSIKA OF KTESIAS. By JOHN GILMORE, M.A. 8vo. 8s. 6d.
LIVY.—BOOKS I.-IV. Translated by Rev. H. M. STEPHENSON, M.A. [*In prep.*
BOOKS XXI.-XXV. Translated by A. J. CHURCH, M.A., and W. J. BRODRIBB, M.A. Cr. 8vo. 7s. 6d.
*INTRODUCTION TO THE STUDY OF LIVY. By Rev. W. W. CAPES, M.A. Fcap. 8vo. 1s. 6d. (*Classical Writers.*)
LONGINUS.—ON THE SUBLIME. Translated by H. L. HAVELL, B.A. With Introduction by ANDREW LANG. Cr. 8vo. 4s. 6d.

MARTIAL.—BOOKS I. AND II. OF THE EPIGRAMS. By Prof. JOHN E. B. MAYOR, M.A. 8vo. [*In the Press.*

MELEAGER.—FIFTY POEMS OF MELEAGER. Translated by WALTER HEADLAM. Fcap. 4to. 7s. 6d.

PAUSANIAS.—DESCRIPTION OF GREECE. Translated with Commentary by J. G. FRAZER, M.A., Fellow of Trinity College, Cambridge. [*In prep.*

PHRYNICHUS.—THE NEW PHRYNICHUS; being a Revised Text of the Ecloga of the Grammarian Phrynichus. With Introduction and Commentary by Rev. W. G. RUTHERFORD, M.A., LL.D., Headmaster of Westminster. 8vo. 18s.

PINDAR.—THE EXTANT ODES OF PINDAR. Translated by ERNEST MYERS, M.A. Cr. 8vo. 5s.

THE OLYMPIAN AND PYTHIAN ODES. Edited, with an Introductory Essay, by BASIL GILDERSLEEVE, Professor of Greek in the Johns Hopkins University, U.S.A. Cr. 8vo. 7s. 6d.

THE NEMEAN ODES. By J. B. BURY, M.A., Fellow of Trinity College, Dublin. 8vo. 12s.

THE ISTHMIAN ODES. By the same Editor. [*In the Press.*

PLATO.—PHÆDO. By R. D. ARCHER-HIND, M.A., Fellow of Trinity College, Cambridge. 8vo. 8s. 6d.

PHÆDO. By W. D. GEDDES, LL.D., Principal of the University of Aberdeen. 8vo. 8s. 6d.

TIMAEUS. With Translation. By R. D. ARCHER-HIND, M.A. 8vo. 16s.

THE REPUBLIC OF PLATO. Translated by J. LL. DAVIES, M.A., and D. J. VAUGHAN, M.A. 18mo. 4s. 6d.

EUTHYPHRO, APOLOGY, CRITO, AND PHÆDO. Translated by F. J. CHURCH. 18mo. 4s. 6d.

PHÆDRUS, LYSIS, AND PROTAGORAS. Translated by J. WRIGHT, M.A. 18mo. 4s. 6d.

PLAUTUS.—THE MOSTELLARIA. By WILLIAM RAMSAY, M.A. Edited by G. G. RAMSAY, M.A., Professor of Humanity in the University of Glasgow. 8vo. 14s.

PLINY.—CORRESPONDENCE WITH TRAJAN. C. Plinii Caecilii Secundi Epistulæ ad Traianum Imperatorem cum Eiusdem Responsis. By E. G. HARDY, M.A. 8vo. 10s. 6d.

POLYBIUS.—THE HISTORIES OF POLYBIUS. Translated by E. S. SHUCKBURGH, M.A. 2 vols. Cr. 8vo. 24s.

SALLUST.—CATILINE AND JUGURTHA. Translated by A. W. POLLARD, B.A. Cr. 8vo. 6s. THE CATILINE (separately). 3s.

SOPHOCLES.—ŒDIPUS THE KING. Translated into English Verse by E. D. A. MORSHEAD, M.A., Assistant Master at Winchester. Fcap. 8vo. 3s. 6d.

TACITUS.—THE ANNALS. By G. O. HOLBROOKE, M.A., Professor of Latin in Trinity College, Hartford, U.S.A. With Maps. 8vo. 16s.

THE ANNALS. Translated by A. J. CHURCH, M.A., and W. J. BRODRIBB, M.A. With Maps. Cr. 8vo. 7s. 6d.

THE HISTORIES. By Rev. W. A. SPOONER, M.A., Fellow and Tutor of New College, Oxford. 8vo. 16s.

THE HISTORY. Translated by A. J. CHURCH, M.A., and W. J. BRODRIBB, M.A. With Map. Cr. 8vo. 6s.

THE AGRICOLA AND GERMANY, WITH THE DIALOGUE ON ORATORY. Translated by A. J. CHURCH, M.A., and W. J. BRODRIBB, M.A. With Maps. Cr. 8vo. 4s. 6d

*INTRODUCTION TO THE STUDY OF TACITUS. By A. J. CHURCH, M.A., and W. J. BRODRIBB, M.A. Fcap. 8vo. 1s. 6d. (*Classical Writers.*)

THEOCRITUS, BION, AND MOSCHUS. Translated by A. LANG, M.A. 18mo. 4s. 6d. Also an Edition on Large Paper. Cr. 8vo. 9s.

THUCYDIDES.—BOOK IV. A Revision of the Text, Illustrating the Principal Causes of Corruption in the Manuscripts of this Author. By Rev. W. G. RUTHERFORD, M.A., LL.D., Headmaster of Westminster. 8vo. 7s. 6d.

BOOK VIII. By H. C. GOODHART, M.A., Fellow of Trinity College, Cambridge.
[*In the Press.*

VIRGIL.—Translated by J. LONSDALE, M.A., and S. LEE, M.A. Gl. 8vo. 3s. 6d.
THE ÆNEID. Translated by J. W. MACKAIL, M.A., Fellow of Balliol College,
Oxford. Cr. 8vo. 7s. 6d.

XENOPHON.—Translated by H. G. DAKYNS, M.A. In four vols. Cr. 8vo. Vol. I.,
containing "The Anabasis" and Books I. and II. of "The Hellenica." 10s. 6d.
Vol. II. "Hellenica" III.-VII., and the two Polities—"Athenian" and
"Laconian," the "Agesilaus," and the tract on "Revenues." With Maps and
Plans.   [*In the Press.*

GRAMMAR, COMPOSITION, & PHILOLOGY.

*BELCHER.—SHORT EXERCISES IN LATIN PROSE COMPOSITION AND
EXAMINATION PAPERS IN LATIN GRAMMAR. Part I. By Rev. H.
BELCHER, LL.D., Rector of the High School, Dunedin, N.Z. 18mo. 1s. 6d.
KEY, for Teachers only. 18mo. 3s. 6d.

*Part II., On the Syntax of Sentences, with an Appendix, including EXERCISES
IN LATIN IDIOMS, etc. 18mo. 2s. KEY, for Teachers only. 18mo. 3s.

BLACKIE.—GREEK AND ENGLISH DIALOGUES FOR USE IN SCHOOLS
AND COLLEGES. By JOHN STUART BLACKIE, Emeritus Professor of Greek
in the University of Edinburgh. New Edition. Fcap. 8vo. 2s. 6d.
A GREEK PRIMER, COLLOQUIAL AND CONSTRUCTIVE. Cr. 8vo. 2s. 6d.

*BRYANS.—LATIN PROSE EXERCISES BASED UPON CÆSAR'S GALLIC
WAR. With a Classification of Cæsar's Chief Phrases and Grammatical Notes
on Cæsar's Usages. By CLEMENT BRYANS, M.A., Assistant Master at Dulwich
College. Ex. fcap. 8vo. 2s. 6d. KEY, for Teachers only. 4s. 6d.
GREEK PROSE EXERCISES based upon Thucydides. By the same.
[*In preparation.*

COOKSON.—A LATIN SYNTAX. By CHRISTOPHER COOKSON, M.A., Assistant
Master at St. Paul's School. 8vo.   [*In preparation.*

CORNELL UNIVERSITY STUDIES IN CLASSICAL PHILOLOGY. Edited by
I. FLAGG, W. G. HALE, and B. I. WHEELER. I. The *CUM*-Constructions: their
History and Functions. By W. G. HALE. Part 1. Critical. 1s. 8d. net. Part
2. Constructive. 3s. 4d. net. II. Analogy and the Scope of its Application
in Language. By B. I. WHEELER. 1s. 3d. net.

*EICKE.—FIRST LESSONS IN LATIN. By K. M. EICKE, B.A., Assistant Master
at Oundle School. Gl. 8vo. 2s. 6d.

*ENGLAND.—EXERCISES ON LATIN SYNTAX AND IDIOM. ARRANGED
WITH REFERENCE TO ROBY'S SCHOOL LATIN GRAMMAR. By E.
B. ENGLAND, Assistant Lecturer at the Owens College, Victoria University,
Manchester. Cr. 8vo. 2s. 6d. KEY, for Teachers only. 2s. 6d.

GILES.—A SHORT MANUAL OF PHILOLOGY FOR CLASSICAL STUDENTS
By P. GILES, M.A., Reader in Comparative Philology in the University of Cam
bridge. Cr. 8vo.   [*In the Press*

GOODWIN.—Works by W. W. GOODWIN, LL.D., D.C.L., Professor of Greek in
Harvard University, U.S.A.
SYNTAX OF THE MOODS AND TENSES OF THE GREEK VERB. New
Ed., revised and enlarged. 8vo. 14s.
*A GREEK GRAMMAR. Cr. 8vo. 6s.
*A GREEK GRAMMAR FOR SCHOOLS. Cr. 8vo. 3s. 6d.

GREENWOOD.—THE ELEMENTS OF GREEK GRAMMAR. Adapted to the
System of Crude Forms. By J. G. GREENWOOD, sometime Principal of the
Owens College, Manchester. Cr. 8vo. 5s. 6d.

HADLEY.—ESSAYS, PHILOLOGICAL AND CRITICAL. By JAMES HADLEY,
late Professor in Yale College. 8vo. 16s.

HADLEY and ALLEN.— A GREEK GRAMMAR FOR SCHOOLS AND
COLLEGES. By JAMES HADLEY, late Professor in Yale College. Revised
and in part rewritten by F. DE F. ALLEN, Professor in Harvard College.
Cr. 8vo. 6s.

HODGSON.—MYTHOLOGY FOR LATIN VERSIFICATION. A brief sketch of the Fables of the Ancients, prepared to be rendered into Latin Verse for Schools. By F. Hodgson, B.D., late Provost of Eton. New Ed., revised by F. C. Hodgson, M.A. 18mo. 3s.

*__JACKSON.__—FIRST STEPS TO GREEK PROSE COMPOSITION By Blomfield Jackson, M.A., Assistant Master at King's College School. 18mo. 1s. 6d. KEY, for Teachers only. 18mo. 3s. 6d.

*SECOND STEPS TO GREEK PROSE COMPOSITION, with Miscellaneous Idioms, Aids to Accentuation, and Examination Papers in Greek Scholarship. By the same. 18mo. 2s. 6d. KEY, for Teachers only. 18mo. 3s. 6d.

KYNASTON.—EXERCISES IN THE COMPOSITION OF GREEK IAMBIC VERSE by Translations from English Dramatists. By Rev. H. Kynaston, D.D., Professor of Classics in the University of Durham. With Vocabulary. Ex. fcap. 8vo. 5s.
KEY, for Teachers only. Ex. fcap. 8vo. 4s. 6d.

LUPTON.—*AN INTRODUCTION TO LATIN ELEGIAC VERSE COMPOSITION. By J. H. Lupton, Sur-Master of St. Paul's School. Gl. 8vo. 2s. 6d. KEY TO PART II. (XXV.-C.) Gl. 8vo. 3s. 6d.

*AN INTRODUCTION TO LATIN LYRIC VERSE COMPOSITION. By the same. Gl. 8vo. 3s. KEY, for Teachers only. Gl. 8vo. 4s. 6d.

MACKIE.—PARALLEL PASSAGES FOR TRANSLATION INTO GREEK AND ENGLISH. With Indexes. By Rev. Ellis C. Mackie, M.A., Classical Master at Heversham Grammar School. Gl. 8vo. 4s. 6d.

*__MACMILLAN.__—FIRST LATIN GRAMMAR. By M. C. Macmillan, M.A. Fcap. 8vo. 1s. 6d.

MACMILLAN'S GREEK COURSE.—Edited by Rev. W. G. Rutherford, M.A., LL.D., Headmaster of Westminster. Gl. 8vo.
*FIRST GREEK GRAMMAR—ACCIDENCE. By the Editor. 2s.
*FIRST GREEK GRAMMAR—SYNTAX. By the same. 2s.
ACCIDENCE AND SYNTAX. In one volume. 3s. 6d.
*EASY EXERCISES IN GREEK ACCIDENCE. By H. G. Underhill, M.A., Assistant Master at St. Paul's Preparatory School. 2s.
*A SECOND GREEK EXERCISE BOOK. By Rev. W. A. Heard, M.A., Headmaster of Fettes College, Edinburgh. 2s. 6d.
EASY EXERCISES IN GREEK SYNTAX. By Rev. G. H. Nall, M.A., Assistant Master at Westminster School.   [In preparation.
MANUAL OF GREEK ACCIDENCE. By the Editor.   [In preparation.
MANUAL OF GREEK SYNTAX. By the Editor.   [In preparation.
ELEMENTARY GREEK COMPOSITION. By the Editor.   [In preparation.

*__MACMILLAN'S GREEK READER.__—STORIES AND LEGENDS. A First Greek Reader, with Notes, Vocabulary, and Exercises. By F. H. Colson, M.A., Headmaster of Plymouth College. Gl. 8vo. 3s.

MACMILLAN'S LATIN COURSE.—By A. M. Cook, M.A., Assistant Master at St. Paul's School.
*FIRST PART. Gl. 8vo. 3s. 6d.
*SECOND PART. 2s. 6d.   [Third Part in preparation.

*__MACMILLAN'S SHORTER LATIN COURSE.__—By A. M. Cook, M.A. Being an abridgment of "Macmillan's Latin Course," First Part. Gl. 8vo. 1s. 6d.

*__MACMILLAN'S LATIN READER.__—A LATIN READER FOR THE LOWER FORMS IN SCHOOLS. By H. J. Hardy, M.A., Assistant Master at Winchester. Gl. 8vo. 2s. 6d.

*__MARSHALL.__—A TABLE OF IRREGULAR GREEK VERBS, classified according to the arrangement of Curtius's Greek Grammar. By J. M. Marshall, M.A., Headmaster of the Grammar School, Durham. 8vo. 1s.

MAYOR.—FIRST GREEK READER. By Prof. John E. B. Mayor, M.A., Fellow of St. John's College, Cambridge. Fcap. 8vo. 4s. 6d.

MAYOR.—GREEK FOR BEGINNERS. By Rev. J. B. MAYOR, M.A., late Professor of Classical Literature in King's College, London. Part I., with Vocabulary, 1s. 6d. Parts II. and III., with Vocabulary and Index. Fcap. 8vo. 3s. 6d. Complete in one Vol. 4s. 6d.

NIXON.—PARALLEL EXTRACTS, Arranged for Translation into English and Latin, with Notes on Idioms. By J. E. NIXON, M.A., Fellow and Classical Lecturer, King's College, Cambridge. Part I.—Historical and Epistolary. Cr. 8vo. 3s. 6d.

PROSE EXTRACTS, Arranged for Translation into English and Latin, with General and Special Prefaces on Style and Idiom. By the same. I. Oratorical. II. Historical. III. Philosophical. IV. Anecdotes and Letters. 2d Ed., enlarged to 280 pp. Cr. 8vo. 4s. 6d. SELECTIONS FROM THE SAME. 3s.
Translations of about 70 Extracts can be supplied to Schoolmasters (2s. 6d.), on application to the Author : and about 40 similarly of "Parallel Extracts." 1s. 6d. post free.

*PANTIN.—A FIRST LATIN VERSE BOOK. By W. E. P. PANTIN, M.A., Assistant Master at St. Paul's School. Gl. 8vo. 1s. 6d.

*PEILE.—A PRIMER OF PHILOLOGY. By J. PEILE, Litt.D., Master of Christ's College, Cambridge. 18mo. 1s.

*POSTGATE.—SERMO LATINUS. A short Guide to Latin Prose Composition. By Prof. J. P. POSTGATE, Litt.D., Fellow of Trinity College, Cambridge. Gl. 8vo. 2s. 6d. KEY to "Selected Passages." Gl. 8vo. 3s. 6d.

POSTGATE and VINCE.—A DICTIONARY OF LATIN ETYMOLOGY. By J. P. POSTGATE and C. A. VINCE. [In preparation.

POTTS.—*HINTS TOWARDS LATIN PROSE COMPOSITION. By A. W. POTTS, M.A., LL.D., late Fellow of St. John's College, Cambridge. Ex. fcap. 8vo. 3s.
*PASSAGES FOR TRANSLATION INTO LATIN PROSE. Edited with Notes and References to the above. Ex. fcap. 8vo. 2s. 6d. KEY, for Teachers only. 2s. 6d.

*PRESTON.—EXERCISES IN LATIN VERSE OF VARIOUS KINDS. By Rev. G. PRESTON. Gl. 8vo. 2s. 6d. KEY, for Teachers only. Gl. 8vo. 5s.

REID.—A GRAMMAR OF TACITUS. By J. S. REID, Litt.D., Fellow of Caius College, Cambridge. [In the Press.
A GRAMMAR OF VIRGIL. By the same. [In preparation.

ROBY.—Works by H. J. ROBY, M.A., late Fellow of St. John's College, Cambridge.
A GRAMMAR OF THE LATIN LANGUAGE, from Plautus to Suetonius. Part I. Sounds, Inflexions, Word-formation, Appendices. Cr. 8vo. 9s. Part II. Syntax, Prepositions, etc. 10s. 6d.
*SCHOOL LATIN GRAMMAR. Cr. 8vo. 5s.
AN ELEMENTARY LATIN GRAMMAR. [In the Press.

*RUSH.—SYNTHETIC LATIN DELECTUS. With Notes and Vocabulary. By E. RUSH, B.A. Ex. fcap. 8vo. 2s. 6d.

*RUST.—FIRST STEPS TO LATIN PROSE COMPOSITION. By Rev. G. RUST, M.A. 18mo. 1s. 6d. KEY, for Teachers only. By W. M. YATES. 18mo. 3s. 6d.

RUTHERFORD.—Works by the Rev. W. G. RUTHERFORD, M.A., LL.D., Headmaster of Westminster.
REX LEX. A Short Digest of the principal Relations between the Latin, Greek, and Anglo-Saxon Sounds. 8vo. [In preparation.
THE NEW PHRYNICHUS; being a Revised Text of the Ecloga of the Grammarian Phrynichus. With Introduction and Commentary. 8vo. 18s. (See also Macmillan's Greek Course.)

SHUCKBURGH.—PASSAGES FROM LATIN AUTHORS FOR TRANSLATION INTO ENGLISH. Selected with a view to the needs of Candidates for the Cambridge Local, and Public Schools' Examinations. By E. S. SHUCKBURGH, M.A. Cr. 8vo. 2s.

*SIMPSON. — LATIN PROSE AFTER THE BEST AUTHORS : Cæsarian Prose. By F. P. SIMPSON, B.A. Ex. fcap. 8vo. 2s. 6d. KEY, for Teachers only. Ex. fcap. 8vo. 5s.

STRACHAN and WILKINS.—ANALECTA. Selected Passages for Translation. By J. S. STRACHAN, M.A., Professor of Greek, and A. S. WILKINS, Litt.D., Professor of Latin in the Owens College, Manchester. Cr. 8vo. 5s. KEY to Latin Passages. Cr. 8vo. Sewed, 6d.

THRING.—Works by the Rev. E. THRING, M.A., late Headmaster of Uppingham.
 A LATIN GRADUAL. A First Latin Construing Book for Beginners. With
 Coloured Sentence Maps. Fcap. 8vo. 2s. 6d.
 A MANUAL OF MOOD CONSTRUCTIONS. Fcap. 8vo. 1s. 6d.
*WELCH and DUFFIELD. — LATIN ACCIDENCE AND EXERCISES AR-
 RANGED FOR BEGINNERS. By W. WELCH and C. G. DUFFIELD,
 Assistant Masters at Cranleigh School. 18mo. 1s. 6d.
WHITE.—FIRST LESSONS IN GREEK. Adapted to GOODWIN'S GREEK GRAM-
 MAR, and designed as an introduction to the ANABASIS OF XENOPHON. By
 JOHN WILLIAMS WHITE, Assistant Professor of Greek in Harvard University,
 U.S.A. Cr. 8vo. 3s. 6d.
WRIGHT.—Works by J. WRIGHT, M.A., late Headmaster of Sutton Coldfield School.
 A HELP TO LATIN GRAMMAR; or, the Form and Use of Words in Latin,
 with Progressive Exercises. Cr. 8vo. 4s. 6d.
 THE SEVEN KINGS OF ROME. An Easy Narrative, abridged from the First
 Book of Livy by the omission of Difficult Passages; being a First Latin Read-
 ing Book, with Grammatical Notes and Vocabulary. Fcap. 8vo. 3s. 6d.
 FIRST LATIN STEPS; OR, AN INTRODUCTION BY A SERIES OF
 EXAMPLES TO THE STUDY OF THE LATIN LANGUAGE. Cr. 8vo. 3s.
 ATTIC PRIMER. Arranged for the Use of Beginners. Ex. fcap. 8vo. 2s. 6d.
 A COMPLETE LATIN COURSE, comprising Rules with Examples, Exercises,
 both Latin and English, on each Rule, and Vocabularies. Cr. 8vo. 2s. 6d.

ANTIQUITIES, ANCIENT HISTORY, AND PHILOSOPHY.

ARNOLD.—A HISTORY OF THE EARLY ROMAN EMPIRE. By W. T. ARNOLD,
 M.A. [In preparation.
ARNOLD.—THE SECOND PUNIC WAR. Being Chapters from THE HISTORY
 OF ROME by the late THOMAS ARNOLD, D.D., Headmaster of Rugby.
 Edited, with Notes, by W. T. ARNOLD, M.A. With 8 Maps. Cr. 8vo. 5s.
*BEESLY.—STORIES FROM THE HISTORY OF ROME. By Mrs. BEESLY.
 Fcap. 8vo. 2s. 6d.
BLACKIE.—HORÆ HELLENICÆ. By JOHN STUART BLACKIE, Emeritus Pro-
 fessor of Greek in the University of Edinburgh. 8vo. 12s.
BURN.—ROMAN LITERATURE IN RELATION TO ROMAN ART. By Rev.
 ROBERT BURN, M.A., late Fellow of Trinity College, Cambridge. Illustrated.
 Ex. cr. 8vo. 14s.
BURY.—A HISTORY OF THE LATER ROMAN EMPIRE FROM ARCADIUS
 TO IRENE, A.D. 395-800. By J. B. BURY, M.A., Fellow of Trinity College,
 Dublin. 2 vols. 8vo. 32s.
*CLASSICAL WRITERS.—Edited by JOHN RICHARD GREEN, M.A., LL.D. Fcap.
 8vo. 1s. 6d. each.
 SOPHOCLES. By Prof. L. CAMPBELL, M.A.
 EURIPIDES. By Prof. MAHAFFY, D.D.
 DEMOSTHENES. By Prof. S. H. BUTCHER, M.A.
 VIRGIL. By Prof. NETTLESHIP, M.A.
 LIVY. By Rev. W. W. CAPES, M.A.
 TACITUS. By Prof. A. J. CHURCH, M.A., and W. J. BRODRIBB, M.A.
 MILTON. By Rev. STOPFORD A. BROOKE, M.A.
DYER.—STUDIES OF THE GODS IN GREECE AT CERTAIN SANCTUARIES
 RECENTLY EXCAVATED. By LOUIS DYER, B.A. Ex. Cr. 8vo. 8s. 6d. net.
FREEMAN.—Works by EDWARD A. FREEMAN, D.C.L., LL.D., Regius Professor of
 Modern History in the University of Oxford.
 HISTORY OF ROME. (Historical Course for Schools.) 18mo. [In preparation.
 HISTORY OF GREECE. (Historical Course for Schools.) 18mo. [In preparation.
 A SCHOOL HISTORY OF ROME. Cr 8vo. [In preparation.
 HISTORICAL ESSAYS. Second Series. [Greek and Roman History.] 8vo.
 10s. 6d.

GARDNER.—SAMOS AND SAMIAN COINS. An Essay. By PERCY GARDNER, Litt.D., Professor of Archæology in the University of Oxford. 8vo. 7s. 6d.

GEDDES.—THE PROBLEM OF THE HOMERIC POEMS. By W. D. GEDDES, Principal of the University of Aberdeen. 8vo. 14s.

GLADSTONE.—Works by the Rt. Hon. W. E. GLADSTONE, M.P.
THE TIME AND PLACE OF HOMER. Cr. 8vo. 6s. 6d.
LANDMARKS OF HOMERIC STUDY. Cr. 8vo. 2s. 6d.
*A PRIMER OF HOMER. 18mo. 1s.

GOW.—A COMPANION TO SCHOOL CLASSICS. By JAMES Gow, Litt.D., Master of the High School, Nottingham. With Illustrations. 2d Ed., revised Cr. 8vo. 6s.

HARRISON and VERRALL.—MYTHOLOGY AND MONUMENTS OF ANCIENT ATHENS. Translation of a portion of the "Attica" of Pausanias. By MARGARET DE G. VERRALL. With Introductory Essay and Archæological Commentary by JANE E. HARRISON. With Illustrations and Plans. Cr. 8vo. 16s.

JEBB.—Works by R. C. JEBB, Litt.D., Professor of Greek in the University of Cambridge.
THE ATTIC ORATORS FROM ANTIPHON TO ISAEOS. 2 vols. 8vo. 25s.
*A PRIMER OF GREEK LITERATURE. 18mo. 1s.
(See also *Classical Series*.)

KIEPERT.—MANUAL OF ANCIENT GEOGRAPHY. By Dr. H. KIEPERT. Cr. 8vo. 5s.

LANCIANI.—ANCIENT ROME IN THE LIGHT OF RECENT DISCOVERIES. By RODOLFO LANCIANI, Professor of Archæology in the University of Rome. Illustrated. 4to. 24s.

LEAF.—INTRODUCTION TO THE ILIAD FOR ENGLISH READERS. By WALTER LEAF, Litt.D. [*In preparation.*

MAHAFFY.—Works by J. P. MAHAFFY, D.D., Fellow of Trinity College, Dublin and Professor of Ancient History in the University of Dublin.
SOCIAL LIFE IN GREECE; from Homer to Menander. Cr. 8vo. 9s.
GREEK LIFE AND THOUGHT; from the Age of Alexander to the Roman Conquest. Cr. 8vo. 12s. 6d.
THE GREEK WORLD UNDER ROMAN SWAY. From Plutarch to Polybius. Cr. 8vo. 10s. 6d.
RAMBLES AND STUDIES IN GREECE. With Illustrations. With Map. Cr. 8vo. 10s. 6d.
A HISTORY OF CLASSICAL GREEK LITERATURE. Cr. 8vo. Vol. I. In two parts. Part I. The Poets, with an Appendix on Homer by Prof. SAYCE. Part II. Dramatic Poets. Vol. II. The Prose Writers. In two parts. Part I. Herodotus to Plato. Part II. Isocrates to Aristotle. 4s. 6d. each.
*A PRIMER OF GREEK ANTIQUITIES. With Illustrations. 18mo. 1s.
*EURIPIDES. 18mo. 1s. 6d. (*Classical Writers*.)

MAYOR.—BIBLIOGRAPHICAL CLUE TO LATIN LITERATURE. Edited after HÜBNER. By Prof. JOHN E. B. MAYOR. Cr. 8vo. 10s. 6d.

NEWTON.—ESSAYS ON ART AND ARCHÆOLOGY. By Sir CHARLES NEWTON, K.C.B., D.C.L. 8vo. 12s. 6d.

PHILOLOGY.—THE JOURNAL OF PHILOLOGY. Edited by W. A. WRIGHT, M.A., I. BYWATER, M.A., and H. JACKSON, Litt.D. 4s. 6d. each (half-yearly).

SAYCE.—THE ANCIENT EMPIRES OF THE EAST. By A. H. SAYCE, M.A., Deputy-Professor of Comparative Philology, Oxford. Cr. 8vo. 6s.

SCHMIDT and WHITE. AN INTRODUCTION TO THE RHYTHMIC AND METRIC OF THE CLASSICAL LANGUAGES. By Dr. J. H. HEINRICH SCHMIDT. Translated by JOHN WILLIAMS WHITE, Ph.D. 8vo. 10s. 6d.

SHUCHHARDT.—DR. SCHLIEMANN'S EXCAVATIONS AT TROY, TIRYNS, MYCENÆ, ORCHOMENOS, ITHACA, presented in the light of recent knowledge. By Dr. CARL SHUCHHARDT. Translated by EUGENIE SELLERS. Introduction by WALTER LEAF, Litt.D. Illustrated. 8vo. 18s. net.

SHUCKBURGH.—A SCHOOL HISTORY OF ROME. By E. S. SHUCKBURGH, M.A. Cr. 8vo. [*In preparation.*

*****STEWART.**—THE TALE OF TROY. Done into English by AUBREY STEWART. Gl. 8vo. 3s. 6d.

*****TOZER.**—A PRIMER OF CLASSICAL GEOGRAPHY. By H. F. TOZER, M.A. 18mo. 1s.

WALDSTEIN.—CATALOGUE OF CASTS IN THE MUSEUM OF CLASSICAL ARCHÆOLOGY, CAMBRIDGE. By CHARLES WALDSTEIN, University Reader in Classical Archæology. Cr. 8vo. 1s. 6d.
   *_*_* Also an Edition on Large Paper, small 4to. 5s.

WILKINS.—Works by Prof. WILKINS, Litt.D., LL.D.
*****A PRIMER OF ROMAN ANTIQUITIES. Illustrated. 18mo. 1s.
*****A PRIMER OF ROMAN LITERATURE. 18mo. 1s.

WILKINS and ARNOLD. — A MANUAL OF ROMAN ANTIQUITIES. By Prof. A. S. WILKINS, Litt.D., and W. T. ARNOLD, M.A. Cr. 8vo. Illustrated. [*In preparation.*

MODERN LANGUAGES AND LITERATURE.

English ; French ; German ; Modern Greek ; Italian ; Spanish.

ENGLISH.

*****ABBOTT.**—A SHAKESPEARIAN GRAMMAR. An Attempt to Illustrate some of the Differences between Elizabethan and Modern English. By the Rev. E. A. ABBOTT, D.D., formerly Headmaster of the City of London School. Ex. fcap. 8vo. 6s.

*****BACON.**—ESSAYS. With Introduction and Notes, by F. G. SELBY, M.A., Professor of Logic and Moral Philosophy, Deccan College, Poona. Gl. 8vo. 3s. ; sewed, 2s. 6d.

*****BURKE.**—REFLECTIONS ON THE FRENCH REVOLUTION. By the same. Gl. 8vo. 5s.

BROOKE.—*PRIMER OF ENGLISH LITERATURE. By Rev. STOPFORD A. BROOKE, M.A. 18mo. 1s.
   EARLY ENGLISH LITERATURE. By the same. 2 vols. 8vo. [*Vol. I. In the Press.*

BUTLER.—HUDIBRAS. With Introduction and Notes, by ALFRED MILNES, M.A. Ex. fcap. 8vo. Part I. 3s. 6d. Parts II. and III. 4s. 6d.

CAMPBELL.—SELECTIONS. With Introduction and Notes, by CECIL M. BARROW, M.A., Principal of Victoria College, Palghât. Gl. 8vo. [*In preparation.*

COWPER.—*THE TASK : an Epistle to Joseph Hill, Esq. ; TIROCINIUM, or a Review of the Schools ; and THE HISTORY OF JOHN GILPIN. Edited, with Notes, by W. BENHAM, B.D. Gl. 8vo. 1s. (*Globe Readings from Standard Authors.*)
   THE TASK. With Introduction and Notes, by F. J. ROWE, M.A., and W. T. WEBB, M.A., Professors of English Literature, Presidency College, Calcutta. [*In preparation.*

*****DOWDEN.**—A PRIMER OF SHAKESPERE. By Prof. DOWDEN. 18mo. 1s.

DRYDEN.—SELECT PROSE WORKS. Edited, with Introduction and Notes, by Prof. C. D. YONGE. Fcap. 8vo. 2s. 6d.

*****GLOBE READERS.** For Standards I.-VI. Edited by A. F. MURISON. Illustrated. Gl. 8vo.

Primer I. (48 pp.)	3d.		Book III. (232 pp.)	1s. 3d.
Primer II. (48 pp.)	3d.		Book IV. (328 pp.)	1s. 9d.
Book I. (132 pp.)	6d.		Book V. (408 pp.)	2s.
Book II. (136 pp.)	9d.		Book VI. (436 pp.)	2s. 6d.

*****THE SHORTER GLOBE READERS.**—Illustrated. Gl. 8vo.

Primer I. (48 pp.)	3d.		Standard III. (178 pp.)	1s.
Primer II. (48 pp.)	3d.		Standard IV. (182 pp.)	1s.
Standard I. (90 pp.)	6d.		Standard V. (216 pp.)	1s. 3d.
Standard II. (124 pp.)	9d.		Standard VI. (228 pp.)	1s. 6d.

*GOLDSMITH.—THE TRAVELLER, or a Prospect of Society ; and THE DESERTED VILLAGE. With Notes, Philological and Explanatory, by J. W. HALES, M.A. Cr. 8vo. 6d.

*THE TRAVELLER AND THE DESERTED VILLAGE. With Introduction and Notes, by A. BARRETT, B.A., Professor of English Literature, Elphinstone College, Bombay. Gl. 8vo. 1s. 9d. ; sewed, 1s. 6d. The Traveller (separately), 1s., sewed.

*THE VICAR OF WAKEFIELD. With a Memoir of Goldsmith, by Prof. MASSON. Gl. 8vo. 1s. (Globe Readings from Standard Authors.)

SELECT ESSAYS. With Introduction and Notes, by Prof. C. D. YONGE. Fcap. 8vo. 2s. 6d.

GOSSE.—A HISTORY OF EIGHTEENTH CENTURY LITERATURE (1660-1780). By EDMUND GOSSE, M.A. Cr. 8vo. 7s. 6d.

*GRAY.—POEMS. With Introduction and Notes, by JOHN BRADSHAW, LL.D. Gl. 8vo. 1s. 9d. ; sewed, 1s. 6d.

*HALES.—LONGER ENGLISH POEMS. With Notes, Philological and Explanatory, and an Introduction on the Teaching of English, by J. W. HALES, M.A., Professor of English Literature at King's College, London. Ex. fcap. 8vo. 4s. 6d.

*HELPS.—ESSAYS WRITTEN IN THE INTERVALS OF BUSINESS. With Introduction and Notes, by F. J. ROWE, M.A., and W. T. WEBB, M.A. Gl. 8vo. 1s. 9d. ; sewed, 1s. 6d.

*JOHNSON.—LIVES OF THE POETS. The Six Chief Lives (Milton, Dryden, Swift, Addison, Pope, Gray), with Macaulay's "Life of Johnson." With Preface and Notes by MATTHEW ARNOLD. Cr. 8vo. 4s. 6d.

KELLNER.— HISTORICAL OUTLINES OF ENGLISH SYNTAX. By L. KELLNER, Ph.D. [In the Press.

*LAMB.—TALES FROM SHAKSPEARE. With Preface by the Rev. CANON AINGER, M.A., LL.D. Gl. 8vo. 2s. (Globe Readings from Standard Authors.)

*LITERATURE PRIMERS.—Edited by JOHN RICHARD GREEN, LL.D. 18mo. 1s. each.

ENGLISH GRAMMAR. By Rev. R. MORRIS, LL.D.

ENGLISH GRAMMAR EXERCISES. By R. MORRIS, LL.D., and H. C. BOWEN, M.A.

EXERCISES ON MORRIS'S PRIMER OF ENGLISH GRAMMAR. By J. WETHERELL, M.A.

ENGLISH COMPOSITION. By Professor NICHOL.

QUESTIONS AND EXERCISES ON ENGLISH COMPOSITION. By Prof. NICHOL and W. S. M'CORMICK.

ENGLISH LITERATURE. By STOPFORD BROOKE, M.A.

SHAKSPERE. By Professor DOWDEN.

THE CHILDREN'S TREASURY OF LYRICAL POETRY. Selected and arranged with Notes by FRANCIS TURNER PALGRAVE. In Two Parts. 1s. each.

PHILOLOGY. By J. PEILE, Litt.D.

ROMAN LITERATURE. By Prof. A. S. WILKINS, Litt.D.

GREEK LITERATURE. By Prof. JEBB, Litt.D.

HOMER. By the Rt. Hon. W. E. GLADSTONE, M.P.

A HISTORY OF ENGLISH LITERATURE IN FOUR VOLUMES. Cr. 8vo.

EARLY ENGLISH LITERATURE. By STOPFORD BROOKE, M.A. [In preparation.

ELIZABETHAN LITERATURE. (1560-1665.) By GEORGE SAINTSBURY. 7s. 6d.

EIGHTEENTH CENTURY LITERATURE. (1660-1780.) By EDMUND GOSSE, M.A. 7s. 6d.

THE MODERN PERIOD. By Prof. DOWDEN. [In preparation.

*MACMILLAN'S READING BOOKS.

PRIMER. 18mo. 48 pp. 2d.	BOOK IV. for Standard IV. 176 pp.
BOOK I. for Standard I. 96 pp. 4d.	8d.
BOOK II. for Standard II. 144 pp. 5d.	BOOK V. for Standard V. 380 pp. 1s.
BOOK III. for Standard III. 160 pp. 6d.	BOOK VI. for Standard VI. Cr. 8vo. 430 pp. 2s.

Book VI. is fitted for Higher Classes, and as an Introduction to English Literature.

*MACMILLAN'S COPY BOOKS.—1. Large Post 4to. Price 4d. each.   2. Post Oblong. Price 2d. each.

   1. INITIATORY EXERCISES AND SHORT LETTERS.
   2. WORDS CONSISTING OF SHORT LETTERS.
   3. LONG LETTERS. With Words containing Long Letters—Figures.
   4. WORDS CONTAINING LONG LETTERS.
   4a. PRACTISING AND REVISING COPY-BOOK. For Nos. 1 to 4.
   5. CAPITALS AND SHORT HALF-TEXT. Words beginning with a Capital.
   6. HALF-TEXT WORDS beginning with Capitals—Figures.
   7. SMALL-HAND AND HALF-TEXT. With Capitals and Figures.
   8. SMALL-HAND AND HALF-TEXT. With Capitals and Figures.
   8a. PRACTISING AND REVISING COPY-BOOK. For Nos. 5 to 8.
   9. SMALL-HAND SINGLE HEADLINES—Figures.
   10. SMALL-HAND SINGLE HEADLINES—Figures.
   11. SMALL-HAND DOUBLE HEADLINES—Figures.
   12. COMMERCIAL AND ARITHMETICAL EXAMPLES, &c.
   12a. PRACTISING AND REVISING COPY-BOOK. For Nos. 8 to 12.
   Nos. 3, 4, 5, 6, 7, 8, 9 may be had with Goodman's Patent Sliding Copies. Large Post 4to. Price 6d. each.

MARTIN.—*THE POET'S HOUR : Poetry selected and arranged for Children. By FRANCES MARTIN. 18mo. 2s. 6d.

   *SPRING-TIME WITH THE POETS. By the same. 18mo. 3s. 6d.

*MILTON.—PARADISE LOST. Books I. and II. With Introduction and Notes, by MICHAEL MACMILLAN, B.A., Professor of Logic and Moral Philosophy, Elphinstone College, Bombay. Gl. 8vo. 1s. 9d. ; sewed, 1s. 6d. Or separately, 1s. 3d. ; sewed, 1s. each.

   *L'ALLEGRO, IL PENSEROSO, LYCIDAS, ARCADES, SONNETS, &c. With Introduction and Notes, by W. BELL, M.A., Professor of Philosophy and Logic, Government College, Lahore. Gl. 8vo. 1s. 9d. ; sewed, 1s. 6d.

   *COMUS. By the same. Gl. 8vo. 1s. 3d. ; sewed, 1s.

   *SAMSON AGONISTES. By H. M. PERCIVAL, M.A., Professor of English Literature, Presidency College, Calcutta. Gl. 8vo. 2s. ; sewed, 1s. 9d.

   *INTRODUCTION TO THE STUDY OF MILTON. By STOPFORD BROOKE, M.A. Fcap. 8vo. 1s. 6d. *(Classical Writers.)*

MORRIS.—Works by the Rev. R. MORRIS, LL.D.

   *PRIMER OF ENGLISH GRAMMAR. 18mo. 1s.

   *ELEMENTARY LESSONS IN HISTORICAL ENGLISH GRAMMAR, containing Accidence and Word-Formation. 18mo. 2s. 6d.

   *HISTORICAL OUTLINES OF ENGLISH ACCIDENCE, comprising Chapters on the History and Development of the Language, and on Word-Formation. Ex. fcap. 8vo. 6s.

NICHOL and M'CORMICK.—A SHORT HISTORY OF ENGLISH LITERATURE. By Prof. JOHN NICHOL and Prof. W. S. M'CORMICK. [*In preparation.*

OLIPHANT.—THE OLD AND MIDDLE ENGLISH. By T. L. KINGTON OLIPHANT. New Ed., revised and enlarged, of "The Sources of Standard English." 2nd Ed. Gl. 8vo. 9s.

   THE NEW ENGLISH. By the same. 2 vols. Cr. 8vo. 21s.

*PALGRAVE.—THE CHILDREN'S TREASURY OF LYRICAL POETRY. Selected and arranged, with Notes, by FRANCIS T. PALGRAVE. 18mo. 2s. 6d. Also in Two Parts. 1s. each.

PATMORE.—THE CHILDREN'S GARLAND FROM THE BEST POETS. Selected and arranged by COVENTRY PATMORE. Gl. 8vo. 2s. *(Globe Readings from Standard Authors.)*

PLUTARCH.—Being a Selection from the Lives which illustrate Shakespeare. North's Translation. Edited, with Introductions, Notes, Index of Names, and Glossarial Index, by Prof. W. W. SKEAT, Litt.D. Cr. 8vo. 6s.

*RANSOME.—SHORT STUDIES OF SHAKESPEARE'S PLOTS. By CYRIL RANSOME, Professor of Modern History and Literature, Yorkshire College, Leeds. Cr. 8vo. 3s. 6d.

*RYLAND.—CHRONOLOGICAL OUTLINES OF ENGLISH LITERATURE. By F. RYLAND, M.A. Cr. 8vo. 6s.

SAINTSBURY.—A HISTORY OF ELIZABETHAN LITERATURE. 1560-1665. By GEORGE SAINTSBURY. Cr. 8vo. 7s. 6d.

SCOTT.—*LAY OF THE LAST MINSTREL, and THE LADY OF THE LAKE. Edited, with Introduction and Notes, by FRANCIS TURNER PALGRAVE. Gl. 8vo. 1s. (Globe Readings from Standard Authors.)

*THE LAY OF THE LAST MINSTREL. With Introduction and Notes, by G. H. STUART, M.A., and E. H. ELLIOT, B.A. Gl. 8vo. 2s.; sewed, 1s. 9d. Introduction and Canto I. 9d. sewed. Cantos I. to III. 1s. 3d. ; sewed, 1s. Cantos IV. to VI. 1s. 3d. ; sewed, 1s.

*MARMION, and THE LORD OF THE ISLES. By F. T. PALGRAVE. Gl. 8vo. 1s. (Globe Readings from Standard Authors.)

*MARMION. With Introduction and Notes, by MICHAEL MACMILLAN, B.A. Gl. 8vo. 3s. ; sewed, 2s. 6d.

*THE LADY OF THE LAKE. By G. H. STUART, M.A. Gl. 8vo. 2s. 6d. ; sewed, 2s.

*ROKEBY. With Introduction and Notes, by MICHAEL MACMILLAN, B.A. Gl. 8vo. 3s. ; sewed, 2s. 6d.

SHAKESPEARE.—*A SHAKESPEARIAN GRAMMAR. By Rev. E. A. ABBOTT, D.D. Gl. 8vo. 6s.

A SHAKESPEARE MANUAL. By F. G. FLEAY, M.A. 2d Ed. Ex. fcap. 8vo. 4s. 6d.

*A PRIMER OF SHAKESPERE. By Prof. DOWDEN. 18mo. 1s.

*SHORT STUDIES OF SHAKESPEARE'S PLOTS. By CYRIL RANSOME, M.A. Cr. 8vo. 3s. 6d.

*THE TEMPEST. With Introduction and Notes, by K. DEIGHTON, late Principal of Agra College. Gl. 8vo. 1s. 9d. ; sewed, 1s. 6d.

*MUCH ADO ABOUT NOTHING. By the same. Gl. 8vo. 1s. 9d. ; sewed, 1s. 6d.

*A MIDSUMMER NIGHT'S DREAM. By the same. Gl. 8vo. 1s. 9d.; sewed, 1s. 6d.

*THE MERCHANT OF VENICE. By the same. Gl. 8vo. 1s. 9d. ; sewed, 1s. 6d.

*AS YOU LIKE IT. By the same. Gl. 8vo. 1s. 9d. ; sewed, 1s. 6d.

*TWELFTH NIGHT. By the same. Gl. 8vo. 1s. 9d. ; sewed, 1s. 6d.

*THE WINTER'S TALE. By the same. Gl. 8vo. 2s. ; sewed, 1s. 9d.

*KING JOHN. By the same. Gl. 8vo. 1s. 9d. ; sewed, 1s. 6d.

*RICHARD II. By the same. Gl. 8vo. 1s. 9d. ; sewed, 1s. 6d.

*HENRY V. By the same. Gl. 8vo. 1s. 9d. ; sewed, 1s. 6d.

*RICHARD III. By C. H. TAWNEY, M.A., Principal and Professor of English Literature, Presidency College, Calcutta. Gl. 8vo. 2s. 6d. ; sewed, 2s.

*CORIOLANUS. By K. DEIGHTON. Gl. 8vo. 2s. 6d. ; sewed, 2s.

*JULIUS CÆSAR. By the same. Gl. 8vo. 1s. 9d. ; sewed, 1s. 6d

*MACBETH. By the same. Gl. 8vo. 1s. 9d. ; sewed, 1s. 6d.

*HAMLET. By the same. Gl. 8vo. 2s. 6d. ; sewed, 2s.

*KING LEAR. By the same. Gl. 8vo. 1s. 9d. ; sewed, 1s. 6d.

*OTHELLO. By the same. Gl. 8vo. 2s. ; sewed, 1s. 9d.

*ANTONY AND CLEOPATRA. By the same. Gl. 8vo. 2s. 6d. ; sewed, 2s.

*CYMBELINE. By the same. Gl. 8vo. 2s. 6d. ; sewed, 2s.

*SONNENSCHEIN and MEIKLEJOHN.—THE ENGLISH METHOD OF TEACHING TO READ. By A. SONNENSCHEIN and J. M. D. MEIKLEJOHN, M.A. Fcap. 8vo.

THE NURSERY BOOK, containing all the Two-Letter Words in the Language. 1d. (Also in Large Type on Sheets for School Walls. 5s.)

B

THE FIRST COURSE, consisting of Short Vowels with Single Consonants. 7d.
THE SECOND COURSE, with Combinations and Bridges, consisting of Short Vowels with Double Consonants. 7d.
THE THIRD AND FOURTH COURSES, consisting of Long Vowels, and all the Double Vowels in the Language. 7d.

*SOUTHEY.—LIFE OF NELSON. With Introduction and Notes, by MICHAEL MACMILLAN, B.A. Gl. 8vo. 3s. ; sewed, 2s. 6d.
SPENSER.—FAIRY QUEEN. Book I. With Introduction and Notes, by H. M. PERCIVAL, M.A. [In the Press.
TAYLOR.—WORDS AND PLACES; or, Etymological Illustrations of History, Ethnology, and Geography. By Rev. ISAAC TAYLOR, Litt.D. With Maps. Gl. 8vo. 6s.
TENNYSON.—THE COLLECTED WORKS OF LORD TENNYSON. An Edition for Schools. In Four Parts. Cr. 8vo. 2s. 6d. each.
TENNYSON FOR THE YOUNG. Edited, with Notes for the Use of Schools, by the Rev. ALFRED AINGER, LL.D., Canon of Bristol. 18mo. 1s. net. [In the Press.
*SELECTIONS FROM TENNYSON. With Introduction and Notes, by F. J. ROWE, M.A., and W. T. WEBB, M.A. Gl. 8vo. 3s. 6d.
This selection contains :—Recollections of the Arabian Nights, The Lady of Shalott, Œnone, The Lotos Eaters, Ulysses, Tithonus, Morte d'Arthur, Sir Galahad, Dora, Ode on the Death of the Duke of Wellington, and The Revenge.
*ENOCH ARDEN. By W. T. WEBB, M.A. Gl. 8vo. 2s.
AYLMER'S FIELD. By W. T. WEBB, M.A. [In the Press.
THE PRINCESS; A MEDLEY. By P. M. WALLACE, B.A. [In the Press.
*THE COMING OF ARTHUR, AND THE PASSING OF ARTHUR. By F. J. ROWE, M.A. Gl. 8vo. 2s.
THRING.—THE ELEMENTS OF GRAMMAR TAUGHT IN ENGLISH. By EDWARD THRING, M.A. With Questions. 4th Ed. 18mo. 2s.
*VAUGHAN.—WORDS FROM THE POETS. By C. M. VAUGHAN. 18mo. 1s.
WARD.—THE ENGLISH POETS. Selections, with Critical Introductions by various Writers and a General Introduction by MATTHEW ARNOLD. Edited by T. H. WARD, M.A. 4 Vols. Vol. I. CHAUCER TO DONNE.—Vol. II. BEN JONSON TO DRYDEN.—Vol. III. ADDISON TO BLAKE.—Vol. IV. WORDSWORTH TO ROSSETTI. 2d Ed. Cr. 8vo. 7s. 6d. each.
*WETHERELL.—EXERCISES ON MORRIS'S PRIMER OF ENGLISH GRAMMAR. By JOHN WETHERELL, M.A., Headmaster of Towcester Grammar School. 18mo. 1s.
WOODS.—*A FIRST POETRY BOOK. By M. A. WOODS, Head Mistress of the Clifton High School for Girls. Fcap. 8vo. 2s. 6d.
*A SECOND POETRY BOOK. By the same. In Two Parts. 2s. 6d. each.
*A THIRD POETRY BOOK. By the same. 4s. 6d.
HYMNS FOR SCHOOL WORSHIP. By the same. 18mo. 1s. 6d.
WORDSWORTH.—SELECTIONS. With Introduction and Notes, by F. J. ROWE, M.A., and W. T. WEBB, M.A. Gl. 8vo. [In preparation.
YONGE.—*A BOOK OF GOLDEN DEEDS. By CHARLOTTE M. YONGE. Gl. 8vo. 2s.
*THE ABRIDGED BOOK OF GOLDEN DEEDS. 18mo. 1s.

FRENCH.

BEAUMARCHAIS.—LE BARBIER DE SEVILLE. With Introduction and Notes. By L. P. BLOUET. Fcap. 8vo. 3s. 6d.
*BOWEN.—FIRST LESSONS IN FRENCH. By H. COURTHOPE BOWEN, M.A. Ex. fcap. 8vo. 1s.
BREYMANN.—Works by HERMANN BREYMANN, Ph.D., Professor of Philology in the University of Munich.
FIRST FRENCH EXERCISE BOOK. Ex. fcap. 8vo. 4s. 6d.
SECOND FRENCH EXERCISE BOOK. Ex. fcap. 8vo. 2s. 6d.
FASNACHT.—Works by G. E. FASNACHT, late Assistant Master at Westminster.
THE ORGANIC METHOD OF STUDYING LANGUAGES. Ex. fcap. 8vo. I. French. 3s. 6d.

A SYNTHETIC FRENCH GRAMMAR FOR SCHOOLS. Cr. 8vo. 3s. 6d.

GRAMMAR AND GLOSSARY OF THE FRENCH LANGUAGE OF THE SEVENTEENTH CENTURY. Cr. 8vo. [*In preparation.*

MACMILLAN'S PRIMARY SERIES OF FRENCH READING BOOKS.—Edited by G. E. FASNACHT. With Illustrations, Notes, Vocabularies, and Exercises. Gl. 8vo.

*FRENCH READINGS FOR CHILDREN. By G. E. FASNACHT. 1s. 6d.

*CORNAZ—NOS ENFANTS ET LEURS AMIS. By EDITH HARVEY. 1s. 6d.

*DE MAISTRE—LA JEUNE SIBÉRIENNE ET LE LÉPREUX DE LA CITÉ D'AOSTE. By STEPHANE BARLET, B.Sc. etc. 1s. 6d.

*FLORIAN—FABLES. By Rev. CHARLES YELD, M.A., Headmaster of University School, Nottingham. 1s. 6d.

*LA FONTAINE—A SELECTION OF FABLES. By L. M. MORIARTY, B.A., Assistant Master at Harrow. 2s. 6d.

*MOLESWORTH—FRENCH LIFE IN LETTERS. By Mrs. MOLESWORTH. 1s. 6d.

*PERRAULT—CONTES DE FÉES. By G. E. FASNACHT. 1s. 6d.

MACMILLAN'S PROGRESSIVE FRENCH COURSE.—By G. E. FASNACHT. Ex. fcap. 8vo.

*FIRST YEAR, containing Easy Lessons on the Regular Accidence. 1s.

*SECOND YEAR, containing an Elementary Grammar with copious Exercises, Notes, and Vocabularies. 2s.

*THIRD YEAR, containing a Systematic Syntax, and Lessons in Composition. 2s. 6d.

THE TEACHER'S COMPANION TO MACMILLAN'S PROGRESSIVE FRENCH COURSE. With Copious Notes, Hints for Different Renderings, Synonyms, Philological Remarks, etc. By G. E. FASNACHT. Ex. fcap. 8vo. Each Year 4s. 6d.

*MACMILLAN'S FRENCH COMPOSITION.—By G. E. FASNACHT. Ex. fcap. 8vo. Part I. Elementary. 2s. 6d. Part II. Advanced. [*In the Press.*

THE TEACHER'S COMPANION TO MACMILLAN'S COURSE OF FRENCH COMPOSITION. By G. E. FASNACHT. Part I. Ex. fcap. 8vo. 4s. 6d.

MACMILLAN'S PROGRESSIVE FRENCH READERS. By G. E. FASNACHT. Ex. fcap. 8vo.

*FIRST YEAR, containing Tales, Historical Extracts, Letters, Dialogues, Ballads, Nursery Songs, etc., with Two Vocabularies: (1) in the order of subjects; (2) in alphabetical order. With Imitative Exercises. 2s. 6d.

*SECOND YEAR, containing Fiction in Prose and Verse, Historical and Descriptive Extracts, Essays, Letters, Dialogues, etc. With Imitative Exercises. 2s. 6d.

MACMILLAN'S FOREIGN SCHOOL CLASSICS. Edited by G. E. FASNACHT. 18mo.

*CORNEILLE—LE CID. By G. E. FASNACHT. 1s.

*DUMAS—LES DEMOISELLES DE ST. CYR. By VICTOR OGER, Lecturer at University College, Liverpool. 1s. 6d.

LA FONTAINE'S FABLES. Books I.-VI. By L. M. MORIARTY, B.A., Assistant Master at Harrow. [*In preparation.*

*MOLIÈRE—L'AVARE. By the same. 1s.

*MOLIÈRE—LE BOURGEOIS GENTILHOMME. By the same. 1s. 6d.

*MOLIÈRE—LES FEMMES SAVANTES. By G. E. FASNACHT. 1s.

*MOLIÈRE—LE MISANTHROPE. By the same. 1s.

*MOLIÈRE—LE MÉDECIN MALGRÉ LUI. By the same. 1s.

*MOLIÈRE—LES PRÉCIEUSES RIDICULES. By the same. 1s.

*RACINE—BRITANNICUS. By E. PELLISSIER, M.A. 2s.

*FRENCH READINGS FROM ROMAN HISTORY. Selected from various Authors, by C. COLBECK, M.A., Assistant Master at Harrow. 4s. 6d.

*SAND, GEORGE—LA MARE AU DIABLE. By W. E. RUSSELL, M.A., Assistant Master at Haileybury. 1s.

*SANDEAU, JULES—MADEMOISELLE DE LA SEIGLIÈRE. By H. C. STEEL, Assistant Master at Winchester. 1s. 6d.

*VOLTAIRE—CHARLES XII. By G. E. FASNACHT. 3s. 6d.

*MASSON.—A COMPENDIOUS DICTIONARY OF THE FRENCH LANGUAGE. Adapted from the Dictionaries of Professor A. ELWALL. By GUSTAVE MASSON. Cr. 8vo. 3s. 6d.

MOLIÈRE.—LE MALADE IMAGINAIRE. With Introduction and Notes, by F. TARVER, M.A., Assistant Master at Eton. Fcap. 8vo. 2s. 6d.

*PELLISSIER.—FRENCH ROOTS AND THEIR FAMILIES. A Synthetic Vocabulary, based upon Derivations. By E. PELLISSIER, M.A., Assistant Master at Clifton College. Gl. 8vo. 6s.

GERMAN.

BEHAGEL.—THE GERMAN LANGUAGE. By Dr. OTTO BEHAGEL. Translated by EMIL TRECHMANN, B.A., Ph.D., Lecturer in Modern Literature in the University of Sydney, N.S.W. Gl. 8vo. [Nearly Ready.

HUSS.—A SYSTEM OF ORAL INSTRUCTION IN GERMAN, by means of Progressive Illustrations and Applications of the leading Rules of Grammar. By H. C. O. HUSS, Ph.D. Cr. 8vo. 5s.

MACMILLAN'S PRIMARY SERIES OF GERMAN READING BOOKS. Edited by G. E. FASNACHT. With Notes, Vocabularies, and Exercises. Gl. 8vo.

*GRIMM—KINDER UND HAUSMÄRCHEN. By G. E. FASNACHT. 2s. 6d.

*HAUFF—DIE KARAVANE. By HERMAN HAGER, Ph.D., Lecturer in the Owens College, Manchester. 3s.

*SCHMID, CHR. VON—H. VON EICHENFELS. By G. E. FASNACHT. 2s. 6d.

MACMILLAN'S PROGRESSIVE GERMAN COURSE. By G. E. FASNACHT. Ex. fcap. 8vo.

*FIRST YEAR. Easy lessons and Rules on the Regular Accidence. 1s. 6d.

*SECOND YEAR. Conversational Lessons in Systematic Accidence and Elementary Syntax. With Philological Illustrations and Etymological Vocabulary. 3s. 6d.

THIRD YEAR. [In the Press.

TEACHER'S COMPANION TO MACMILLAN'S PROGRESSIVE GERMAN COURSE. With copious Notes, Hints for Different Renderings, Synonyms, Philological Remarks, etc. By G. E. FASNACHT. Ex. fcap. 8vo. FIRST YEAR. 4s. 6d. SECOND YEAR. 4s. 6d.

MACMILLAN'S GERMAN COMPOSITION. By G. E. FASNACHT. Ex. fcap. 8vo.

*I. FIRST COURSE. Parallel German-English Extracts and Parallel English-German Syntax. 2s. 6d.

TEACHER'S COMPANION TO MACMILLAN'S GERMAN COMPOSITION. By G. E. FASNACHT. FIRST COURSE. Gl. 8vo. 4s. 6d.

MACMILLAN'S PROGRESSIVE GERMAN READERS. By G. E. FASNACHT. Ex. fcap. 8vo.

*FIRST YEAR, containing an Introduction to the German order of Words, with Copious Examples, extracts from German Authors in Prose and Poetry; Notes, and Vocabularies. 2s. 6d.

MACMILLAN'S FOREIGN SCHOOL CLASSICS.—Edited by G. E. FASNACHT. 18mo.

FREYTAG (G.)—DOKTOR LUTHER. By F. STORR, M.A., Headmaster of the Modern Side, Merchant Taylors' School. [In preparation.

*GOETHE—GÖTZ VON BERLICHINGEN. By H. A. BULL, M.A., Assistant Master at Wellington. 2s.

*GOETHE—FAUST. PART I., followed by an Appendix on PART II. By JANE LEE, Lecturer in German Literature at Newnham College, Cambridge. 4s. 6d.

*HEINE—SELECTIONS FROM THE REISEBILDER AND OTHER PROSE WORKS. By C. COLBECK, M.A., Assistant Master at Harrow. 2s. 6d.

LESSING—MINNA VON BARNHELM. By JAMES SIME, M.A. [In preparation.

*SCHILLER—SELECTIONS FROM SCHILLER'S LYRICAL POEMS. With a Memoir of Schiller. By E. J. TURNER, B.A., and E. D. A. MORSHEAD, M.A., Assistant Masters at Winchester. 2s. 6d.

*SCHILLER—DIE JUNGFRAU VON ORLEANS. By JOSEPH GOSTWICK. 2s. 6d.

*SCHILLER—MARIA STUART. By C. SHELDON, D.Litt., of the Royal Academical Institution, Belfast. 2s. 6d.

*SCHILLER—WILHELM TELL. By G. E. FASNACHT. 2s. 6d.

*SCHILLER—WALLENSTEIN. Part I. DAS LAGER. By H. B. COTTERILL, M.A. 2s.

*UHLAND—SELECT BALLADS. Adapted as a First Easy Reading Book for Beginners. With Vocabulary. By G. E. FASNACHT. 1s.

*PYLODET.—NEW GUIDE TO GERMAN CONVERSATION; containing an Alphabetical List of nearly 800 Familiar Words; followed by Exercises, Vocabulary of Words in frequent use, Familiar Phrases and Dialogues, a Sketch of German Literature, Idiomatic Expressions, etc. By L. PYLODET. 18mo. 2s. 6d.

SMITH.—COMMERCIAL GERMAN. By F. C. SMITH, M.A. [In the Press.

WHITNEY.—A COMPENDIOUS GERMAN GRAMMAR. By W. D. WHITNEY, Professor of Sanskrit and Instructor in Modern Languages in Yale College. Cr. 8vo. 4s. 6d.

A GERMAN READER IN PROSE AND VERSE. By the same. With Notes and Vocabulary. Cr. 8vo. 5s.

*WHITNEY and EDGREN.—A COMPENDIOUS GERMAN AND ENGLISH DICTIONARY, with Notation of Correspondences and Brief Etymologies. By Prof. W. D. WHITNEY, assisted by A. H. EDGREN. Cr. 8vo. 7s. 6d.

THE GERMAN-ENGLISH PART, separately, 5s.

MODERN GREEK.

VINCENT and DICKSON.—HANDBOOK TO MODERN GREEK. By Sir EDGAR VINCENT, K.C.M.G., and T. G. DICKSON, M.A. With Appendix on the relation of Modern and Classical Greek by Prof. JEBB. Cr. 8vo. 6s.

ITALIAN.

DANTE.—THE INFERNO OF DANTE. With Translation and Notes, by A. J. BUTLER, M.A. Cr. 8vo. [In the Press.

THE PURGATORIO OF DANTE With Translations and Notes, by the same. Cr. 8vo. 12s. 6d.

THE PARADISO OF DANTE. With Translation and Notes, by the same. 2d. Ed. Cr. 8vo. 12s. 6d.

READINGS ON THE PURGATORIO OF DANTE. Chiefly based on the Commentary of Benvenuto Da Imola. By the Hon. W. WARREN VERNON, M.A. With an Introduction by the Very Rev. the DEAN OF ST. PAUL'S. 2 vols. Cr. 8vo. 24s.

SPANISH.

CALDERON.—FOUR PLAYS OF CALDERON. With Introduction and Notes. By NORMAN MACCOLL, M.A. Cr. 8vo. 14s.

The four plays here given are *El Principe Constante, La Vida es Sueno, El Alcalde de Zalamea*, and *El Escondido y La Tapada*.

MATHEMATICS.

Arithmetic, Book-keeping, Algebra, Euclid and Pure Geometry, Geometrical
Drawing, Mensuration, Trigonometry, Analytical Geometry (Plane and
Solid), Problems and Questions in Mathematics,· Higher Pure Mathematics, Mechanics (Statics, Dynamics, Hydrostatics, Hydrodynamics: see
also Physics), Physics (Sound, Light, Heat, Electricity, Elasticity, Attractions, &c.), Astronomy, Historical.

ARITHMETIC.

*ALDIS.—THE GREAT GIANT ARITHMOS. A most Elementary Arithmetic
for Children. By MARY STEADMAN ALDIS. Illustrated. Gl. 8vo. 2s. 6d.

ARMY PRELIMINARY EXAMINATION, SPECIMENS OF PAPERS SET AT
THE, 1882-89.—With Answers to the Mathematical Questions. Subjects:
Arithmetic, Algebra, Euclid, Geometrical Drawing, Geography, French,
English Dictation. Cr. 8vo. 3s. 6d.

*BRADSHAW.—A COURSE OF EASY ARITHMETICAL EXAMPLES FOR
BEGINNERS. By J. G. BRADSHAW, B.A., Assistant Master at Clifton College.
Gl. 8vo. 2s. With Answers, 2s. 6d.

*BROOKSMITH.—ARITHMETIC IN THEORY AND PRACTICE. By J. BROOK-
SMITH, M.A. Cr. 8vo. 4s. 6d. KEY. Crown 8vo. 10s. 6d.

*BROOKSMITH.—ARITHMETIC FOR BEGINNERS. By J. and E. J. BROOK-
SMITH. Gl. 8vo. 1s. 6d.

CANDLER.—HELP TO ARITHMETIC. Designed for the use of Schools. By H.
CANDLER, Mathematical Master of Uppingham School. 2d Ed. Ex. fcap. 8vo.
2s. 6d.

*DALTON.—RULES AND EXAMPLES IN ARITHMETIC. By the Rev. T. DAL-
TON, M.A., Senior Mathematical Master at Eton. New Ed., with Answers.
18mo. 2s. 6d.

*GOYEN.—HIGHER ARITHMETIC AND ELEMENTARY MENSURATION.
By P. GOYEN, Inspector of Schools, Dunedin, New Zealand. Cr. 8vo. 5s.

*HALL and KNIGHT.—ARITHMETICAL EXERCISES AND EXAMINATION
PAPERS. With an Appendix containing Questions in LOGARITHMS and
MENSURATION. By H. S. HALL, M.A., Master of the Military and Engineering
Side, Clifton College, and S. R. KNIGHT, B.A. Gl. 8vo. 2s. 6d.

LOCK.—Works by Rev. J. B. LOCK, M.A., Senior Fellow and Bursar of Gonville
and Caius College, Cambridge.

*ARITHMETIC FOR SCHOOLS. With Answers and 1000 additional Examples
for Exercise. 3d Ed., revised. Gl. 8vo. 4s. 6d. Or, Part I. 2s. Part II. 3s.
KEY. Cr. 8vo. 10s. 6d.

*ARITHMETIC FOR BEGINNERS. A School Class-Book of Commercial Arith-
metic. Gl. 8vo. 2s. 6d. KEY. Cr. 8vo. 8s. 6d.

*A SHILLING BOOK OF ARITHMETIC, FOR ELEMENTARY SCHOOLS.
18mo. 1s. With Answers. 1s. 6d.

*PEDLEY.—EXERCISES IN ARITHMETIC for the Use of Schools. Containing
more than 7000 original Examples. By SAMUEL PEDLEY. Cr. 8vo. 5s.
Also in Two Parts, 2s. 6d. each.

SMITH.—Works by Rev. BARNARD SMITH, M.A., late Fellow and Senior Bursar of
St. Peter's College, Cambridge.

ARITHMETIC AND ALGEBRA, in their Principles and Application; with
numerous systematically arranged Examples taken from the Cambridge Examination Papers, with especial reference to the Ordinary Examination for the
B.A. Degree. New Ed., carefully revised. Cr. 8vo. 10s. 6d.

*ARITHMETIC FOR SCHOOLS. Cr. 8vo. 4s. 6d. KEY. Cr. 8vo. 8s. 6d.
New Edition. Revised by Prof W. H. HUDSON. [In preparation.

EXERCISES IN ARITHMETIC. Cr. 8vo. 2s. With Answers, 2s. 6d. Answers separately, 6d.

SCHOOL CLASS-BOOK OF ARITHMETIC. 18mo. 3s. Or separately, in Three Parts, 1s. each. KEYS. Parts I., II., and III., 2s. 6d. each.

SHILLING BOOK OF ARITHMETIC. 18mo. Or separately, Part I., 2d.; Part II., 3d.; Part III., 7d. Answers, 6d. KEY. 18mo. 4s. 6d.

*THE SAME, with Answers. 18mo, cloth. 1s. 6d.

EXAMINATION PAPERS IN ARITHMETIC. 18mo. 1s. 6d. The Same, with Answers. 18mo. 2s. Answers, 6d. KEY. 18mo. 4s. 6d.

THE METRIC SYSTEM OF ARITHMETIC, ITS PRINCIPLES AND APPLICATIONS, with Numerous Examples. 18mo. 3d.

A CHART OF THE METRIC SYSTEM, on a Sheet, size 42 in. by 34 in. on Roller. 3s. 6d. Also a Small Chart on a Card. Price 1d.

EASY LESSONS IN ARITHMETIC, combining Exercises in Reading, Writing, Spelling, and Dictation. Part I. Cr. 8vo. 9d.

EXAMINATION CARDS IN ARITHMETIC. With Answers and Hints. Standards I. and II., in box, 1s. Standards III., IV., and V., in boxes, 1s. each. Standard VI. in Two Parts, in boxes, 1s. each.

A and B papers, of nearly the same difficulty, are given so as to prevent copying, and the colours of the A and B papers differ in each Standard, and from those of every other Standard, so that a master or mistress can see at a glance whether the children have the proper papers.

BOOK-KEEPING.

*THORNTON.—FIRST LESSONS IN BOOK-KEEPING. By J. THORNTON. Cr. 8vo. 2s. 6d. KEY. Oblong 4to. 10s. 6d.

*PRIMER OF BOOK-KEEPING. 18mo. 1s. KEY. Demy 8vo. 2s. 6d.

ALGEBRA.

*DALTON.—RULES AND EXAMPLES IN ALGEBRA. By Rev. T. DALTON, Senior Mathematical Master at Eton. Part I. 18mo. 2s. KEY. Cr. 8vo. 7s. 6d. Part II. 18mo. 2s. 6d.

HALL and KNIGHT.—Works by H. S. HALL, M.A., Master of the Military and Engineering Side, Clifton College, and S. R. KNIGHT, B.A.

*ELEMENTARY ALGEBRA FOR SCHOOLS. 6th Ed., revised and corrected. Gl. 8vo, bound in maroon coloured cloth, 3s. 6d.; with Answers, bound in green coloured cloth, 4s. 6d. KEY. 8s. 6d.

*ALGEBRAICAL EXERCISES AND EXAMINATION PAPERS. To accompany ELEMENTARY ALGEBRA. 2d Ed., revised. Gl. 8vo. 2s. 6d.

*HIGHER ALGEBRA. 3d Ed. Cr. 8vo. 7s. 6d. KEY. Cr. 8vo. 10s. 6d.

*JONES and CHEYNE.—ALGEBRAICAL EXERCISES. Progressively Arranged. By Rev. C. A. JONES and C. H. CHEYNE, M.A., late Mathematical Masters at Westminster School. 18mo. 2s. 6d.

KEY. By Rev. W. FAILES, M.A., Mathematical Master at Westminster School. Cr. 8vo. 7s. 6d.

SMITH.—ARITHMETIC AND ALGEBRA, in their Principles and Application; with numerous systematically arranged Examples taken from the Cambridge Examination Papers, with especial reference to the Ordinary Examination for the B.A. Degree. By Rev. BARNARD SMITH, M.A. New Edition, carefully revised. Cr. 8vo. 10s. 6d.

SMITH.—Works by CHARLES SMITH, M.A., Master of Sidney Sussex College, Cambridge.

*ELEMENTARY ALGEBRA. 2d Ed., revised. Gl. 8vo. 4s. 6d. KEY. By A. G. CRACKNELL, B.A. Cr. 8vo. 10. 6d.

*A TREATISE ON ALGEBRA. 2d Ed. Cr. 8vo. 7s. 6d. KEY. Cr. 8vo. 10s. 6d.

TODHUNTER.—Works by ISAAC TODHUNTER, F.R.S.

*ALGEBRA FOR BEGINNERS. 18mo. 2s. 6d. KEY. Cr. 8vo. 6s. 6d.

*ALGEBRA FOR COLLEGES AND SCHOOLS. By ISAAC TODHUNTER, F.R.S. Cr. 8vo. 7s. 6d. KEY. Cr. 8vo. 10s. 6d.

EUCLID AND PURE GEOMETRY.

COCKSHOTT and WALTERS.—A TREATISE ON GEOMETRICAL CONICS. In accordance with the Syllabus of the Association for the Improvement of Geometrical Teaching. By A. COCKSHOTT, M.A., Assistant Master at Eton, and Rev. F. B. WALTERS, M.A., Principal of King William's College, Isle of Man. Cr. 8vo. 5s.

CONSTABLE.—GEOMETRICAL EXERCISES FOR BEGINNERS. By SAMUEL CONSTABLE. Cr. 8vo. 3s. 6d.

CUTHBERTSON.—EUCLIDIAN GEOMETRY. By FRANCIS CUTHBERTSON, M.A., LL.D. Ex. fcap. 8vo. 4s. 6d.

DAY.—PROPERTIES OF CONIC SECTIONS PROVED GEOMETRICALLY. By Rev. H. G. DAY, M.A. Part I. The Ellipse, with an ample collection of Problems. Cr. 8vo. 3s. 6d.

˙DEAKIN.—RIDER PAPERS ON EUCLID. BOOKS I. AND II. By RUPERT DEAKIN, M.A. 18mo. 1s.

DODGSON.—Works by CHARLES L. DODGSON, M.A., Student and late Mathematical Lecturer, Christ Church, Oxford.

EUCLID, BOOKS I. AND II. 6th Ed., with words substituted for the Algebraical Symbols used in the 1st Ed. Cr. 8vo. 2s.

EUCLID AND HIS MODERN RIVALS. 2d Ed. Cr. 8vo. 6s.

CURIOSA MATHEMATICA. Part I. A New Theory of Parallels. 3d Ed. Cr. 8vo. 2s.

DREW.—GEOMETRICAL TREATISE ON CONIC SECTIONS. By W. H. DREW, M.A. New Ed., enlarged. Cr. 8vo. 5s.

DUPUIS.—ELEMENTARY SYNTHETIC GEOMETRY OF THE POINT, LINE AND CIRCLE IN THE PLANE. By N. F. DUPUIS, M.A., Professor of Pure Mathematics in the University of Queen's College, Kingston, Canada. Gl. 8vo. 4s. 6d.

*HALL and STEVENS.—A TEXT-BOOK OF EUCLID'S ELEMENTS. Including Alternative Proofs, together with additional Theorems and Exercises, classified and arranged. By H. S. HALL, M.A., and F. H. STEVENS, M.A., Masters of the Military and Engineering Side, Clifton College. Gl. 8vo. Book I., 1s.; Books I. and II., 1s. 6d.; Books I.-IV., 3s.; Books III.-IV., 2s.; Books III.-VI., 3s.; Books V.-VI. and XI., 2s. 6d.; Books I.-VI. and XI., 4s. 6d.; Book XI., 1s. [KEY. In preparation.

HALSTED.—THE ELEMENTS OF GEOMETRY. By G. B. HALSTED, Professor of Pure and Applied Mathematics in the University of Texas. 8vo. 12s. 6d.

HAYWARD.—THE ELEMENTS OF SOLID GEOMETRY. By R. B. HAYWARD, M.A., F.R.S. Gl. 8vo. 3s.

LOCK.—EUCLID FOR BEGINNERS. Being an Introduction to existing Text-Books. By Rev. J. B. LOCK, M.A. [In the Press.

MILNE and DAVIS.—GEOMETRICAL CONICS. Part I. The Parabola. By Rev. J. J. MILNE, M.A., and R. F. DAVIS, M.A. Cr. 8vo. 2s.

*RICHARDSON.—THE PROGRESSIVE EUCLID. Books I. and II. With Notes, Exercises, and Deductions. Edited by A. T. RICHARDSON, M.A., Senior Mathematical Master at the Isle of Wight College. Gl. 8vo. 2s. 6d.

SYLLABUS OF PLANE GEOMETRY (corresponding to Euclid, Books I.-VI.)—Prepared by the Association for the Improvement of Geometrical Teaching. Cr. 8vo. Sewed, 1s.

SYLLABUS OF MODERN PLANE GEOMETRY.—Prepared by the Association for the Improvement of Geometrical Teaching. Cr. 8vo. Sewed. 1s.

*TODHUNTER.—THE ELEMENTS OF EUCLID. By I. TODHUNTER, F.R.S. 18mo. 3s. 6d. *Books I. and II. 1s. KEY. Cr. 8vo. 6s. 6d.

WILSON.—Works by Ven. Archdeacon WILSON, M.A., formerly Headmaster of Clifton College.

ELEMENTARY GEOMETRY. BOOKS I.-V. Containing the Subjects of Euclid's first Six Books. Following the Syllabus of the Geometrical Association. Ex. fcap. 8vo. 4s. 6d.

WILSON.—Works by Ven. Archdeacon WILSON—*continued.*
SOLID GEOMETRY AND CONIC SECTIONS.   With Appendices on Transversals and Harmonic Division.   Ex. fcap. 8vo.   3s. 6d.

GEOMETRICAL DRAWING.

EAGLES.—CONSTRUCTIVE GEOMETRY OF PLANE CURVES.   By T. H. EAGLES, M.A., Instructor in Geometrical Drawing and Lecturer in Architecture at the Royal Indian Engineering College, Cooper's Hill.   Cr. 8vo.   12s.

EDGAR and PRITCHARD. — NOTE - BOOK ON PRACTICAL SOLID OR DESCRIPTIVE GEOMETRY.   Containing Problems with help for Solutions. By J. H. EDGAR and G. S. PRITCHARD.   4th Ed., revised by A. MEEZE.   Gl. 8vo.   4s. 6d.

*KITCHENER.—A GEOMETRICAL NOTE-BOOK.   Containing Easy Problems in Geometrical Drawing preparatory to the Study of Geometry.   For the Use of Schools.   By F. E. KITCHENER, M.A., Headmaster of the Newcastle-under-Lyme High School.   4to.   2s.

MILLAR.—ELEMENTS OF DESCRIPTIVE GEOMETRY.   By J. B. MILLAR, Civil Engineer, Lecturer on Engineering in the Victoria University, Manchester. 2d Ed.   Cr. 8vo.   6s.

PLANT.—PRACTICAL PLANE AND DESCRIPTIVE GEOMETRY.   By E. C. PLANT.   Globe 8vo.   [*In preparation.*

MENSURATION.

STEVENS.—ELEMENTARY MENSURATION.   With Exercises on the Mensuration of Plane and Solid Figures.   By F. H. STEVENS, M.A.   Gl. 8vo.
                                                        [*In preparation.*

TEBAY.—ELEMENTARY MENSURATION FOR SCHOOLS.   By S. TEBAY. Ex. fcap. 8vo.   3s. 6d.

*TODHUNTER.—MENSURATION FOR BEGINNERS.   By ISAAC TODHUNTER, F.R.S.   18mo.   2s. 6d.   KEY.   By Rev. FR. L. McCARTHY.   Cr. 8vo.   7s. 6d.

TRIGONOMETRY.

BEASLEY.—AN ELEMENTARY TREATISE ON PLANE TRIGONOMETRY. With Examples.   By R. D. BEASLEY, M.A.   9th Ed., revised and enlarged. Cr. 8vo.   3s. 6d.

BOTTOMLEY.—FOUR-FIGURE MATHEMATICAL TABLES.   Comprising Logarithmic and Trigonometrical Tables, and Tables of Squares, Square Roots, and Reciprocals.   By J. T. BOTTOMLEY, M.A., Lecturer in Natural Philosophy in the University of Glasgow.   8vo.   2s. 6d.

HAYWARD.—THE ALGEBRA OF CO-PLANAR VECTORS AND TRIGONO-METRY.   By R. B. HAYWARD, M.A., F.R.S., Assistant Master at Harrow.
                                                        [*In preparation.*

JOHNSON.—A TREATISE ON TRIGONOMETRY.   By W. E. JOHNSON, M.A., late Scholar and Assistant Mathematical Lecturer at King's College, Cambridge.   Cr. 8vo.   8s. 6d.

LEVETT and DAVISON.—ELEMENTS OF TRIGONOMETRY.   By RAWDON LEVETT and A. F. DAVISON, Assistant Masters at King Edward's School, Birmingham.   [*In the Press.*

LOCK.—Works by Rev. J. B. LOCK, M.A., Senior Fellow and Bursar of Gonville and Caius College, Cambridge.

*THE TRIGONOMETRY OF ONE ANGLE.   Gl. 8vo.   2s. 6d.

*TRIGONOMETRY FOR BEGINNERS, as far as the Solution of Triangles.   3d Ed.   Gl. 8vo.   2s. 6d.   KEY.   Cr. 8vo.   6s. 6d.

*ELEMENTARY TRIGONOMETRY.   6th Ed. (in this edition the chapter on logarithms has been carefully revised).   Gl. 8vo.   4s. 6d.   KEY.   Cr. 8vo.   8s. 6d.

HIGHER TRIGONOMETRY. 5th Ed. Gl. 8vo. 4s. 6d. Both Parts complete in One Volume. Gl. 8vo. 7s. 6d.

M'CLELLAND and PRESTON.—A TREATISE ON SPHERICAL TRIGONO-METRY. With applications to Spherical Geometry and numerous Examples. By W. J. M'CLELLAND, M.A., Principal of the Incorporated Society's School, Santry, Dublin, and T. PRESTON, M.A. Cr. 8vo. 8s. 6d., or: Part I. To the End of Solution of Triangles, 4s. 6d. Part II., 5s.

MATTHEWS.—MANUAL OF LOGARITHMS. By G. F. MATTHEWS, B.A. 8vo. 5s. net.

PALMER.—TEXT-BOOK OF PRACTICAL LOGARITHMS AND TRIGONO-METRY. By J. H. PALMER, Headmaster, R.N., H.M.S. *Cambridge*, Devonport. Gl. 8vo. 4s. 6d.

SNOWBALL.—THE ELEMENTS OF PLANE AND SPHERICAL TRIGONO-METRY. By J. C. SNOWBALL. 14th Ed. Cr. 8vo. 7s. 6d.

TODHUNTER.—Works by ISAAC TODHUNTER, F.R.S.
*TRIGONOMETRY FOR BEGINNERS. 18mo. 2s. 6d. KEY. Cr. 8vo. 8s. 6d.
PLANE TRIGONOMETRY. Cr. 8vo. 5s. A New Edition, revised by R. W. HOGG, M.A. Cr. 8vo. 5s. KEY. Cr. 8vo. 10s. 6d.
A TREATISE ON SPHERICAL TRIGONOMETRY. Cr. 8vo. 4s. 6d.

WOLSTENHOLME.—EXAMPLES FOR PRACTICE IN THE USE OF SEVEN-FIGURE LOGARITHMS. By JOSEPH WOLSTENHOLME, D.Sc., late Professor of Mathematics in the Royal Indian Engineering Coll., Cooper's Hill. 8vo. 5s.

ANALYTICAL GEOMETRY (Plane and Solid).

DYER.—EXERCISES IN ANALYTICAL GEOMETRY. By J. M. DYER, M.A., Assistant Master at Eton. Illustrated. Cr. 8vo. 4s. 6d.

FERRERS.—AN ELEMENTARY TREATISE ON TRILINEAR CO-ORDIN-ATES, the Method of Reciprocal Polars, and the Theory of Projectors. By the Rev. N. M. FERRERS, D.D., F.R.S., Master of Gonville and Caius College, Cambridge. 4th Ed., revised. Cr. 8vo. 6s. 6d.

FROST.—Works by PERCIVAL FROST, D.Sc., F.R.S., Fellow and Mathematical Lecturer at King's College, Cambridge.
AN ELEMENTARY TREATISE ON CURVE TRACING. 8vo. 12s.
SOLID GEOMETRY. 3d Ed. Demy 8vo. 16s.
HINTS FOR THE SOLUTION OF PROBLEMS in the Third Edition of SOLID GEOMETRY. 8vo. 8s. 6d.

JOHNSON.—CURVE TRACING IN CARTESIAN CO-ORDINATES. By W. WOOLSEY JOHNSON, Professor of Mathematics at the U.S. Naval Academy, Annapolis, Maryland. Cr. 8vo. 4s. 6d.

M'CLELLAND.—THE GEOMETRY OF THE CIRCLE. By W. J. M'CLELLAND, M.A. Cr. 8vo. [*In the Press.*

PUCKLE.—AN ELEMENTARY TREATISE ON CONIC SECTIONS AND AL-GEBRAIC GEOMETRY. With Numerous Examples and Hints for their Solution. By G. H. PUCKLE, M.A. 5th Ed., revised and enlarged. Cr. 8vo. 7s. 6d.

SMITH.—Works by CHARLES SMITH, M.A., Master of Sidney Sussex College, Cambridge.
CONIC SECTIONS. 7th Ed. Cr. 8vo. 7s. 6d.
SOLUTIONS TO CONIC SECTIONS. Cr. 8vo. 10s. 6d.
AN ELEMENTARY TREATISE ON SOLID GEOMETRY. 2d Ed. Cr. 8vo. 9s. 6d.

TODHUNTER.—Works by ISAAC TODHUNTER, F.R.S.
PLANE CO-ORDINATE GEOMETRY, as applied to the Straight Line and the Conic Sections. Cr. 8vo. 7s. 6d.
KEY. By C. W. BOURNE. M.A., Headmaster of King's College School. Cr. 8vo. 10s. 6d.

TODHUNTER.—Works by ISAAC TODHUNTER, F.R.S.—*continued.*
EXAMPLES OF ANALYTICAL GEOMETRY OF THREE DIMENSIONS.
New Ed., revised. Cr. 8vo. 4s.

PROBLEMS AND QUESTIONS IN MATHEMATICS.

ARMY PRELIMINARY EXAMINATION, 1882-1890, Specimens of Papers set at
the. With Answers to the Mathematical Questions. Subjects: Arithmetic,
Algebra, Euclid, Geometrical Drawing, Geography, French, English Dictation.
Cr. 8vo. 3s. 6d.
**CAMBRIDGE SENATE-HOUSE PROBLEMS AND RIDERS, WITH SOLU-
TIONS:—**
1875—PROBLEMS AND RIDERS. By A. G. GREENHILL, F.R.S. Cr. 8vo. 8s. 6d.
1878—SOLUTIONS OF SENATE-HOUSE PROBLEMS. By the Mathematical
Moderators and Examiners. Edited by J. W. L. GLAISHER, F.R.S., Fellow of
Trinity College, Cambridge. 12s.
CHRISTIE.—A COLLECTION OF ELEMENTARY TEST-QUESTIONS IN PURE
AND MIXED MATHEMATICS; with Answers and Appendices on Synthetic
Division, and on the Solution of Numerical Equations by Horner's Method.
By JAMES R. CHRISTIE, F.R.S. Cr. 8vo. 8s. 6d.
CLIFFORD.—MATHEMATICAL PAPERS. By W. K. CLIFFORD. Edited by R.
TUCKER. With an Introduction by H. J. STEPHEN SMITH, M.A. 8vo. 30s.
MILNE.—Works by Rev. JOHN J. MILNE, Private Tutor.
WEEKLY PROBLEM PAPERS. With Notes intended for the use of Students
preparing for Mathematical Scholarships, and for Junior Members of the Uni-
versities who are reading for Mathematical Honours. Pott 8vo. 4s. 6d.
SOLUTIONS TO WEEKLY PROBLEM PAPERS. Cr. 8vo. 10s. 6d.
COMPANION TO WEEKLY PROBLEM PAPERS. Cr. 8vo. 10s. 6d.
RICHARDSON.—MISCELLANEOUS MATHEMATICAL PAPERS. Elementary
and Advanced. By A. T. RICHARDSON, M.A., Senior Mathematical Master at
the Isle of Wight College. [*In the Press.*
SANDHURST MATHEMATICAL PAPERS, for admission into the Royal Military
College, 1881-1889. Edited by E. J. BROOKSMITH, B.A., Instructor in Mathe-
matics at the Royal Military Academy, Woolwich. Cr. 8vo. 3s. 6d.
WOOLWICH MATHEMATICAL PAPERS, for Admission into the Royal Military
Academy, Woolwich, 1880-1888 inclusive. By the same Editor. Cr. 8vo. 6s.
WOLSTENHOLME.—Works by JOSEPH WOLSTENHOLME, D.Sc., late Professor of
Mathematics in the Royal Engineering Coll., Cooper's Hill.
MATHEMATICAL PROBLEMS, on Subjects included in the First and Second
Divisions of the Schedule of Subjects for the Cambridge Mathematical Tripos
Examination. New Ed., greatly enlarged. 8vo. 18s.
EXAMPLES FOR PRACTICE IN THE USE OF SEVEN-FIGURE LOG-
ARITHMS. 8vo. 5s.

HIGHER PURE MATHEMATICS.

AIRY.—Works by Sir G. B. AIRY, K.C.B., formerly Astronomer-Royal.
ELEMENTARY TREATISE ON PARTIAL DIFFERENTIAL EQUATIONS.
With Diagrams. 2d Ed. Cr. 8vo. 5s. 6d.
ON THE ALGEBRAICAL AND NUMERICAL THEORY OF ERRORS OF
OBSERVATIONS AND THE COMBINATION OF OBSERVATIONS.
2d Ed., revised. Cr. 8vo. 6s. 6d.
BOOLE.—THE CALCULUS OF FINITE DIFFERENCES. By G. BOOLE. 3d Ed.,
revised by J. F. MOULTON, Q.C. Cr. 8vo. 10s. 6d.
EDWARDS.—THE DIFFERENTIAL CALCULUS. By JOSEPH EDWARDS, M.A.
With Applications and numerous Examples. Cr. 8vo. 10s. 6d.
FERRERS.—AN ELEMENTARY TREATISE ON SPHERICAL HARMONICS,
AND SUBJECTS CONNECTED WITH THEM. By Rev. N. M. FERRERS,
D.D F.R.S., Master of Gonville and Caius College, Cambridge. Cr. 8vo. 7s. 6d.

FORSYTH.—A TREATISE ON DIFFERENTIAL EQUATIONS. By ANDREW RUSSELL FORSYTH, F.R.S., Fellow and Assistant Tutor of Trinity College, Cambridge. 2d Ed. 8vo. 14s.

FROST.—AN ELEMENTARY TREATISE ON CURVE TRACING. By PERCIVAL FROST, M.A., D.Sc. 8vo. 12s.

GRAHAM.—GEOMETRY OF POSITION. By R. H. GRAHAM. Cr. 8vo. 7s. 6d.

GREENHILL.—DIFFERENTIAL AND INTEGRAL CALCULUS. By A. G. GREENHILL, Professor of Mathematics to the Senior Class of Artillery Officers, Woolwich. New Ed. Cr. 8vo. 10s. 6d.

APPLICATIONS OF ELLIPTIC FUNCTIONS. By the same. [In the Press.

JOHNSON.—Works by WILLIAM WOOLSEY JOHNSON, Professor of Mathematics at the U.S. Naval Academy, Annapolis, Maryland.

INTEGRAL CALCULUS, an Elementary Treatise on the. Founded on the Method of Rates or Fluxions. 8vo. 9s.

CURVE TRACING IN CARTESIAN CO-ORDINATES. Cr. 8vo. 4s. 6d.

A TREATISE ON ORDINARY AND DIFFERENTIAL EQUATIONS. Ex. cr. 8vo. 15s.

KELLAND and TAIT.—INTRODUCTION TO QUATERNIONS, with numerous examples. By P. KELLAND and P. G. TAIT, Professors in the Department of Mathematics in the University of Edinburgh. 2d Ed. Cr. 8vo. 7s. 6d.

KEMPE.—HOW TO DRAW A STRAIGHT LINE: a Lecture on Linkages. By A. B. KEMPE. Illustrated. Cr. 8vo. 1s. 6d.

KNOX.—DIFFERENTIAL CALCULUS FOR BEGINNERS. By ALEXANDER KNOX. Fcap. 8vo. 3s. 6d.

MUIR.—THE THEORY OF DETERMINANTS IN THE HISTORICAL ORDER OF ITS DEVELOPMENT. Part I. Determinants in General. Leibnitz (1693) to Cayley (1841). By THOS. MUIR, Mathematical Master in the High School of Glasgow. 8vo. 10s. 6d.

RICE and JOHNSON.—AN ELEMENTARY TREATISE ON THE DIFFEREN-TIAL CALCULUS. Founded on the Method of Rates or Fluxions. By J. M. RICE, Professor of Mathematics in the United States Navy, and W. W. JOHNSON, Professor of Mathematics at the United States Naval Academy. 3d Ed., revised and corrected. 8vo. 18s. Abridged Ed. 9s.

TODHUNTER.—Works by ISAAC TODHUNTER, F.R.S.

AN ELEMENTARY TREATISE ON THE THEORY OF EQUATIONS. Cr. 8vo. 7s. 6d.

A TREATISE ON THE DIFFERENTIAL CALCULUS. Cr. 8vo. 10s. 6d. KEY. Cr. 8vo. 10s. 6d.

A TREATISE ON THE INTEGRAL CALCULUS AND ITS APPLICATIONS. Cr. 8vo. 10s. 6d. KEY. Cr. 8vo. 10s. 6d.

A HISTORY OF THE MATHEMATICAL THEORY OF PROBABILITY, from the time of Pascal to that of Laplace. 8vo. 18s.

AN ELEMENTARY TREATISE ON LAPLACE'S, LAME'S, AND BESSEL'S FUNCTIONS. Cr. 8vo. 10s. 6d.

MECHANICS : Statics, Dynamics, Hydrostatics, Hydrodynamics. (See also Physics.)

ALEXANDER and THOMSON.—ELEMENTARY APPLIED MECHANICS. By Prof. T. ALEXANDER and A. W. THOMSON. Part II. Transverse Stress. Cr. 8vo. 10s. 6d.

BALL.—EXPERIMENTAL MECHANICS. A Course of Lectures delivered at the Royal College of Science for Ireland. By Sir R. S. BALL, F.R.S. 2d Ed. Illustrated. Cr. 8vo. 6s.

CLIFFORD.—THE ELEMENTS OF DYNAMIC. An Introduction to the Study of Motion and Rest in Solid and Fluid Bodies. By W. K. CLIFFORD. Part I.— Kinematic. Cr. 8vo. Books I.-III. 7s. 6d. ; Book IV. and Appendix, 6s.

COTTERILL.—APPLIED MECHANICS : An Elementary General Introduction to the Theory of Structures and Machines. By J. H. COTTERILL, F.R.S., Professor of Applied Mechanics in the Royal Naval College, Greenwich. 8vo. 18s.

COTTERILL and SLADE.—LESSONS IN APPLIED MECHANICS. By Prof. J. H. COTTERILL and J. H. SLADE. Fcap. 8vo. 5s. 6d.

DYNAMICS, SYLLABUS OF ELEMENTARY. Part I. Linear Dynamics. With an Appendix on the Meanings of the Symbols in Physical Equations. Prepared by the Association for the Improvement of Geometrical Teaching. 4to. 1s.

GANGUILLET and KUTTER.—A GENERAL FORMULA FOR THE UNIFORM FLOW OF WATER IN RIVERS AND OTHER CHANNELS. By E. GANGUILLET and W. R. KUTTER. Translated, with Additions, including Tables and Diagrams, and the Elements of over 1200 Gaugings of Rivers, Small Channels, and Pipes in English Measure, by R. HERING, Assoc. Am. Soc., C.E., M. Inst. C.E., and J. C. TRAUTWINE Jun., Assoc. Am. Soc. C.E., Assoc. Inst. C.E. 8vo. 17s.

GRAHAM.—GEOMETRY OF POSITION. By R. H. GRAHAM. Cr. 8vo. 7s. 6d.

GREAVES.—Works by JOHN GREAVES, M.A., Fellow and Mathematical Lecturer at Christ's College, Cambridge.

*STATICS FOR BEGINNERS. Gl. 8vo. 3s. 6d.

A TREATISE ON ELEMENTARY STATICS. 2d Ed. Cr. 8vo. 6s. 6d.

GREENHILL.—HYDROSTATICS. By A. G. GREENHILL, Professor of Mathematics to the Senior Class of Artillery Officers, Woolwich. Cr. 8vo. [In preparation.

*HICKS.—ELEMENTARY DYNAMICS OF PARTICLES AND SOLIDS. By W. M. HICKS, D.Sc., Principal and Professor of Mathematics and Physics, Firth College, Sheffield. Cr. 8vo. 6s. 6d.

JELLETT.—A TREATISE ON THE THEORY OF FRICTION. By JOHN H. JELLETT, B.D., late Provost of Trinity College, Dublin. 8vo. 8s. 6d.

KENNEDY.—THE MECHANICS OF MACHINERY. By A. B. W. KENNEDY, F.R.S. Illustrated. Cr. 8vo. 12s. 6d.

LOCK.—Works by Rev. J. B. LOCK, M.A.

*ELEMENTARY STATICS. 2d Ed. Gl. 8vo. 4s. 6d.

*ELEMENTARY DYNAMICS. 3d Ed. Gl. 8vo. 4s. 6d.

ELEMENTARY HYDROSTATICS. Gl. 8vo. [In preparation.

MECHANICS FOR BEGINNERS. Gl. 8vo. Part I. MECHANICS OF SOLIDS. [In the Press. Part II. MECHANICS OF FLUIDS. [In preparation.

MACGREGOR.—KINEMATICS AND DYNAMICS. An Elementary Treatise. By J. G. MACGREGOR, D.Sc., Munro Professor of Physics in Dalhousie College, Halifax, Nova Scotia. Illustrated. Cr. 8vo. 10s. 6d.

PARKINSON.—AN ELEMENTARY TREATISE ON MECHANICS. By S. PARKINSON, D.D., F.R.S., late Tutor and Prælector of St. John's College, Cambridge. 6th Ed., revised. Cr. 8vo. 9s. 6d.

PIRIE.—LESSONS ON RIGID DYNAMICS. By Rev. G. PIRIE, M.A., Professor of Mathematics in the University of Aberdeen. Cr. 8vo. 6s.

ROUTH.—Works by EDWARD JOHN ROUTH, D.Sc., LL.D., F.R.S., Hon. Fellow of St. Peter's College, Cambridge.

A TREATISE ON THE DYNAMICS OF THE SYSTEM OF RIGID BODIES. With numerous Examples. Two Vols. 8vo. Vol. I.—Elementary Parts. 5th Ed. 14s. Vol. II.—The Advanced Parts. 4th Ed. 14s.

STABILITY OF A GIVEN STATE OF MOTION, PARTICULARLY STEADY MOTION. Adams Prize Essay for 1877. 8vo. 8s. 6d.

*SANDERSON.—HYDROSTATICS FOR BEGINNERS. By F. W. SANDERSON, M.A., Assistant Master at Dulwich College. Gl. 8vo. 4s. 6d.

TAIT and STEELE.—A TREATISE ON DYNAMICS OF A PARTICLE. By Professor TAIT, M.A., and W. J. STEELE, B.A. 6th Ed., revised. Cr. 8vo. 12s.

TODHUNTER.—Works by ISAAC TODHUNTER, F.R.S.

*MECHANICS FOR BEGINNERS. 18mo. 4s. 6d. KEY. Cr. 8vo. 6s. 6d.

A TREATISE ON ANALYTICAL STATICS. 5th Ed. Edited by Prof. J. D. EVERETT, F.R.S. Cr. 8vo. 10s. 6d.

PHYSICS: Sound, Light, Heat, Electricity, Elasticity, Attractions, etc. (See also Mechanics.)

AIRY.—Works by Sir G. B. AIRY, K.C.B., formerly Astronomer-Royal.
ON SOUND AND ATMOSPHERIC VIBRATIONS. With the Mathematical Elements of Music. 2d Ed., revised and enlarged. Cr. 8vo. 9s.
GRAVITATION: An Elementary Explanation of the Principal Perturbations in the Solar System. 2d Ed. Cr. 8vo. 7s. 6d.

CLAUSIUS.—MECHANICAL THEORY OF HEAT. By R. CLAUSIUS. Translated by W. R. BROWNE, M.A. Cr. 8vo. 10s. 6d.

CUMMING.—AN INTRODUCTION TO THE THEORY OF ELECTRICITY. By LINNÆUS CUMMING, M.A., Assistant Master at Rugby. Illustrated. Cr. 8vo. 8s. 6d.

DANIELL.—A TEXT-BOOK OF THE PRINCIPLES OF PHYSICS. By ALFRED DANIELL, D.Sc. Illustrated. 2d Ed., revised and enlarged. 8vo. 21s.

DAY.—ELECTRIC LIGHT ARITHMETIC. By R. E. DAY, Evening Lecturer in Experimental Physics at King's College, London. Pott 8vo. 2s.

EVERETT.—ILLUSTRATIONS OF THE C. G. S. SYSTEM OF UNITS WITH TABLES OF PHYSICAL CONSTANTS. By J. D. EVERETT, F.R.S., Professor of Natural Philosophy, Queen's College, Belfast. New Ed. Ex. fcap. 8vo. 5s.

FERRERS.—AN ELEMENTARY TREATISE ON SPHERICAL HARMONICS, and Subjects connected with them. By Rev. N. M. FERRERS, D.D., F.R.S., Master of Gonville and Caius College, Cambridge. Cr. 8vo. 7s. 6d.

FESSENDEN.—PHYSICS FOR PUBLIC SCHOOLS. By C. FESSENDEN. Illustrated. Fcap. 8vo.   [In the Press.

GRAY.—THE THEORY AND PRACTICE OF ABSOLUTE MEASUREMENTS IN ELECTRICITY AND MAGNETISM. By A. GRAY, F.R.S.E., Professor of Physics in the University College of North Wales. Two Vols. Cr. 8vo. Vol. I. 12s. 6d.   [Vol. II. In the Press.
ABSOLUTE MEASUREMENTS IN ELECTRICITY AND MAGNETISM. 2d Ed., revised and greatly enlarged. Fcap. 8vo. 5s. 6d.

IBBETSON.—THE MATHEMATICAL THEORY OF PERFECTLY ELASTIC SOLIDS, with a Short Account of Viscous Fluids. By W. J. IBBETSON, late Senior Scholar of Clare College, Cambridge. 8vo. 21s.

*JONES.—EXAMPLES IN PHYSICS. Containing over 1000 Problems with Answers and numerous solved Examples. Suitable for candidates preparing for the Intermediate, Science, Preliminary, Scientific, and other Examinations of the University of London. By D. E. JONES, B.Sc., Professor of Physics in the University College of Wales, Aberystwyth. Fcap. 8vo. 3s. 6d.
***ELEMENTARY LESSONS IN HEAT, LIGHT, AND SOUND. By the same. Gl. 8vo. 2s. 6d.

LOCKYER.—CONTRIBUTIONS TO SOLAR PHYSICS. By J. NORMAN LOCKYER, F.R.S. With Illustrations. Royal 8vo. 31s. 6d.

LODGE.—MODERN VIEWS OF ELECTRICITY. By OLIVER J. LODGE, F.R.S., Professor of Experimental Physics in University College, Liverpool. Illustrated. Cr. 8vo. 6s. 6d.

LOEWY.—*QUESTIONS AND EXAMPLES ON EXPERIMENTAL PHYSICS: Sound, Light, Heat, Electricity, and Magnetism. By B. LOEWY, Examiner in Experimental Physics to the College of Preceptors. Fcap. 8vo. 2s.
*A GRADUATED COURSE OF NATURAL SCIENCE FOR ELEMENTARY AND TECHNICAL SCHOOLS AND COLLEGES. By the same. In Three Parts. Part I. FIRST YEAR'S COURSE. Gl. 8vo. 2s. Part II. [In preparation.

LUPTON.—NUMERICAL TABLES AND CONSTANTS IN ELEMENTARY SCIENCE. By S. LUPTON, M.A., late Assistant Master at Harrow. Ex. fcap. 8vo. 2s. 6d.

MACFARLANE.—PHYSICAL ARITHMETIC. By A. MACFARLANE, D.Sc., late Examiner in Mathematics at the University of Edinburgh. Cr. 8vo. 7s. 6d.

*MAYER.—SOUND: A Series of Simple, Entertaining, and Inexpensive Experiments in the Phenomena of Sound. By A. M. MAYER, Professor of Physics in the Stevens Institute of Technology. Illustrated. Cr. 8vo. 3s. 6d.

*MAYER and BARNARD.—LIGHT: A Series of Simple, Entertaining, and Inexpensive Experiments in the Phenomena of Light. By A. M. MAYER and C. BARNARD. Illustrated. Cr. 8vo. 2s. 6d.

MOLLOY.—GLEANINGS IN SCIENCE : Popular Lectures on Scientific Subjects. By the Rev. GERALD MOLLOY, D.Sc., Rector of the Catholic University of Ireland. 8vo. 7s. 6d.

NEWTON.—PRINCIPIA. Edited by Prof. Sir W. THOMSON, P.R.S., and Prof. BLACKBURNE. 4to. 31s. 6d.

THE FIRST THREE SECTIONS OF NEWTON'S PRINCIPIA. With Notes and Illustrations. Also a Collection of Problems, principally intended as Examples of Newton's Methods. By P. FROST, M.A., D.Sc. 3d Ed. 8vo. 12s.

PARKINSON.—A TREATISE ON OPTICS. By S. PARKINSON, D.D., F.R.S., late Tutor and Prælector of St. John's College, Cambridge. 4th Ed., revised and enlarged. Cr. 8vo. 10s. 6d.

PEABODY.—THERMODYNAMICS OF THE STEAM-ENGINE AND OTHER HEAT-ENGINES. By CECIL H. PEABODY, Associate Professor of Steam Engineering, Massachusetts Institute of Technology. 8vo. 21s.

PERRY. — STEAM: An Elementary Treatise. By JOHN PERRY, Professor of Mechanical Engineering and Applied Mechanics at the Technical College, Finsbury. 18mo. 4s. 6d.

PICKERING.—ELEMENTS OF PHYSICAL MANIPULATION. By Prof. EDWARD C. PICKERING. Medium 8vo. Part I., 12s. 6d. Part II., 14s.

PRESTON.—THE THEORY OF LIGHT. By THOMAS PRESTON, M.A. Illustrated. 8vo. 12s. 6d.

THE THEORY OF HEAT. By the same Author. 8vo. [In preparation.

RAYLEIGH.—THE THEORY OF SOUND. By Lord RAYLEIGH, F.R.S. 8vo. Vol. I., 12s. 6d. Vol. II., 12s. 6d. [Vol. III. In the Press.

SHANN.—AN ELEMENTARY TREATISE ON HEAT, IN RELATION TO STEAM AND THE STEAM - ENGINE. By G. SHANN, M.A. Illustrated. Cr. 8vo. 4s. 6d.

SPOTTISWOODE.—POLARISATION OF LIGHT. By the late W. SPOTTISWOODE, F.R.S. Illustrated. Cr. 8vo. 3s. 6d.

STEWART.—Works by BALFOUR STEWART, F.R.S., late Langworthy Professor of Physics in the Owens College, Victoria University, Manchester.

*PRIMER OF PHYSICS. Illustrated. With Questions. 18mo. 1s.
*LESSONS IN ELEMENTARY PHYSICS. Illustrated. Fcap. 8vo. 4s. 6d.
*QUESTIONS. By Prof. T. H. CORE. Fcap. 8vo. 2s.

STEWART and GEE.—LESSONS IN ELEMENTARY PRACTICAL PHYSICS. By BALFOUR STEWART, F.R.S., and W. W. HALDANE GEE, B.Sc. Cr. 8vo. Vol. I. GENERAL PHYSICAL PROCESSES. 6s. Vol. II. ELECTRICITY AND MAGNETISM. 7s. 6d. [Vol. III. OPTICS, HEAT, AND SOUND. In the Press.

*PRACTICAL PHYSICS FOR SCHOOLS AND THE JUNIOR STUDENTS OF COLLEGES. Gl. 8vo. Vol. I. ELECTRICITY AND MAGNETISM. 2s. 6d. [Vol. II. OPTICS, HEAT, AND SOUND. In the Press.

STOKES.—ON LIGHT. Burnett Lectures, delivered in Aberdeen in 1883-4-5. By Sir G. G. STOKES, F.R.S., Lucasian Professor of Mathematics in the University of Cambridge. First Course : ON THE NATURE OF LIGHT. Second Course : ON LIGHT AS A MEANS OF INVESTIGATION. Third Course : ON THE BENEFICIAL EFFECTS OF LIGHT. Cr. 8vo. 7s. 6d.

*** The 2d and 3d Courses may be had separately. Cr. 8vo. 2s. 6d. each.

STONE.—AN ELEMENTARY TREATISE ON SOUND. By W. H. STONE. Illustrated. Fcap. 8vo. 3s. 6d.

TAIT.—HEAT. By P. G. TAIT, Professor of Natural Philosophy in the University of Edinburgh. Cr. 8vo. 6s.

LECTURES ON SOME RECENT ADVANCES IN PHYSICAL SCIENCE. By the same. 3d Edition. Crown 8vo. 9s.

TAYLOR.—SOUND AND MUSIC. An Elementary Treatise on the Physical Constitution of Musical Sounds and Harmony, including the Chief Acoustical Discoveries of Professor Helmholtz. By SEDLEY TAYLOR, M.A. Illustrated. 2d Ed. Ex. cr. 8vo. 8s. 6d.

*THOMPSON. — ELEMENTARY LESSONS IN ELECTRICITY AND MAGNETISM. By SILVANUS P. THOMPSON, Principal and Professor of Physics in the Technical College, Finsbury. Illustrated. New Ed., revised. Fcap. 8vo. 4s. 6d.

THOMSON.—Works by J. J. THOMSON, Professor of Experimental Physics in the University of Cambridge.
A TREATISE ON THE MOTION OF VORTEX RINGS. Adams Prize Essay 1882. 8vo. 6s.
APPLICATIONS OF DYNAMICS TO PHYSICS AND CHEMISTRY. Cr. 8vo. 7s. 6d.

THOMSON.—Works by Sir W. THOMSON, P.R.S., Professor of Natural Philosophy in the University of Glasgow.
ELECTROSTATICS AND MAGNETISM, REPRINTS OF PAPERS ON. 2d Ed. 8vo. 18s.
POPULAR LECTURES AND ADDRESSES. 3 Vols. Illustrated. Cr. 8vo. Vol. I. CONSTITUTION OF MATTER. 7s. 6d. Vol. III. NAVIGATION. 7s. 6d.

TODHUNTER.—Works by ISAAC TODHUNTER, F.R.S.
AN ELEMENTARY TREATISE ON LAPLACE'S, LAME'S, AND BESSEL'S FUNCTIONS. Crown 8vo. 10s. 6d.
A HISTORY OF THE MATHEMATICAL THEORIES OF ATTRACTION, AND THE FIGURE OF THE EARTH, from the time of Newton to that of Laplace. 2 vols. 8vo. 24s.

TURNER.—A COLLECTION OF EXAMPLES ON HEAT AND ELECTRICITY. By H. H. TURNER, Fellow of Trinity College, Cambridge. Cr. 8vo. 2s. 6d.

WRIGHT.—LIGHT: A Course of Experimental Optics, chiefly with the Lantern. By LEWIS WRIGHT. Illustrated. Cr. 8vo. 7s. 6d.

ASTRONOMY. •

AIRY.—Works by Sir G. B. AIRY, K.C.B., formerly Astronomer-Royal.
*POPULAR ASTRONOMY. 7th Ed. Revised by H. H. TURNER, M.A. 18mo. 4s. 6d.
GRAVITATION: An Elementary Explanation of the Principal Perturbations in the Solar System. 2d Ed. Cr. 8vo. 7s. 6d.

CHEYNE.—AN ELEMENTARY TREATISE ON THE PLANETARY THEORY. By C. H. H. CHEYNE. With Problems. 3d Ed. Edited by Rev. A. FREEMAN, M.A., F.R.A.S. Cr. 8vo. 7s. 6d.

CLARK and SADLER.—THE STAR GUIDE. By L. CLARK and H. SADLER. Roy. 8vo. 5s.

CROSSLEY, GLEDHILL, and WILSON.—A HANDBOOK OF DOUBLE STARS. By E. CROSSLEY, J. GLEDHILL, and J. M. WILSON. 8vo. 21s.
CORRECTIONS TO THE HANDBOOK OF DOUBLE STARS. 8vo. 1s.

FORBES.—TRANSIT OF VENUS. By G. FORBES, Professor of Natural Philosophy in the Andersonian University, Glasgow. Illustrated. Cr. 8vo. 3s. 6d.

GODFRAY.—Works by HUGH GODFRAY, M.A., Mathematical Lecturer at Pembroke College, Cambridge.
A TREATISE ON ASTRONOMY. 4th Ed. 8vo. 12s. 6d.
AN ELEMENTARY TREATISE ON THE LUNAR THEORY, with a brief Sketch of the Problem up to the time of Newton. 2d Ed., revised. Cr. 8vo. 5s. 6d.

LOCKYER.—Works by J. NORMAN LOCKYER, F.R.S.
*PRIMER OF ASTRONOMY. Illustrated. 18mo. 1s.
*ELEMENTARY LESSONS IN ASTRONOMY. With Spectra of the Sun, Stars, and Nebulæ, and numerous Illustrations. 36th Thousand. Revised throughout. Fcap. 8vo. 5s. 6d.

*QUESTIONS ON LOCKYER'S ELEMENTARY LESSONS IN ASTRONOMY.
By J. FORBES ROBERTSON. 18mo. 1s. 6d.

THE CHEMISTRY OF THE SUN. Illustrated. 8vo. 14s.

THE METEORITIC HYPOTHESIS OF THE ORIGIN OF COSMICAL
SYSTEMS. Illustrated. 8vo. 17s. net.

THE EVOLUTION OF THE HEAVENS AND THE EARTH. Cr. 8vo. Illustrated.   [In the Press.

LOCKYER and SEABROKE.—STAR-GAZING PAST AND PRESENT. By J.
NORMAN LOCKYER, F.R.S. Expanded from Shorthand Notes with the
assistance of G. M. SEABROKE, F.R.A.S. Royal 8vo. 21s.

NEWCOMB.—POPULAR ASTRONOMY. By S. NEWCOMB, LL.D., Professor
U.S. Naval Observatory. Illustrated. 2d Ed., revised. 8vo. 18s.

HISTORICAL.

BALL.—A SHORT ACCOUNT OF THE HISTORY OF MATHEMATICS. By W.
W. R. BALL, M.A. Cr. 8vo. 10s. 6d.

NATURAL SCIENCES.

Chemistry ; Physical Geography, Geology, and Mineralogy ; Biology ;
Medicine.

(For MECHANICS, PHYSICS, and ASTRONOMY, see
MATHEMATICS.)

CHEMISTRY.

ARMSTRONG.—A MANUAL OF INORGANIC CHEMISTRY. By HENRY ARM-
STRONG, F.R.S., Professor of Chemistry in the City and Guilds of London Technical Institute. Cr. 8vo.   [In preparation.

*COHEN.—THE OWENS COLLEGE COURSE OF PRACTICAL ORGANIC
CHEMISTRY. By JULIUS B. COHEN, Ph.D., Assistant Lecturer on Chemistry
in the Owens College, Manchester. With a Preface by Sir HENRY ROSCOE,
F.R.S., and C. SCHORLEMMER, F.R.S. Fcap. 8vo. 2s. 6d.

COOKE.—ELEMENTS OF CHEMICAL PHYSICS. By JOSIAH P. COOKE, Jun.,
Erving Professor of Chemistry and Mineralogy in Harvard University. 4th Ed.
8vo. 21s.

FLEISCHER.—A SYSTEM OF VOLUMETRIC ANALYSIS. By EMIL FLEISCHER.
Translated, with Notes and Additions, by M. M. P. MUIR, F.R.S.E. Illustrated.
Cr. 8vo. 7s. 6d.

FRANKLAND.—A HANDBOOK OF AGRICULTURAL CHEMICAL ANALYSIS.
By P. F. FRANKLAND, F.R.S., Professor of Chemistry in University College,
Dundee. Cr. 8vo. 7s. 6d.

HARTLEY.—A COURSE OF QUANTITATIVE ANALYSIS FOR STUDENTS.
By W. NOEL HARTLEY, F.R.S., Professor of Chemistry and of Applied Chemistry, Science and Art Department, Royal College of Science, Dublin. Gl.
8vo. 5s.

HEMPEL.—METHODS OF GAS ANALYSIS. By Dr. WALTHER HEMPEL. Translated by Dr. L. M. DENNIS.   [In preparation.

HIORNS.—PRACTICAL METALLURGY AND ASSAYING. A Text-Book for
the use of Teachers, Students, and Assayers. By ARTHUR H. HIORNS, Principal of the School of Metallurgy, Birmingham and Midland Institute. Illustrated. Gl. 8vo. 6s.

A TEXT-BOOK OF ELEMENTARY METALLURGY FOR THE USE OF
STUDENTS. To which is added an Appendix of Examination Questions, em-
bracing the whole of the Questions set in the three stages of the subject by the
Science and Art Department for the past twenty years. By the same. Gl. 8vo. 4s.

IRON AND STEEL MANUFACTURE. A Text-Book for Beginners. By the same. Illustrated. Gl. 8vo. 3s. 6d.

MIXED METALS OR METALLIC ALLOYS. By the same. Gl. 8vo. 6s.

JONES.—*THE OWENS COLLEGE JUNIOR COURSE OF PRACTICAL CHEM-ISTRY. By FRANCIS JONES, F.R.S.E., Chemical Master at the Grammar School, Manchester. With Preface by Sir HENRY ROSCOE, F.R.S. Illustrated. Fcap. 8vo. 2s. 6d.

*QUESTIONS ON CHEMISTRY. A Series of Problems and Exercises in Inorganic and Organic Chemistry. By the same. Fcap. 8vo. 3s.

LANDAUER.—BLOWPIPE ANALYSIS. By J. LANDAUER. Authorised English Edition by J. TAYLOR and W. E. KAY, of Owens College, Manchester.
[New Edition in the Press.

LOCKYER.—THE CHEMISTRY OF THE SUN. By J. NORMAN LOCKYER, F.R.S. Illustrated. 8vo. 14s.

LUPTON.—CHEMICAL ARITHMETIC. With 1200 Problems. By S. LUPTON, M.A. 2d Ed., revised and abridged. Fcap. 8vo. 4s. 6d.

MANSFIELD.—A THEORY OF SALTS. By C. B. MANSFIELD. Crown 8vo. 14s.

MELDOLA.—THE CHEMISTRY OF PHOTOGRAPHY. By RAPHAEL MELDOLA, F.R.S., Professor of Chemistry in the Technical College, Finsbury. Cr. 8vo. 6s.

MEYER.—HISTORY OF CHEMISTRY FROM THE EARLIEST TIMES TO THE PRESENT DAY. By ERNST VON MEYER, Ph.D. Translated by GEORGE McGOWAN, Ph.D. 8vo. 14s. net.

MIXTER.—AN ELEMENTARY TEXT-BOOK OF CHEMISTRY. By WILLIAM G. MIXTER, Professor of Chemistry in the Sheffield Scientific School of Yale College. 2d and revised Ed. Cr. 8vo. 7s. 6d.

MUIR.—PRACTICAL CHEMISTRY FOR MEDICAL STUDENTS. Specially ar-ranged for the first M.B. Course. By M. M. P. MUIR, F.R.S.E., Fellow and Præ-lector in Chemistry at Gonville and Caius College, Cambridge. Fcap. 8vo. 1s. 6d.

MUIR and WILSON.—THE ELEMENTS OF THERMAL CHEMISTRY. By M. M. P. MUIR, F.R.S.E.; assisted by D. M. WILSON. 8vo. 12s. 6d.

OSTWALD.— OUTLINES OF GENERAL CHEMISTRY (PHYSICAL AND THEORETICAL). By Prof. W. OSTWALD. Translated by JAMES WALKER, D.Sc., Ph.D. 8vo. 10s. net.

RAMSAY.—EXPERIMENTAL PROOFS OF CHEMICAL THEORY FOR BE-GINNERS. By WILLIAM RAMSAY, F.R.S., Professor of Chemistry in Univer-sity College, London. Pott 8vo. 2s. 6d.

REMSEN.—Works by IRA REMSEN, Professor of Chemistry in the Johns Hopkins University, U.S.A.

COMPOUNDS OF CARBON: or, Organic Chemistry, an Introduction to the Study of. Cr. 8vo. 6s. 6d.

AN INTRODUCTION TO THE STUDY OF CHEMISTRY (INORGANIC CHEMISTRY). Cr. 8vo. 6s. 6d.

*THE ELEMENTS OF CHEMISTRY. A Text-Book for Beginners. Fcap. 8vo. 2s. 6d.

A TEXT-BOOK OF INORGANIC CHEMISTRY. 8vo. 16s.

ROSCOE.—Works by Sir HENRY E. ROSCOE, F.R.S., formerly Professor of Chemistry in the Owens College, Victoria University, Manchester.

*PRIMER OF CHEMISTRY. Illustrated. With Questions. 18mo. 1s.

*LESSONS IN ELEMENTARY CHEMISTRY, INORGANIC AND ORGANIC. With Illustrations and Chromolitho of the Solar Spectrum, and of the Alkalies and Alkaline Earths. Fcap. 8vo. 4s. 6d.

ROSCOE and SCHORLEMMER.—INORGANIC AND ORGANIC CHEMISTRY. A Complete Treatise on Inorganic and Organic Chemistry. By Sir HENRY E. ROSCOE, F.R.S., and Prof. C. SCHORLEMMER, F.R.S. Illustrated. 8vo.

Vols. I. and II. INORGANIC CHEMISTRY. Vol. I.—The Non-Metallic Ele-ments. 2d Ed. 21s. Vol. II. Part I.—Metals. 18s. Part II.—Metals. 18s.

Vol. III.—ORGANIC CHEMISTRY. THE CHEMISTRY OF THE HYDRO-CARBONS and their Derivatives. Five Parts. Parts I., II., and IV. 21s. Parts III. and V. 18s. each.

ROSCOE and SCHUSTER.—SPECTRUM ANALYSIS. Lectures delivered in 1868. By Sir HENRY ROSCOE, F.R.S. 4th Ed., revised and considerably enlarged by the Author and by A. SCHUSTER, F.R.S., Ph.D., Professor of Applied Mathematics in the Owens College, Victoria University. With Appendices, Illustrations, and Plates. 8vo. 21s.

*THORPE.—A SERIES OF CHEMICAL PROBLEMS. With Key. For use in Colleges and Schools. By T. E. THORPE, B.Sc. (Vic.), Ph.D., F.R.S. Revised and Enlarged by W. TATE, Assoc.N.S.S. With Preface by Sir H. E. ROSCOE, F.R.S. New Ed. Fcap. 8vo. 2s.

THORPE and RÜCKER.—A TREATISE ON CHEMICAL PHYSICS. By Prof. T. E. THORPE, F.R.S., and Prof. A. W. RÜCKER, F.R.S. Illustrated. 8vo.
[In preparation.

WURTZ.—A HISTORY OF CHEMICAL THEORY. By AD. WURTZ. Translated by HENRY WATTS, F.R.S. Crown 8vo. 6s.

PHYSICAL GEOGRAPHY, GEOLOGY, AND MINERALOGY.

BLANFORD.—THE RUDIMENTS OF PHYSICAL GEOGRAPHY FOR THE USE OF INDIAN SCHOOLS; with a Glossary of Technical Terms employed. By H. F. BLANFORD, F.G.S. Illustrated. Cr. 8vo. 2s. 6d.

FERREL.—A POPULAR TREATISE ON THE WINDS. Comprising the General Motions of the Atmosphere, Monsoons, Cyclones, Tornadoes, Waterspouts, Hailstorms, etc. By WILLIAM FERREL, M.A., Member of the American National Academy of Sciences. 8vo. 18s.

FISHER.—PHYSICS OF THE EARTH'S CRUST. By the Rev. OSMOND FISHER, M.A., F.G.S., Hon. Fellow of King's College, London. 2d Ed., altered and enlarged. 8vo. 12s.

GEIKIE.—Works by Sir ARCHIBALD GEIKIE, F.R.S., Director-General of the Geological Survey of the United Kingdom.

*PRIMER OF PHYSICAL GEOGRAPHY. Illustrated. With Questions. 18mo. 1s.

*ELEMENTARY LESSONS IN PHYSICAL GEOGRAPHY. Illustrated. Fcap. 8vo. 4s. 6d. *QUESTIONS ON THE SAME. 1s. 6d.

*PRIMER OF GEOLOGY. Illustrated. 18mo. 1s.

*CLASS-BOOK OF GEOLOGY. Illustrated. New and Cheaper Ed. Cr. 8vo. 4s. 6d.

TEXT-BOOK OF GEOLOGY. Illustrated. 2d Ed., 7th Thousand, revised and enlarged. 8vo. 28s.

OUTLINES OF FIELD GEOLOGY. Illustrated. New Ed., revised and enlarged. Gl. 8vo. 3s. 6d.

THE SCENERY AND GEOLOGY OF SCOTLAND, VIEWED IN CONNEXION WITH ITS PHYSICAL GEOLOGY. Illustrated. Cr. 8vo. 12s. 6d.

HUXLEY.—PHYSIOGRAPHY. An Introduction to the Study of Nature. By T. H. HUXLEY, F.R.S. Illustrated. New and Cheaper Edition. Cr. 8vo. 6s.

LOCKYER.—OUTLINES OF PHYSIOGRAPHY—THE MOVEMENTS OF THE EARTH. By J. NORMAN LOCKYER, F.R.S., Examiner in Physiography for the Science and Art Department. Illustrated. Cr. 8vo. Sewed, 1s. 6d.

MIERS.—A TREATISE ON MINERALOGY. By H. A. MIERS, of the British Museum. 8vo.
[In preparation.

PHILLIPS. A TREATISE ON ORE DEPOSITS. By J. ARTHUR PHILLIPS, F.R.S. Illustrated. 8vo. 25s.

ROSENBUSCH and IDDINGS.—MICROSCOPICAL PHYSIOGRAPHY OF THE ROCK-MAKING MINERALS: AN AID TO THE MICROSCOPICAL STUDY OF ROCKS. By H. ROSENBUSCH. Translated and Abridged by J. P. IDDINGS. Illustrated. 8vo. 24s.

WILLIAMS.—ELEMENTS OF CRYSTALLOGRAPHY FOR STUDENTS OF CHEMISTRY, PHYSICS, AND MINERALOGY. By G. H. WILLIAMS, Ph.D., Cr. 8vo. 6s.

BIOLOGY.

ALLEN.—ON THE COLOURS OF FLOWERS, as Illustrated in the British Flora. By GRANT ALLEN. Illustrated. Cr. 8vo. 3s. 6d.

BALFOUR.—A TREATISE ON COMPARATIVE EMBRYOLOGY. By F. M. BALFOUR, F.R.S., Fellow and Lecturer of Trinity College, Cambridge. Illustrated. 2d Ed., reprinted without alteration from the 1st Ed. 2 vols. 8vo. Vol. I. 18s. Vol. II. 21s.

BALFOUR and WARD.—A GENERAL TEXT-BOOK OF BOTANY. By ISAAC BAYLEY BALFOUR, F.R.S., Professor of Botany in the University of Edinburgh, and H. MARSHALL WARD, F.R.S., Professor of Botany in the Royal Indian Engineering College, Cooper's Hill. 8vo. [In preparation.

*BETTANY.—FIRST LESSONS IN PRACTICAL BOTANY. By G. T. BETTANY. 18mo. 1s.

*BOWER.—A COURSE OF PRACTICAL INSTRUCTION IN BOTANY. By F. O. BOWER, D.Sc., F.R.S., Regius Professor of Botany in the University of Glasgow. New Ed., revised. Cr. 8vo. 10s. 6d. Abridged Ed. [In preparation.

BUCKTON.—MONOGRAPH OF THE BRITISH CICADÆ, OR TETTIGIDÆ. By G. B. BUCKTON. In 8 parts, Quarterly. Part I. January, 1890. 8vo. Parts I.-VI. ready. 8s. each, net. Vol. I. 33s. 6d. net.

CHURCH and SCOTT.—MANUAL OF VEGETABLE PHYSIOLOGY. By Professor A. H. CHURCH, and D. H. SCOTT, D.Sc., Lecturer in the Normal School of Science. Illustrated. Cr. 8vo. [In preparation.

COPE.—THE ORIGIN OF THE FITTEST. Essays on Evolution. By E. D COPE, M.A., Ph.D. 8vo. 12s. 6d.

COUES.—HANDBOOK OF FIELD AND GENERAL ORNITHOLOGY. By Prof. ELLIOTT COUES, M.A. Illustrated. 8vo. 10s. net.

DARWIN.—MEMORIAL NOTICES OF CHARLES DARWIN, F.R.S., etc. By T. H. HUXLEY, F.R.S., G. J. ROMANES, F.R.S., ARCHIBALD GEIKIE, F.R.S., and W. THISELTON DYER, F.R.S. Reprinted from *Nature*. With a Portrait. Cr. 8vo. 2s. 6d.

EIMER.—ORGANIC EVOLUTION AS THE RESULT OF THE INHERITANCE OF ACQUIRED CHARACTERS ACCORDING TO THE LAWS OF ORGANIC GROWTH. By Dr. G. H. THEODOR EIMER. Translated by J. T. CUNNINGHAM, F.R.S.E., late Fellow of University College, Oxford. 8vo. 12s. 6d.

FEARNLEY.—A MANUAL OF ELEMENTARY PRACTICAL HISTOLOGY. By WILLIAM FEARNLEY. Illustrated. Cr. 8vo. 7s. 6d.

FLOWER and GADOW.—AN INTRODUCTION TO THE OSTEOLOGY OF THE MAMMALIA. By W. H. FLOWER, F.R.S., Director of the Natural History Departments of the British Museum. Illustrated. 3d Ed. Revised with the assistance of HANS GADOW, Ph.D., Lecturer on the Advanced Morphology of Vertebrates in the University of Cambridge. Cr. 8vo. 10s. 6d.

FOSTER.—Works by MICHAEL FOSTER, M.D., F.R.S., Professor of Physiology in the University of Cambridge.

    *PRIMER OF PHYSIOLOGY. Illustrated. 18mo. 1s.

    A TEXT-BOOK OF PHYSIOLOGY. Illustrated. 5th Ed., largely revised. 8vo. Part I., comprising Book I. Blood—The Tissues of Movement, The Vascular Mechanism. 10s. 6d. Part II., comprising Book II. The Tissues of Chemical Action, with their Respective Mechanisms—Nutrition. 10s. 6d. Part III. The Central Nervous System. 7s. 6d.

FOSTER and BALFOUR.—THE ELEMENTS OF EMBRYOLOGY. By Prof. MICHAEL FOSTER, M.D., F.R.S., and the late F. M. BALFOUR, F.R.S., Professor of Animal Morphology in the University of Cambridge. 2d Ed., revised. Edited by A. SEDGWICK, M.A., Fellow and Assistant Lecturer of Trinity College, Cambridge, and W. HEAPE, M.A., late Demonstrator in the Morphological Laboratory of the University of Cambridge. Illustrated. Cr. 8vo. 10s. 6d.

FOSTER and LANGLEY.—A COURSE OF ELEMENTARY PRACTICAL PHYSIOLOGY AND HISTOLOGY. By Prof. MICHAEL FOSTER, M.D., F.R.S., and J. N. LANGLEY, F.R.S., Fellow of Trinity College, Cambridge. 6th Ed. Cr. 8vo. 7s. 6d.

GAMGEE.—A TEXT-BOOK OF THE PHYSIOLOGICAL CHEMISTRY OF THE ANIMAL BODY. Including an Account of the Chemical Changes occurring in Disease. By A. GAMGEE, M.D., F.R.S. Illustrated. 8vo. Vol. I. 18s.

GOODALE.—PHYSIOLOGICAL BOTANY. I. Outlines of the Histology of Phænogamous Plants. II. Vegetable Physiology. By GEORGE LINCOLN GOODALE, M.A., M.D., Professor of Botany in Harvard University. 8vo. 10s. 6d.

GRAY.—STRUCTURAL BOTANY, OR ORGANOGRAPHY ON THE BASIS OF MORPHOLOGY. To which are added the Principles of Taxonomy and Phytography, and a Glossary of Botanical Terms. By Prof. ASA GRAY, LL.D. 8vo. 10s. 6d.

THE SCIENTIFIC PAPERS OF ASA GRAY. Selected by C. SPRAGUE SARGENT. 2 vols. Vol. I. Reviews of Works on Botany and Related Subjects, 1834-1887. Vol. II. Essays, Biographical Sketches, 1841-1886. 8vo. 21s.

HAMILTON.—A SYSTEMATIC AND PRACTICAL TEXT-BOOK OF PATHOLOGY. By D. J. HAMILTON, F.R.S.E., Professor of Pathological Anatomy in the University of Aberdeen. Illustrated. 8vo. Vol. I. 25s.

HARTIG.—TEXT-BOOK OF THE DISEASES OF TREES. By Dr. ROBERT HARTIG. Translated by WM. SOMERVILLE, B.Sc., D.Œ., Professor of Agriculture and Forestry, Durham College of Science, Newcastle-on-Tyne. Edited, with Introduction, by Prof. H. MARSHALL WARD. 8vo. [In preparation.

HOOKER.—Works by Sir JOSEPH HOOKER, F.R.S., &c.
*PRIMER OF BOTANY. Illustrated. 18mo. 1s.
THE STUDENT'S FLORA OF THE BRITISH ISLANDS. 3d Ed., revised. Gl. 8vo. 10s. 6d.

HOWES.—AN ATLAS OF PRACTICAL ELEMENTARY BIOLOGY. By G. B. HOWES, Assistant Professor of Zoology, Normal School of Science and Royal School of Mines. With a Preface by Prof. T. H. HUXLEY, F.R.S. 4to. 14s.

HUXLEY.—Works by Prof. T. H. HUXLEY, F.R.S.
*INTRODUCTORY PRIMER OF SCIENCE. 18mo. 1s.
*LESSONS IN ELEMENTARY PHYSIOLOGY. Illustrated. Fcap. 8vo. 4s. 6d.
*QUESTIONS ON HUXLEY'S PHYSIOLOGY. By T. ALCOCK, M.D. 18mo. 1s. 6d.

HUXLEY and MARTIN.—A COURSE OF PRACTICAL INSTRUCTION IN ELEMENTARY BIOLOGY. By Prof. T. H. HUXLEY, F.R.S., assisted by H. N. MARTIN, F.R.S., Professor of Biology in the Johns Hopkins University, U.S.A. New Ed., revised and extended by G. B. HOWES and D. H. SCOTT, Ph.D., Assistant Professors, Normal School of Science and Royal School of Mines. With a Preface by T. H. HUXLEY, F.R.S. Cr. 8vo. 10s. 6d.

KLEIN.—Works by E. KLEIN, F.R.S., Lecturer on General Anatomy and Physiology in the Medical School of St. Bartholomew's Hospital, Professor of Bacteriology at the College of State Medicine, London.
MICRO-ORGANISMS AND DISEASE. An Introduction into the Study of Specific Micro-Organisms. Illustrated. 3d Ed., revised. Cr. 8vo. 6s.
THE BACTERIA IN ASIATIC CHOLERA. Cr. 8vo. 5s.

LANG.—TEXT-BOOK OF COMPARATIVE ANATOMY. By Dr. ARNOLD LANG. Professor of Zoology in the University of Zurich. Translated by H. M. BERNARD, M.A., and M BERNARD. Introduction by Prof. E. HAECKEL. 2 vols. Illustrated. 8vo. [In the Press.

LANKESTER.—Works by E. RAY LANKESTER, F.R.S., Linacre Professor of Human and Comparative Anatomy in the University of Oxford.
A TEXT-BOOK OF ZOOLOGY. 8vo. [In preparation.
THE ADVANCEMENT OF SCIENCE. Occasional Essays and Addresses. 8vo. 10s. 6d.

LUBBOCK.—Works by the Right Hon. Sir JOHN LUBBOCK, F.R.S., D.C.L.
THE ORIGIN AND METAMORPHOSES OF INSECTS. Illustrated. Cr. 8vo. 3s. 6d.
ON BRITISH WILD FLOWERS CONSIDERED IN RELATION TO INSECTS. Illustrated. Cr. 8vo. 4s. 6d.

LUBBOCK.—Works by the Right Hon. Sir JOHN LUBBOCK, F.R.S., D.C.L.—*cont.*
FLOWERS, FRUITS, AND LEAVES. Illustrated. 2d Ed. Cr. 8vo. 4s. 6d.
SCIENTIFIC LECTURES. 2d Ed. 8vo. 8s. 6d.
FIFTY YEARS OF SCIENCE. Being the Address delivered at York to the British Association, August 1881. 5th Ed. Cr. 8vo. 2s. 6d.

MARTIN and MOALE.—ON THE DISSECTION OF VERTEBRATE ANIMALS. By Prof. H. N. MARTIN and W. A. MOALE. Cr. 8vo. [*In preparation.*

MIVART.—LESSONS IN ELEMENTARY ANATOMY. By ST. GEORGE MIVART, F.R.S., Lecturer on Comparative Anatomy at St. Mary's Hospital. Illustrated. Fcap. 8vo. 6s. 6d.

MÜLLER.—THE FERTILISATION OF FLOWERS. By HERMANN MÜLLER. Translated and Edited by D'ARCY W. THOMPSON, B.A., Professor of Biology in University College, Dundee. With a Preface by C. DARWIN, F.R.S. Illustrated. 8vo. 21s.

OLIVER.—Works by DANIEL OLIVER, F.R.S., late Professor of Botany in University College, London.
*LESSONS IN ELEMENTARY BOTANY. Illustrated. Fcap. 8vo. 4s. 6d.
FIRST BOOK OF INDIAN BOTANY. Illustrated. Ex. fcap. 8vo. 6s. 6d.

PARKER.—Works by T. JEFFERY PARKER, F.R.S., Professor of Biology in the University of Otago, New Zealand.
A COURSE OF INSTRUCTION IN ZOOTOMY (VERTEBRATA). Illustrated. Cr. 8vo. 8s. 6d.
LESSONS IN ELEMENTARY BIOLOGY. Illustrated. Cr. 8vo. 10s. 6d.

PARKER and BETTANY.—THE MORPHOLOGY OF THE SKULL. By Prof. W. K. PARKER, F.R.S., and G. T. BETTANY. Illustrated. Cr. 8vo. 10s. 6d.

ROMANES.—THE SCIENTIFIC EVIDENCES OF ORGANIC EVOLUTION. By GEORGE J. ROMANES, F.R.S., Zoological Secretary of the Linnean Society. Cr. 8vo. 2s. 6d.

SEDGWICK.—TREATISE ON EMBRYOLOGY. By ADAM SEDGWICK, F.R.S., Fellow and Lecturer of Trinity College, Cambridge. Illustrated. 8vo.
[*In preparation.*

SHUFELDT.—THE MYOLOGY OF THE RAVEN (*Corvus corax sinuatus*). A Guide to the Study of the Muscular System in Birds. By R. W. SHUFELDT. Illustrated. 8vo. 13s. net.

SMITH.—DISEASES OF FIELD AND GARDEN CROPS, CHIEFLY SUCH AS ARE CAUSED BY FUNGI. By W. G. SMITH, F.L.S. Illustrated. Fcap. 8vo. 4s. 6d.

STEWART and CORRY.—A FLORA OF THE NORTH-EAST OF IRELAND. Including the Phanerogamia, the Cryptogamia Vascularia, and the Muscineæ. By S. A. STEWART, Curator of the Collections in the Belfast Museum, and the late T. H. CORRY, M.A., Lecturer on Botany in the University Medical and Science Schools, Cambridge. Cr. 8vo. 5s. 6d.

WALLACE.—DARWINISM: An Exposition of the Theory of Natural Selection, with some of its Applications. By ALFRED RUSSEL WALLACE, LL.D., F.R.S. 3d Ed. Cr. 8vo. 9s.
NATURAL SELECTION: AND TROPICAL NATURE. By the same. New Ed. Cr. 8vo. 6s.
ISLAND LIFE. By the same. New Ed. Cr. 8vo. 6s.

WARD.—TIMBER AND SOME OF ITS DISEASES. By H. MARSHALL WARD, F.R.S., Professor of Botany in the Royal Indian Engineering College, Cooper's Hill. Illustrated. Cr. 8vo. 6s.

WIEDERSHEIM.—ELEMENTS OF THE COMPARATIVE ANATOMY OF VERTEBRATES. By Prof. R. WIEDERSHEIM. Adapted by W. NEWTON PARKER, Professor of Biology in the University College of South Wales and Monmouthshire. With Additions. Illustrated. 8vo. 12s. 6d.

MEDICINE.

BLYTH.—A MANUAL OF PUBLIC HEALTH. By A. WYNTER BLYTH, M.R.C.S. 8vo. 17s. net.

BRUNTON.—Works by T. LAUDER BRUNTON, M.D., F.R.S., Examiner in Materia Medica in the University of London, in the Victoria University, and in the Royal College of Physicians, London.

A TEXT-BOOK OF PHARMACOLOGY, THERAPEUTICS, AND MATERIA MEDICA. Adapted to the United States Pharmacopœia by F. H. WILLIAMS, M.D., Boston, Mass. 3d Ed. Adapted to the New British Pharmacopœia, 1885, and additions, 1891. 8vo. 21s. Or in 2 Vols. 22s. 6d.

TABLES OF MATERIA MEDICA: A Companion to the Materia Medica Museum. Illustrated. Cheaper Issue. 8vo. 5s.

ON THE CONNECTION BETWEEN CHEMICAL CONSTITUTION AND PHYSIOLOGICAL ACTION, BEING AN INTRODUCTION TO MODERN THERAPEUTICS. Croonian Lectures. 8vo. [In the Press.

GRIFFITHS.—LESSONS ON PRESCRIPTIONS AND THE ART OF PRESCRIBING. By W. HANDSEL GRIFFITHS. Adapted to the Pharmacopœia, 1885. 18mo. 3s. 6d.

HAMILTON.—A TEXT-BOOK OF PATHOLOGY, SYSTEMATIC AND PRACTICAL. By D. J. HAMILTON, F.R.S.E., Professor of Pathological Anatomy, University of Aberdeen. Illustrated. Vol. I. 8vo. 25s.

KLEIN.—Works by E. KLEIN, F.R.S., Lecturer on General Anatomy and Physiology in the Medical School of St. Bartholomew's Hospital, London.

MICRO-ORGANISMS AND DISEASE. An Introduction into the Study of Specific Micro-Organisms. Illustrated. 3d Ed., revised. Cr. 8vo. 6s.

THE BACTERIA IN ASIATIC CHOLERA. Cr. 8vo. 5s.

WHITE.—A TEXT-BOOK OF GENERAL THERAPEUTICS. By W. HALE WHITE, M.D., Senior Assistant Physician to and Lecturer in Materia Medica at Guy's Hospital. Illustrated. Cr. 8vo. 8s. 6d.

ZIEGLER—MACALISTER.—TEXT-BOOK OF PATHOLOGICAL ANATOMY AND PATHOGENESIS. By Prof. E. ZIEGLER. Translated and Edited by DONALD MACALISTER, M.A., M.D., Fellow and Medical Lecturer of St. John's College, Cambridge. Illustrated. 8vo.

Part I.—GENERAL PATHOLOGICAL ANATOMY. 2d Ed. 12s. 6d.

Part II.—SPECIAL PATHOLOGICAL ANATOMY. Sections I.-VIII. 2d Ed. 12s. 6d. Sections IX.-XII. 12s. 6d.

HUMAN SCIENCES.

Mental and Moral Philosophy ; Political Economy ; Law and Politics ; Anthropology ; Education.

MENTAL AND MORAL PHILOSOPHY.

BALDWIN.—HANDBOOK OF PSYCHOLOGY: SENSES AND INTELLECT. By Prof. J. M. BALDWIN, M.A., LL.D. 2d Ed., revised. 8vo. 12s. 6d.

BOOLE.—THE MATHEMATICAL ANALYSIS OF LOGIC. Being an Essay towards a Calculus of Deductive Reasoning. By GEORGE BOOLE. 8vo. 5s.

CALDERWOOD.—HANDBOOK OF MORAL PHILOSOPHY. By Rev. HENRY CALDERWOOD, LL.D., Professor of Moral Philosophy in the University of Edinburgh. 14th Ed., largely rewritten. Cr. 8vo. 6s.

CLIFFORD.—SEEING AND THINKING. By the late Prof. W. K. CLIFFORD, F.R.S. With Diagrams. Cr. 8vo. 3s. 6d.

HÖFFDING.—OUTLINES OF PSYCHOLOGY. By Prof. H. HÖFFDING. Translated by M. E. LOWNDES. Cr. 8vo. 6s.

JAMES.—THE PRINCIPLES OF PSYCHOLOGY. By WM. JAMES, Professor of Psychology in Harvard University. 2 vols. 8vo. 25s. net.

JARDINE.—THE ELEMENTS OF THE PSYCHOLOGY OF COGNITION. By Rev. ROBERT JARDINE, D.Sc. 3d Ed., revised. Cr. 8vo. 6s. 6d.

JEVONS.—Works by W. STANLEY JEVONS, F.R.S.

*PRIMER OF LOGIC. 18mo. 1s.

*ELEMENTARY LESSONS IN LOGIC, Deductive and Inductive, with Copious Questions and Examples, and a Vocabulary of Logical Terms. Fcap. 8vo. 3s. 6d.

THE PRINCIPLES OF SCIENCE. A Treatise on Logic and Scientific Method. New and revised Ed. Cr. 8vo. 12s. 6d.

STUDIES IN DEDUCTIVE LOGIC. 2d Ed. Cr. 8vo. 6s.

PURE LOGIC: AND OTHER MINOR WORKS. Edited by R. ADAMSON, M.A., LL.D., Professor of Logic at Owens College, Manchester, and HARRIET A. JEVONS. With a Preface by Prof. ADAMSON. 8vo. 10s. 6d.

KANT—MAX MÜLLER.—CRITIQUE OF PURE REASON. By IMMANUEL KANT. 2 vols. 8vo. 16s. each. Vol. I. HISTORICAL INTRODUCTION, by LUDWIG NOIRÉ; Vol. II. CRITIQUE OF PURE REASON, translated by F. MAX MÜLLER.

KANT—MAHAFFY and BERNARD.—KANT'S CRITICAL PHILOSOPHY FOR ENGLISH READERS. By J. P. MAHAFFY, D.D., Professor of Ancient History in the University of Dublin, and JOHN H. BERNARD, B.D., Fellow of Trinity College, Dublin. A new and complete Edition in 2 vols. Cr. 8vo.

Vol. I. THE KRITIK OF PURE REASON EXPLAINED AND DEFENDED. 7s. 6d.

Vol. II. THE PROLEGOMENA. Translated with Notes and Appendices. 6s.

KEYNES.—FORMAL LOGIC, Studies and Exercises in. Including a Generalisation of Logical Processes in their application to Complex Inferences. By JOHN NEVILLE KEYNES, D.Sc. 2d Ed., revised and enlarged. Cr. 8vo. 10s. 6d.

McCOSH.—Works by JAMES McCOSH, D.D., President of Princeton College.

PSYCHOLOGY. Cr. 8vo.

I. THE COGNITIVE POWERS. 6s. 6d.

II. THE MOTIVE POWERS. 6s. 6d.

FIRST AND FUNDAMENTAL TRUTHS: being a Treatise on Metaphysics. Ex. cr. 8vo. 9s.

THE PREVAILING TYPES OF PHILOSOPHY. CAN THEY LOGICALLY REACH REALITY? 8vo. 3s. 6d.

MAURICE.—MORAL AND METAPHYSICAL PHILOSOPHY. By F. D. MAURICE, M.A., late Professor of Moral Philosophy in the University of Cambridge. Vol. I.—Ancient Philosophy and the First to the Thirteenth Centuries. Vol. II.—Fourteenth Century and the French Revolution, with a glimpse into the Nineteenth Century. 4th Ed. 2 vols. 8vo. 16s.

*RAY.—A TEXT-BOOK OF DEDUCTIVE LOGIC FOR THE USE OF STUDENTS. By P. K. RAY, D.Sc., Professor of Logic and Philosophy, Presidency College, Calcutta. 4th Ed. Globe 8vo. 4s. 6d.

SIDGWICK.—Works by HENRY SIDGWICK, LL.D., D.C.L., Knightbridge Professor of Moral Philosophy in the University of Cambridge.

THE METHODS OF ETHICS. 4th Ed. 8vo. 14s. A Supplement to the 2d Ed., containing all the important Additions and Alterations in the 3d Ed. 8vo. 6s.

OUTLINES OF THE HISTORY OF ETHICS, for English Readers. 2d Ed., revised. Cr. 8vo. 3s. 6d.

VENN.—Works by JOHN VENN, F.R.S., Examiner in Moral Philosophy in the University of London.

THE LOGIC OF CHANCE. An Essay on the Foundations and Province of the Theory of Probability, with special Reference to its Logical Bearings and its Application to Moral and Social Science. 3d Ed., rewritten and greatly enlarged. Cr. 8vo. 10s. 6d.

SYMBOLIC LOGIC. Cr. 8vo. 10s. 6d.

THE PRINCIPLES OF EMPIRICAL OR INDUCTIVE LOGIC. 8vo. 18s.

POLITICAL ECONOMY.

BÖHM-BAWERK.—CAPITAL AND INTEREST. Translated by WILLIAM SMART, M.A. 8vo. 12s. net.

THE POSITIVE THEORY OF CAPITAL. By the same Author and Translator. 8vo. 12s. net.

CAIRNES.—THE CHARACTER AND LOGICAL METHOD OF POLITICAL ECONOMY. By J. E. CAIRNES. Cr. 8vo. 6s.

SOME LEADING PRINCIPLES OF POLITICAL ECONOMY NEWLY EXPOUNDED. By the same. 8vo. 14s.

COSSA.—GUIDE TO THE STUDY OF POLITICAL ECONOMY. By Dr. L. COSSA. Translated. With a Preface by W. S. JEVONS, F.R.S. Cr. 8vo. 4s. 6d.

'FAWCETT.—POLITICAL ECONOMY FOR BEGINNERS, WITH QUESTIONS. By Mrs. HENRY FAWCETT. 7th Ed. 18mo. 2s. 6d.

FAWCETT.—A MANUAL OF POLITICAL ECONOMY. By the Right Hon. HENRY FAWCETT, F.R.S. 7th Ed., revised. With a Chapter on "State Socialism and the Nationalisation of the Land," and an Index. Cr. 8vo. 12s. 6d.

AN EXPLANATORY DIGEST of the above. By C. A. WATERS, B.A. Cr. 8vo. 2s. 6d.

GILMAN.—PROFIT-SHARING BETWEEN EMPLOYER AND EMPLOYEE. A Study in the Evolution of the Wages System. By N. P. GILMAN. Cr. 8vo. 7s. 6d.

GUNTON.—WEALTH AND PROGRESS: A Critical Examination of the Wages Question and its Economic Relation to Social Reform. By GEORGE GUNTON. Cr. 8vo. 6s.

HOWELL.—THE CONFLICTS OF CAPITAL AND LABOUR HISTORICALLY AND ECONOMICALLY CONSIDERED. Being a History and Review of the Trade Unions of Great Britain, showing their Origin, Progress, Constitution, and Objects, in their varied Political, Social, Economical, and Industrial Aspects. By GEORGE HOWELL, M.P. 2d Ed., revised. Cr. 8vo. 7s. 6d.

JEVONS.— Works by W. STANLEY JEVONS, F.R.S.

*PRIMER OF POLITICAL ECONOMY. 18mo. 1s.

THE THEORY OF POLITICAL ECONOMY. 3d Ed., revised. 8vo. 10s. 6d.

KEYNES.—THE SCOPE AND METHOD OF POLITICAL ECONOMY. By J. N. KEYNES, D.Sc. 7s. net.

MARSHALL.—PRINCIPLES OF ECONOMICS. By ALFRED MARSHALL, M.A. 2 vols. 8vo. Vol. I. 2d Ed. 12s. 6d. net.

MARSHALL.—THE ECONOMICS OF INDUSTRY. By A. MARSHALL, M.A., Professor of Political Economy in the University of Cambridge, and MARY P. MARSHALL. Ex. fcap. 8vo. 2s. 6d.

PALGRAVE.—A DICTIONARY OF POLITICAL ECONOMY. By various Writers. Edited by R. H. INGLIS PALGRAVE, F.R.S. 3s. 6d. each, net. No. I. July 1891.

PANTALEONI.—MANUAL OF POLITICAL ECONOMY. By Prof. M. PANTALEONI. Translated by T. BOSTON BRUCE. [In preparation.*

SIDGWICK.—THE PRINCIPLES OF POLITICAL ECONOMY. By HENRY SIDGWICK, LL.D., D.C.L., Knightbridge Professor of Moral Philosophy in the University of Cambridge. 2d Ed., revised. 8vo. 16s.

SMART.—AN INTRODUCTION TO THE THEORY OF POLITICAL ECONOMY. By WILLIAM SMART, M.A. Crown 8vo.

WALKER.—Works by FRANCIS A. WALKER, M.A.

FIRST LESSONS IN POLITICAL ECONOMY. Cr. 8vo. 5s.

A BRIEF TEXT-BOOK OF POLITICAL ECONOMY. Cr. 8vo. 6s. 6d.

POLITICAL ECONOMY. 2d Ed., revised and enlarged. 8vo. 12s. 6d.

THE WAGES QUESTION. Ex. Cr. 8vo. 8s. 6d. net.

MONEY. Ex. Cr. 8vo. 8s. 6d. net.

*WICKSTEED.—ALPHABET OF ECONOMIC SCIENCE. By PHILIP H. WICKSTEED, M.A. Part I. Elements of the Theory of Value or Worth. Gl. 8vo. 2s. 6d.

LAW AND POLITICS.

ADAMS and CUNNINGHAM.—THE SWISS CONFEDERATION. By Sir F. O. ADAMS and C. CUNNINGHAM. 8vo. 14s.

ANGLO-SAXON LAW, ESSAYS ON.—Contents: Anglo-Saxon Law Courts, Land and Family Law, and Legal Procedure. 8vo. 18s.

BALL.—THE STUDENT'S GUIDE TO THE BAR. By WALTER W. R. BALL, M.A., Fellow and Assistant Tutor of Trinity College, Cambridge. 4th Ed., revised. Cr. 8vo. 2s. 6d.

BIGELOW.—HISTORY OF PROCEDURE IN ENGLAND FROM THE NORMAN CONQUEST. The Norman Period, 1066-1204. By MELVILLE M. BIGELOW, Ph.D., Harvard University. 8vo. 16s.

BOUTMY. — STUDIES IN CONSTITUTIONAL LAW. By EMILE BOUTMY. Translated by Mrs. DICEY, with Preface by Prof. A. V. DICEY. Cr. 8vo. 6s.

THE ENGLISH CONSTITUTION. By the same. Translated by Mrs. EADEN, with Introduction by Sir F. POLLOCK, Bart. Cr. 8vo. 6s.

BRYCE.—THE AMERICAN COMMONWEALTH. By JAMES BRYCE, M.P., D.C.L.; Regius Professor of Civil Law in the University of Oxford. Two Volumes. Ex. cr. 8vo. 25s. Part I. The National Government. Part II. The State Governments. Part III. The Party System. Part IV. Public Opinion. Part V. Illustrations and Reflections. Part VI. Social Institutions.

BUCKLAND.—OUR NATIONAL INSTITUTIONS. A Short Sketch for Schools. By ANNA BUCKLAND. With Glossary. 18mo. 1s.

CHERRY.—LECTURES ON THE GROWTH OF CRIMINAL LAW IN ANCIENT COMMUNITIES. By R. R. CHERRY, LL.D., Reid Professor of Constitutional and Criminal Law in the University of Dublin. 8vo. 5s. net.

DICEY.—INTRODUCTION TO THE STUDY OF THE LAW OF THE CONSTITUTION. By A. V. DICEY, B.C.L., Vinerian Professor of English Law in the University of Oxford. 3d Ed. 8vo. 12s. 6d.

DILKE.—PROBLEMS OF GREATER BRITAIN. By the Right Hon. Sir CHARLES WENTWORTH DILKE. With Maps. 4th Ed. Ex. cr. 8vo. 12s. 6d.

DONISTHORPE.—INDIVIDUALISM: A System of Politics. By WORDSWORTH DONISTHORPE. 8vo. 14s.

ENGLISH CITIZEN, THE.—A Series of Short Books on his Rights and Responsibilities. Edited by HENRY CRAIK, LL.D. Cr. 8vo. 3s. 6d. each.

CENTRAL GOVERNMENT. By H. D. TRAILL, D.C.L.

THE ELECTORATE AND THE LEGISLATURE. By SPENCER WALPOLE.

THE POOR LAW. By Rev. T. W. FOWLE, M.A. New Ed. With Appendix.

THE NATIONAL BUDGET; THE NATIONAL DEBT; TAXES AND RATES. By A. J. WILSON.

THE STATE IN RELATION TO LABOUR. By W. STANLEY JEVONS, LL.D.

THE STATE AND THE CHURCH. By the Hon. ARTHUR ELLIOT.

FOREIGN RELATIONS. By SPENCER WALPOLE.

THE STATE IN ITS RELATION TO TRADE. By Sir T. H. FARRER, Bart.

LOCAL GOVERNMENT. By M. D. CHALMERS, M.A.

THE STATE IN ITS RELATION TO EDUCATION. By HENRY CRAIK, LL.D.

THE LAND LAWS. By Sir F. POLLOCK, Bart., Professor of Jurisprudence in the University of Oxford.

COLONIES AND DEPENDENCIES. Part I. INDIA. By J. S. COTTON, M.A. II. THE COLONIES. By E. J. PAYNE, M.A.

JUSTICE AND POLICE. By F. W. MAITLAND.

THE PUNISHMENT AND PREVENTION OF CRIME. By Colonel Sir EDMUND DU CANE, K.C.B., Chairman of Commissioners of Prisons.

FISKE.—CIVIL GOVERNMENT IN THE UNITED STATES CONSIDERED WITH SOME REFERENCE TO ITS ORIGINS. By JOHN FISKE, formerly Lecturer on Philosophy at Harvard University. Cr. 8vo. 6s. 6d.

HOLMES.—THE COMMON LAW. By O. W. HOLMES, Jun. Demy 8vo. 12s.

JENKS.—THE GOVERNMENT OF VICTORIA. By EDWARD JENKS, B.A., LL.B., Professor of Law in the University of Melbourne. [In preparation.

MAITLAND.—PLEAS OF THE CROWN FOR THE COUNTY OF GLOUCESTER BEFORE THE ABBOT OF READING AND HIS FELLOW JUSTICES ITINERANT, IN THE FIFTH YEAR OF THE REIGN OF KING HENRY THE THIRD, AND THE YEAR OF GRACE 1221. By F. W. MAITLAND. 8vo. 7s. 6d.

MUNRO.—COMMERCIAL LAW. By J. E. C. MUNRO, LL.D., Professor of Law and Political Economy in the Owens College, Manchester. [In preparation.

PATERSON.—Works by JAMES PATERSON, Barrister-at-Law.

COMMENTARIES ON THE LIBERTY OF THE SUBJECT, AND THE LAWS OF ENGLAND RELATING TO THE SECURITY OF THE PERSON. Cheaper Issue. Two Vols. Cr. 8vo. 21s.

THE LIBERTY OF THE PRESS, SPEECH, AND PUBLIC WORSHIP. Being Commentaries on the Liberty of the Subject and the Laws of England. Cr. 8vo. 12s.

PHILLIMORE.—PRIVATE LAW AMONG THE ROMANS. From the Pandects. By J. G. PHILLIMORE, Q.C. 8vo. 16s.

POLLOCK.—ESSAYS IN JURISPRUDENCE AND ETHICS. By Sir FREDERICK POLLOCK, Bart., Corpus Christi Professor of Jurisprudence in the University of Oxford. 8vo. 10s. 6d.

INTRODUCTION TO THE HISTORY OF THE SCIENCE OF POLITICS. By the same. Cr. 8vo. 2s. 6d.

RICHEY.—THE IRISH LAND LAWS. By ALEX. G. RICHEY, Q.C., Deputy Regius Professor of Feudal English Law in the University of Dublin. Cr. 8vo. 3s. 6d.

SIDGWICK.—THE ELEMENTS OF POLITICS. By HENRY SIDGWICK, LL.D. 8vo. 14s. net.

STEPHEN.—Works by Sir J. FITZJAMES STEPHEN, Bart.

A DIGEST OF THE LAW OF EVIDENCE. 5th Ed., revised and enlarged. Cr. 8vo. 6s.

A DIGEST OF THE CRIMINAL LAW : CRIMES AND PUNISHMENTS. 4th Ed., revised. 8vo. 16s.

A DIGEST OF THE LAW OF CRIMINAL PROCEDURE IN INDICTABLE OFFENCES. By Sir J. F. STEPHEN, Bart., and H. STEPHEN, LL.M., of the Inner Temple, Barrister-at-Law. 8vo. 12s. 6d.

A HISTORY OF THE CRIMINAL LAW OF ENGLAND. Three Vols. 8vo. 48s.

GENERAL VIEW OF THE CRIMINAL LAW OF ENGLAND. 8vo. 14s.

ANTHROPOLOGY.

DAWKINS.—EARLY MAN IN BRITAIN AND HIS PLACE IN THE TERTIARY PERIOD. By Prof. W. BOYD DAWKINS. Medium 8vo. 25s.

FRAZER.—THE GOLDEN BOUGH. A Study in Comparative Religion. By J. G. FRAZER, M.A., Fellow of Trinity College, Cambridge. 2 vols. 8vo. 28s.

M'LENNAN.—THE PATRIARCHAL THEORY. Based on the papers of the late JOHN F. M'LENNAN. Edited by DONALD M'LENNAN, M.A., Barrister-at-Law. 8vo. 14s.

STUDIES IN ANCIENT HISTORY. By the same. Comprising a Reprint of "Primitive Marriage." An inquiry into the origin of the form of capture in Marriage Ceremonies. 8vo. 16s.

TYLOR.—ANTHROPOLOGY. An Introduction to the Study of Man and Civilisation. By E. B. TYLOR, F.R.S. Illustrated. Cr. 8vo. 7s. 6d.

WESTERMARCK.—THE HISTORY OF HUMAN MARRIAGE. By Dr. EDWARD WESTERMARCK. With Preface by A. R. WALLACE. 8vo. 14s. net.

WILSON.—THE RIGHT HAND : LEFT-HANDEDNESS. By Sir D. WILSON. Cr. 8vo. 4s. 6d.

EDUCATION.

ARNOLD.—REPORTS ON ELEMENTARY SCHOOLS. 1852-1882. By MATTHEW ARNOLD, D.C.L. Edited by the Right Hon. Sir FRANCIS SANDFORD, K.C.B. Cheaper Issue. Cr. 8vo. 3s. 6d.

HIGHER SCHOOLS AND UNIVERSITIES IN GERMANY. By the same. Crown 8vo. 6s.

BALL.—THE STUDENT'S GUIDE TO THE BAR. By WALTER W. R. BALL, M.A., Fellow and Assistant Tutor of Trinity College, Cambridge. 4th Ed., revised. Cr. 8vo. 2s. 6d.

*BLAKISTON.—THE TEACHER. Hints on School Management. A Handbook for Managers, Teachers' Assistants, and Pupil Teachers. By J. R. BLAKISTON. Cr. 8vo. 2s. 6d. (Recommended by the London, Birmingham, and Leicester School Boards.)

CALDERWOOD.—ON TEACHING. By Prof. HENRY CALDERWOOD. New Ed. Ex. fcap. 8vo. 2s. 6d.

FEARON.—SCHOOL INSPECTION. By D. R. FEARON. 6th Ed. Cr. 8vo. 2s. 6d.

FITCH.—NOTES ON AMERICAN SCHOOLS AND TRAINING COLLEGES. Reprinted from the Report of the English Education Department for 1888-89, with permission of the Controller of H.M.'s Stationery Office. By J. G. FITCH, M.A. Gl. 8vo. 2s. 6d.

GEIKIE.—THE TEACHING OF GEOGRAPHY. A Practical Handbook for the use of Teachers. By Sir ARCHIBALD GEIKIE, F R.S., Director-General of the Geological Survey of the United Kingdom. Cr. 8vo. 2s.

GLADSTONE.—SPELLING REFORM FROM A NATIONAL POINT OF VIEW. By J. H. GLADSTONE. Cr. 8vo. 1s. 6d.

HERTEL.—OVERPRESSURE IN HIGH SCHOOLS IN DENMARK. By Dr. HERTEL. Translated by C. G. SÖRENSEN. With Introduction by Sir J. CRICHTON-BROWNE, F.R.S. Cr. 8vo. 3s. 6d.

TODHUNTER.—THE CONFLICT OF STUDIES. By ISAAC TODHUNTER, F.R.S. 8vo. 10s. 6d.

TECHNICAL KNOWLEDGE.

(See also MECHANICS, LAW, and MEDICINE.)

Civil and Mechanical Engineering; Military and Naval Science; Agriculture; Domestic Economy; Book-Keeping; Commerce.

CIVIL AND MECHANICAL ENGINEERING.

ALEXANDER and THOMSON.—ELEMENTARY APPLIED MECHANICS. By T. ALEXANDER, Professor of Civil Engineering, Trinity College, Dublin, and A. W. THOMSON, Professor at College of Science, Poona, India. Part II. TRANSVERSE STRESS. Cr. 8vo. 10s. 6d.

CHALMERS.—GRAPHICAL DETERMINATION OF FORCES IN ENGINEERING STRUCTURES. By J. B. CHALMERS, C.E. Illustrated. 8vo. 24s.

COTTERILL.—APPLIED MECHANICS: An Elementary General Introduction to the Theory of Structures and Machines. By J. H. COTTERILL, F.R.S., Professor of Applied Mechanics in the Royal Naval College, Greenwich. 2d Ed. 8vo. 18s.

COTTERILL and SLADE.—LESSONS IN APPLIED MECHANICS. By Prof. J. H. COTTERILL and J. H. SLADE. Fcap. 8vo. 5s. 6d.

GRAHAM.—GEOMETRY OF POSITION. By R. H. GRAHAM. Cr. 8vo. 7s. 6d.

KENNEDY.—THE MECHANICS OF MACHINERY. By A. B. W. KENNEDY, F.R.S. Illustrated. Cr. 8vo. 12s. 6d.

WHITHAM.—STEAM-ENGINE DESIGN. For the Use of Mechanical Engineers, Students, and Draughtsmen. By J. M. WHITHAM, Professor of Engineering, Arkansas Industrial University. Illustrated. 8vo. 25s.

YOUNG.—SIMPLE PRACTICAL METHODS OF CALCULATING STRAINS ON GIRDERS, ARCHES, AND TRUSSES. With a Supplementary Essay on Economy in Suspension Bridges. By E. W. YOUNG, C.E. With Diagrams. 8vo. 7s. 6d.

MILITARY AND NAVAL SCIENCE.

AITKEN.—THE GROWTH OF THE RECRUIT AND YOUNG SOLDIER. With a view to the selection of "Growing Lads" for the Army, and a Regulated System of Training for Recruits. By Sir W. AITKEN, F.R.S., Professor of Pathology in the Army Medical School. Cr. 8vo. 8s. 6d.

ARMY PRELIMINARY EXAMINATION, 1882-1890, Specimens of Papers set at the. With Answers to the Mathematical Questions. Subjects: Arithmetic, Algebra, Euclid, Geometrical Drawing, Geography, French, English Dictation. Cr. 8vo. 3s. 6d.

MATTHEWS.—MANUAL OF LOGARITHMS. By G. F. MATTHEWS, B.A. 8vo. 5s. net.

MAURICE.—WAR. By FREDERICK MAURICE, Colonel C.B., R.A. 8vo. 5s. net.

MERCUR.—ELEMENTS OF THE ART OF WAR. Prepared for the use of Cadets of the United States Military Academy. By JAMES MERCUR, Professor of Civil Engineering at the United States Academy, West Point, New York. 2d Ed., revised and corrected. 8vo. 17s.

PALMER.—TEXT-BOOK OF PRACTICAL LOGARITHMS AND TRIGONO-METRY. By J. H. PALMER, Head Schoolmaster, R.N., H.M.S. *Cambridge*, Devonport. Gl. 8vo. 4s. 6d.

ROBINSON.—TREATISE ON MARINE SURVEYING. Prepared for the use of younger Naval Officers. With Questions for Examinations and Exercises principally from the Papers of the Royal Naval College. With the results. By Rev. JOHN L. ROBINSON, Chaplain and Instructor in the Royal Naval College, Greenwich. Illustrated. Cr. 8vo. 7s. 6d.

SANDHURST MATHEMATICAL PAPERS, for Admission into the Royal Military College, 1881-1889. Edited by E. J. BROOKSMITH, B.A., Instructor in Mathematics at the Royal Military Academy, Woolwich. Cr. 8vo. 3s. 6d.

SHORTLAND.—NAUTICAL SURVEYING. By the late Vice-Admiral SHORTLAND, LL.D. 8vo. 21s.

THOMSON.—POPULAR LECTURES AND ADDRESSES. By Sir WILLIAM THOMSON, LL.D., P.R.S. In 3 vols. Illustrated. Cr. 8vo. Vol. III. Navigation. 7s. 6d.

WILKINSON.—THE BRAIN OF AN ARMY. A Popular Account of the German General Staff. By SPENSER WILKINSON. Cr. 8vo. 2s. 6d.

WOLSELEY.—Works by General Viscount WOLSELEY, G.C.M.G.
THE SOLDIER'S POCKET-BOOK FOR FIELD SERVICE. 5th Ed., revised and enlarged. 16mo. Roan. 5s.
FIELD POCKET-BOOK FOR THE AUXILIARY FORCES. 16mo. 1s. 6d.

WOOLWICH MATHEMATICAL PAPERS, for Admission into the Royal Military Academy, Woolwich, 1880-1888 inclusive. Edited by E. J. BROOKSMITH, B.A., Instructor in Mathematics at the Royal Military Academy, Woolwich. Cr. 8vo. 6s.

AGRICULTURE.

FRANKLAND.—AGRICULTURAL CHEMICAL ANALYSIS, A Handbook of. By PERCY F. FRANKLAND, F.R.S., Professor of Chemistry, University College, Dundee. Founded upon *Leitfaden für die Agriculture Chemiche Analyse*, von Dr. F. KROCKER. Cr. 8vo. 7s. 6d.

HARTIG.—TEXT-BOOK OF THE DISEASES OF TREES. By Dr. ROBERT HARTIG. Translated by WM. SOMERVILLE, B.Sc., D.Œ., Professor of Agriculture and Forestry, Durham College of Science, Newcastle-on-Tyne. Edited, with Introduction, by Prof. H. MARSHALL WARD. 8vo. [*In preparation.*]

LASLETT.—TIMBER AND TIMBER TREES, NATIVE AND FOREIGN. By THOMAS LASLETT. Cr. 8vo. 8s. 6d.

SMITH.—DISEASES OF FIELD AND GARDEN CROPS, CHIEFLY SUCH AS ARE CAUSED BY FUNGI. By WORTHINGTON G. SMITH, F.L.S. Illustrated. Fcap. 8vo. 4s. 6d.

TANNER.—*ELEMENTARY LESSONS IN THE SCIENCE OF AGRICULTURAL PRACTICE. By HENRY TANNER, F.C.S., M.R.A.C., Examiner in the Principles of Agriculture under the Government Department of Science. Fcap. 8vo. 3s. 6d.

*FIRST PRINCIPLES OF AGRICULTURE. By the same. 18mo. 1s.
THE PRINCIPLES OF AGRICULTURE. By the same. A Series of Reading Books for use in Elementary Schools. Ex. fcap. 8vo.
  *I. The Alphabet of the Principles of Agriculture. 6d.
  *II. Further Steps in the Principles of Agriculture. 1s.
  *III. Elementary School Readings on the Principles of Agriculture for the third stage. 1s.

WARD.—TIMBER AND SOME OF ITS DISEASES. By H. Marshall Ward, M.A., F.L.S., F.R.S., Fellow of Christ's College, Cambridge, Professor of Botany at the Royal Indian Engineering College, Cooper's Hill. With Illustrations. Cr. 8vo. 6s.

DOMESTIC ECONOMY.

*BARKER.—FIRST LESSONS IN THE PRINCIPLES OF COOKING. By Lady Barker. 18mo. 1s.

*BERNERS.—FIRST LESSONS ON HEALTH. By J. Berners. 18mo. 1s.

*COOKERY BOOK.—THE MIDDLE CLASS COOKERY BOOK. Edited by the Manchester School of Domestic Cookery. Fcap. 8vo. 1s. 6d.

CRAVEN.—A GUIDE TO DISTRICT NURSES. By Mrs. Dacre Craven (née Florence Sarah Lees), Hon. Associate of the Order of St. John of Jerusalem, etc. Cr. 8vo. 2s. 6d.

FREDERICK.—HINTS TO HOUSEWIVES ON SEVERAL POINTS, PARTICULARLY ON THE PREPARATION OF ECONOMICAL AND TASTEFUL DISHES. By Mrs. Frederick. Cr. 8vo. 1s.

*GRAND'HOMME.—CUTTING-OUT AND DRESSMAKING. From the French of Mdlle. E. Grand'homme. With Diagrams. 18mo. 1s.

JEX-BLAKE.—THE CARE OF INFANTS. A Manual for Mothers and Nurses. By Sophia Jex-Blake, M.D., Lecturer on Hygiene at the London School of Medicine for Women. 18mo. 1s.

RATHBONE.—THE HISTORY AND PROGRESS OF DISTRICT NURSING FROM ITS COMMENCEMENT IN THE YEAR 1859 TO THE PRESENT DATE, including the foundation by the Queen of the Queen Victoria Jubilee Institute for Nursing the Poor in their own Homes. By William Rathbone, M.P. Cr. 8vo. 2s. 6d.

*TEGETMEIER.—HOUSEHOLD MANAGEMENT AND COOKERY. With an Appendix of Recipes used by the Teachers of the National School of Cookery. By W. B. Tegetmeier. Compiled at the request of the School Board for London. 18mo. 1s.

*WRIGHT.—THE SCHOOL COOKERY-BOOK. Compiled and Edited by C. E. Guthrie Wright, Hon. Sec. to the Edinburgh School of Cookery. 18mo. 1s.

BOOK-KEEPING.

*THORNTON.—FIRST LESSONS IN BOOK-KEEPING. By J. Thornton. Cr. 8vo. 2s. 6d. KEY. Oblong 4to. 10s. 6d.

*PRIMER OF BOOK-KEEPING. By the same. 18mo. 1s. KEY. 8vo. 2s. 6d.

COMMERCE.

MACMILLAN'S ELEMENTARY COMMERCIAL CLASS BOOKS. Edited by James Gow, Litt.D., Headmaster of Nottingham School. Globe 8vo.

The following volumes are arranged for :—

*THE HISTORY OF COMMERCE IN EUROPE. By H. de B. Gibbins, M.A. 3s. 6d. [*Ready.*

COMMERCIAL GERMAN. By F. C. Smith, B.A., formerly scholar of Magdalene College, Cambridge. [*In the Press.*

COMMERCIAL GEOGRAPHY. By E. C. K. Gonner, M.A., Professor of Political Economy in University College, Liverpool. [*In preparation.*

COMMERCIAL FRENCH.

COMMERCIAL ARITHMETIC. By A. W. Sunderland, M.A., late Scholar of Trinity College, Cambridge ; Fellow of the Institute of Actuaries. [*In prep.*

COMMERCIAL LAW. By J. E. C. Munro, LL.D., Professor of Law and Political Economy in the Owens College, Manchester.

GEOGRAPHY.

(See also PHYSICAL GEOGRAPHY.)

BARTHOLOMEW.—*THE ELEMENTARY SCHOOL ATLAS. By JOHN BAR-THOLOMEW, F.R.G.S. 4to. 1s.

*MACMILLAN'S SCHOOL ATLAS, PHYSICAL AND POLITICAL. Consisting of 80 Maps and complete Index. By the same. Prepared for the use of Senior Pupils. Royal 4to. 8s. 6d. Half-morocco. 10s. 6d.

THE LIBRARY REFERENCE ATLAS OF THE WORLD. By the same. A Complete Series of 84 Modern Maps. With Geographical Index to 100,000 places. Half-morocco. Gilt edges. Folio. £2:12:6 net. Also issued in parts, 5s. each net. Geographical Index, 7s. 6d. net. Part I., April 1891.

*CLARKE.**—CLASS-BOOK OF GEOGRAPHY. By C. B. CLARKE, F.R.S. New Ed., revised 1889, with 18 Maps. Fcap. 8vo. 3s. Sewed, 2s. 6d.

GEIKIE.—Works by Sir ARCHIBALD GEIKIE, F.R.S., Director-General of the Geological Survey of the United Kingdom.

*THE TEACHING OF GEOGRAPHY. A Practical Handbook for the use of Teachers. Cr. 8vo. 2s.

*GEOGRAPHY OF THE BRITISH ISLES. 18mo. 1s.

*GREEN.**—A SHORT GEOGRAPHY OF THE BRITISH ISLANDS. By JOHN RICHARD GREEN and A. S. GREEN. With Maps. Fcap. 8vo. 3s. 6d.

*GROVE.**—A PRIMER OF GEOGRAPHY. By Sir GEORGE GROVE, D.C.L. Illustrated. 18mo. 1s.

KIEPERT.—A MANUAL OF ANCIENT GEOGRAPHY. By Dr. H. KIEPERT. Cr. 8vo. 5s.

MACMILLAN'S GEOGRAPHICAL SERIES.—Edited by Sir ARCHIBALD GEIKIE, F.R.S., Director-General of the Geological Survey of the United Kingdom.

*THE TEACHING OF GEOGRAPHY. A Practical Handbook for the Use of Teachers. By Sir ARCHIBALD GEIKIE, F.R.S. Cr. 8vo. 2s.

*MAPS AND MAP-DRAWING. By W. A. ELDERTON. 18mo. 1s.

*GEOGRAPHY OF THE BRITISH ISLES. By Sir A. GEIKIE, F.R.S. 18mo. 1s.

*AN ELEMENTARY CLASS-BOOK OF GENERAL GEOGRAPHY. By H. R. MILL, D.Sc., Lecturer on Physiography and on Commercial Geography in the Heriot-Watt College, Edinburgh. Illustrated. Cr. 8vo. 3s. 6d.

*GEOGRAPHY OF EUROPE. By J. SIME, M.A. Illustrated. Gl. 8vo. 3s.

*ELEMENTARY GEOGRAPHY OF INDIA, BURMA, AND CEYLON. By H. F. BLANFORD, F.G.S. Gl. 8vo. 2s. 6d.

GEOGRAPHY OF NORTH AMERICA. By Prof. N. S. SHALER. [In preparation.

GEOGRAPHY OF THE BRITISH COLONIES. By G. M. DAWSON and A. SUTHERLAND. [In the Press.

STRACHEY.—LECTURES ON GEOGRAPHY. By General RICHARD STRACHEY, R.E. Cr. 8vo. 4s. 6d.

*TOZER.**—A PRIMER OF CLASSICAL GEOGRAPHY. By H. F. TOZER, M.A. 18mo. 1s.

HISTORY.

ARNOLD.—THE SECOND PUNIC WAR. Being Chapters from THE HISTORY OF ROME, by the late THOMAS ARNOLD, D.D., Headmaster of Rugby. Edited, with Notes, by W. T. ARNOLD, M.A. With 8 Maps. Cr. 8vo. 5s.

ARNOLD.—A HISTORY OF THE EARLY ROMAN EMPIRE. By W. T. ARNOLD, M.A. Cr. 8vo. [In preparation.

*BEESLY.**—STORIES FROM THE HISTORY OF ROME. By Mrs. BEESLY. Fcap. 8vo. 2s. 6d.

BRYCE.—Works by JAMES BRYCE, M.P., D.C.L., Regius Professor of Civil Law in the University of Oxford.

THE HOLY ROMAN EMPIRE. 9th Ed. Cr. 8vo. 7s. 6d.
    *** Also a *Library Edition.* Demy 8vo. 14s.
THE AMERICAN COMMONWEALTH. 2 vols. Ex. cr. 8vo. 25s. Part I.
The National Government. Part II. The State Governments. Part III.
The Party System. Part IV. Public Opinion. Part V. Illustrations and
Reflections. Part VI. Social Institutions.

*BUCKLEY.—A HISTORY OF ENGLAND FOR BEGINNERS. By ARABELLA
B. BUCKLEY. With Maps and Tables. Gl. 8vo. 3s.

BURY.—A HISTORY OF THE LATER ROMAN EMPIRE FROM ARCADIUS
TO IRENE, A.D. 395-800. By JOHN B. BURY, M.A., Fellow of Trinity College,
Dublin. 2 vols. 8vo. 32s.

CASSEL.—MANUAL OF JEWISH HISTORY AND LITERATURE. By Dr. D.
CASSEL. Translated by Mrs. HENRY LUCAS. Fcap. 8vo. 2s. 6d.

ENGLISH STATESMEN, TWELVE. Cr. 8vo. 2s. 6d. each.
    WILLIAM THE CONQUEROR. By EDWARD A. FREEMAN, D.C.L., LL.D.
    HENRY II. By Mrs. J. R. GREEN.
    EDWARD I. By F. YORK POWELL.   *[In preparation.*
    HENRY VII. By JAMES GAIRDNER.
    CARDINAL WOLSEY. By Bishop CREIGHTON.
    ELIZABETH. By E. S. BEESLY.   *[In preparation.*
    OLIVER CROMWELL. By FREDERIC HARRISON.
    WILLIAM III. By H. D. TRAILL.
    WALPOLE. By JOHN MORLEY.
    CHATHAM. By JOHN MORLEY.   *[In preparation.*
    PITT. By JOHN MORLEY.   *[In preparation.*
    PEEL. By J. R. THURSFIELD.

FISKE.—Works by JOHN FISKE, formerly Lecturer on Philosophy at Harvard
University.
    THE CRITICAL PERIOD IN AMERICAN HISTORY, 1783-1789. Ex. cr.
    8vo. 10s. 6d.
    THE BEGINNINGS OF NEW ENGLAND; or, The Puritan Theocracy in its
    Relations to Civil and Religious Liberty. Cr. 8vo. 7s. 6d.
    THE AMERICAN REVOLUTION. 2 vols. Cr. 8vo. 18s.

FREEMAN.—Works by EDWARD A. FREEMAN, D.C.L., Regius Professor of Modern
History in the University of Oxford, etc.
    *OLD ENGLISH HISTORY. With Maps. Ex. fcap. 8vo. 6s.
    A SCHOOL HISTORY OF ROME. Cr. 8vo.   *[In preparation.*
    METHODS OF HISTORICAL STUDY. 8vo. 10s. 6d.
    THE CHIEF PERIODS OF EUROPEAN HISTORY. Six Lectures. With an
    Essay on Greek Cities under Roman Rule. 8vo. 10s. 6d.
    HISTORICAL ESSAYS. First Series. 4th Ed. 8vo. 10s. 6d.
    HISTORICAL ESSAYS. Second Series. 3d Ed., with additional Essays. 8vo.
    10s. 6d.
    HISTORICAL ESSAYS. Third Series. 8vo. 12s.
    THE GROWTH OF THE ENGLISH CONSTITUTION FROM THE EARLIEST
    TIMES. 4th Ed. Cr. 8vo. 5s.
    *GENERAL SKETCH OF EUROPEAN HISTORY. Enlarged, with Maps, etc.
    18mo. 3s. 6d.
    *PRIMER OF EUROPEAN HISTORY. 18mo. 1s. (*History Primers.*)

FRIEDMANN.—ANNE BOLEYN. A Chapter of English History, 1527-1536. By
PAUL FRIEDMANN. 2 vols. 8vo. 28s.

*GIBBINS.—THE HISTORY OF COMMERCE IN EUROPE. By H. de B.
GIBBINS, M.A. With Maps. Globe 8vo. 3s. 6d.

GREEN.—Works by JOHN RICHARD GREEN, LL.D., late Honorary Fellow of
Jesus College, Oxford.
    *A SHORT HISTORY OF THE ENGLISH PEOPLE. New and Revised Ed.
    With Maps, Genealogical Tables, and Chronological Annals. Cr. 8vo. 8s. 6d.
    159th Thousand.
    *Also the same in Four Parts. With the corresponding portion of Mr. Tait's
    "Analysis." Crown 8vo. 3s. each. Part I. 607-1265. Part II. 1204-1553.
    Part III. 1540-1689   Part IV. 1660-1873.

HISTORY OF THE ENGLISH PEOPLE. In four vols. 8vo. 16s. each.
> Vol. I.—Early England, 449-1071; Foreign Kings, 1071-1214; The Charter, 1214-1291; The Parliament, 1307-1461. With 8 Maps.
> Vol. II.—The Monarchy, 1461-1540; The Reformation, 1540-1603.
> Vol. III.—Puritan England, 1603-1660; The Revolution, 1660-1688. With four Maps.
> Vol. IV.—The Revolution, 1688-1760; Modern England, 1760-1815. With Maps and Index.

THE MAKING OF ENGLAND. With Maps. 8vo. 16s.

THE CONQUEST OF ENGLAND. With Maps and Portrait. 8vo. 18s.

*ANALYSIS OF ENGLISH HISTORY, based on Green's "Short History of the English People." By C. W. A. TAIT, M.A., Assistant Master at Clifton College. Revised and Enlarged Ed. Crown 8vo. 4s. 6d.

*READINGS FROM ENGLISH HISTORY. Selected and Edited by JOHN RICHARD GREEN. Three Parts. Gl. 8vo. 1s. 6d. each. I. Hengist to Cressy. II. Cressy to Cromwell. III. Cromwell to Balaklava.

GUEST.—LECTURES ON THE HISTORY OF ENGLAND. By M. J. GUEST. With Maps. Cr. 8vo. 6s.

*HISTORICAL COURSE FOR SCHOOLS.—Edited by E. A. FREEMAN, D.C.L., Regius Professor of Modern History in the University of Oxford. 18mo.

GENERAL SKETCH OF EUROPEAN HISTORY. By E. A. FREEMAN, D.C.L. New Ed., revised and enlarged. With Chronological Table, Maps, and Index. 3s. 6d.

HISTORY OF ENGLAND. By EDITH THOMPSON. New Ed., revised and enlarged. With Coloured Maps. 2s. 6d.

HISTORY OF SCOTLAND. By MARGARET MACARTHUR. 2s.

HISTORY OF ITALY. By Rev. W. HUNT, M.A. New Ed. With Coloured Maps. 3s. 6d.

HISTORY OF GERMANY. By J. SIME, M.A. New Ed., revised. 3s.

HISTORY OF AMERICA. By JOHN A. DOYLE. With Maps. 4s. 6d.

HISTORY OF EUROPEAN COLONIES. By E. J. PAYNE, M.A. With Maps. 4s. 6d.

HISTORY OF FRANCE. By CHARLOTTE M. YONGE. With Maps. 3s. 6d.

HISTORY OF GREECE. By EDWARD A. FREEMAN, D.C.L. [In preparation.

HISTORY OF ROME. By EDWARD A. FREEMAN, D.C.L. [In preparation.

*HISTORY PRIMERS.—Edited by JOHN RICHARD GREEN, LL.D. 18mo. 1s. each.

ROME. By Bishop CREIGHTON. Maps.

GREECE. By C. A. FYFFE, M.A., late Fellow of University College, Oxford. Maps.

EUROPE. By E. A. FREEMAN, D.C.L. Maps.

FRANCE. By CHARLOTTE M. YONGE.

GREEK ANTIQUITIES. By Rev. J. P. MAHAFFY, D.D. Illustrated.

CLASSICAL GEOGRAPHY. By H. F. TOZER, M.A.

GEOGRAPHY. By Sir G. GROVE, D.C.L. Maps.

ROMAN ANTIQUITIES. By Prof. WILKINS, Litt.D. Illustrated.

ANALYSIS OF ENGLISH HISTORY. By Prof. T. F. TOUT, M.A.

INDIAN HISTORY: ASIATIC AND EUROPEAN. By J. TALBOYS WHEELER.

HOLE.—A GENEALOGICAL STEMMA OF THE KINGS OF ENGLAND AND FRANCE. By Rev. C. HOLE. On Sheet. 1s.

JENNINGS.—CHRONOLOGICAL TABLES. A synchronistic arrangement of the events of Ancient History (with an Index). By Rev. ARTHUR C. JENNINGS. 8vo. 5s.

LABBERTON.—NEW HISTORICAL ATLAS AND GENERAL HISTORY. By R. H. LABBERTON. 4to. New Ed., revised and enlarged. 15s.

LETHBRIDGE.—A SHORT MANUAL OF THE HISTORY OF INDIA. With an Account of INDIA AS IT IS. The Soil, Climate, and Productions; the People, their Races, Religions, Public Works, and Industries; the Civil Services, and System of Administration. By Sir ROPER LETHBRIDGE, Fellow of the Calcutta University. With Maps. Cr. 8vo. 5s.

D

MAHAFFY.—GREEK LIFE AND THOUGHT FROM THE AGE OF ALEX-
ANDER TO THE ROMAN CONQUEST. By Rev. J. P. MAHAFFY, D.D.,
Fellow of Trinity College, Dublin. Cr. 8vo. 12s. 6d.
THE GREEK WORLD UNDER ROMAN SWAY. From Plutarch to Polybius.
By the same Author. Cr. 8vo. 10s. 6d.
MARRIOTT.—THE MAKERS OF MODERN ITALY: MAZZINI, CAVOUR, GARI-
BALDI. Three Lectures. By J. A. R. MARRIOTT, M.A., Lecturer in Modern
History and Political Economy, Oxford. Cr. 8vo. 1s. 6d.
MICHELET.—A SUMMARY OF MODERN HISTORY. By M. Michelet. Trans-
lated by M. C. M. SIMPSON. Gl. 8vo. 4s. 6d.
NORGATE.—ENGLAND UNDER THE ANGEVIN KINGS. By KATE NORGATE.
With Maps and Plans. 2 vols. 8vo. 32s.
OTTÉ.—SCANDINAVIAN HISTORY. By E. C. OTTÉ. With Maps. Gl. 8vo. 6s.
SEELEY.—Works by J. R. SEELEY, M.A., Regius Professor of Modern History in
the University of Cambridge.
THE EXPANSION OF ENGLAND. Crown 8vo. 4s. 6d.
OUR COLONIAL EXPANSION. Extracts from the above. Cr. 8vo. Sewed. 1s.
*TAIT.—ANALYSIS OF ENGLISH HISTORY, based on Green's "Short
History of the English People." By C. W. A. TAIT, M.A., Assistant Master
at Clifton. Revised and Enlarged Ed. Cr. 8vo. 4s. 6d.
WHEELER.—Works by J. TALBOYS WHEELER.
*A PRIMER OF INDIAN HISTORY. Asiatic and European. 18mo. 1s.
*COLLEGE HISTORY OF INDIA, ASIATIC AND EUROPEAN. With Maps.
Cr. 8vo. 3s. ; sewed, 2s. 6d.
A SHORT HISTORY OF INDIA AND OF THE FRONTIER STATES OF
AFGHANISTAN, NEPAUL, AND BURMA. With Maps. Cr. 8vo. 12s.
YONGE.—Works by CHARLOTTE M. YONGE.
CAMEOS FROM ENGLISH HISTORY. Ex. fcap. 8vo. 5s. each. (1)
FROM ROLLO TO EDWARD II. (2) THE WARS IN FRANCE. (3)
THE WARS OF THE ROSES. (4) REFORMATION TIMES. (5) ENG-
LAND AND SPAIN. (6) FORTY YEARS OF STUART RULE (1603-1643).
(7) REBELLION AND RESTORATION (1642-1678).
EUROPEAN HISTORY. Narrated in a Series of Historical Selections from the
Best Authorities. Edited and arranged by E. M. SEWELL and C. M. YONGE.
Cr. 8vo. First Series, 1003-1154. 6s. Second Series, 1088-1228. 6s.
THE VICTORIAN HALF CENTURY—A JUBILEE BOOK. With a New
Portrait of the Queen. Cr. 8vo. Paper covers, 1s. Cloth, 1s. 6d.

ART.

*ANDERSON.—LINEAR PERSPECTIVE AND MODEL DRAWING. A School
and Art Class Manual, with Questions and Exercises for Examination, and
Examples of Examination Papers. By LAURENCE ANDERSON. Illustrated.
8vo. 2s.
COLLIER.—A PRIMER OF ART. By the Hon. JOHN COLLIER. Illustrated.
18mo. 1s.
COOK.—THE NATIONAL GALLERY, A POPULAR HANDBOOK TO. By
EDWARD T. COOK, with a preface by JOHN RUSKIN, LL.D., and Selections
from his Writings. 3d Ed. Cr. 8vo. Half-morocco, 14s.
   ⁎ Also an Edition on large paper, limited to 250 copies. 2 vols. 8vo.
DELAMOTTE.—A BEGINNER'S DRAWING BOOK. By P. H. DELAMOTTE,
F.S.A. Progressively arranged. New Ed., improved. Cr. 8vo. 3s. 6d.
ELLIS.—SKETCHING FROM NATURE. A Handbook for Students and
Amateurs. By TRISTRAM J. ELLIS. Illustrated by H. STACY MARKS, R.A.,
and the Author. New Ed., revised and enlarged. Cr. 8vo. 3s. 6d.
GROVE.—A DICTIONARY OF MUSIC AND MUSICIANS. A.D. 1450-1889.
Edited by Sir GEORGE GROVE, D.C.L. In four vols. 8vo. Price 21s. each.
Also in Parts.
Parts I.-XIV., Parts XIX.-XXII., 3s. 6d. each. Parts XV., XVI., 7s.
Parts XVII., XVIII., 7s. Parts XXIII.-XXV. (Appendix), 9s.

A COMPLETE INDEX TO THE ABOVE. By Mrs. E. WODEHOUSE. 8vo. 7s. 6d.

HUNT.—TALKS ABOUT ART. By WILLIAM HUNT. With a Letter from Sir J. E. MILLAIS, Bart., R.A. Cr. 8vo. 3s. 6d.

MELDOLA.—THE CHEMISTRY OF PHOTOGRAPHY. By RAPHAEL MELDOLA, F.R.S., Professor of Chemistry in the Technical College, Finsbury. Cr. 8vo. 6s.

TAYLOR.—A PRIMER OF PIANOFORTE-PLAYING. By FRANKLIN TAYLOR. Edited by Sir GEORGE GROVE. 18mo. 1s.

TAYLOR.—A SYSTEM OF SIGHT-SINGING FROM THE ESTABLISHED MUSICAL NOTATION; based on the Principle of Tonic Relation, and Illustrated by Extracts from the Works of the Great Masters. By SEDLEY TAYLOR. 8vo. 5s. net.

TYRWHITT.—OUR SKETCHING CLUB. Letters and Studies on Landscape Art. By Rev. R. ST. JOHN TYRWHITT. With an authorised Reproduction of the Lessons and Woodcuts in Prof. Ruskin's "Elements of Drawing." 5th Ed. Cr. 8vo. 7s. 6d.

DIVINITY.

ABBOTT.—BIBLE LESSONS. By Rev. EDWIN A. ABBOTT, D.D. Cr. 8vo. 4s. 6d.

ABBOTT—RUSHBROOKE.—THE COMMON TRADITION OF THE SYNOPTIC GOSPELS, in the Text of the Revised Version. By Rev. EDWIN A. ABBOTT, D.D., and W. G. RUSHBROOKE, M.L. Cr. 8vo. 3s. 6d.

ARNOLD.—Works by MATTHEW ARNOLD.
    A BIBLE-READING FOR SCHOOLS,—THE GREAT PROPHECY OF ISRAEL'S RESTORATION (Isaiah, Chapters xl.-lxvi.) Arranged and Edited for Young Learners. 18mo. 1s.
    ISAIAH XL.-LXVI. With the Shorter Prophecies allied to it. Arranged and Edited, with Notes. Cr. 8vo. 5s.
    ISAIAH OF JERUSALEM, IN THE AUTHORISED ENGLISH VERSION. With Introduction, Corrections and Notes. Cr. 8vo. 4s. 6d.

BENHAM.—A COMPANION TO THE LECTIONARY. Being a Commentary on the Proper Lessons for Sundays and Holy Days. By Rev. W. BENHAM, B.D Cr. 8vo. 4s. 6d.

CASSEL.—MANUAL OF JEWISH HISTORY AND LITERATURE; preceded by a BRIEF SUMMARY OF BIBLE HISTORY. By Dr. D. CASSEL. Translated by Mrs. H. LUCAS. Fcap. 8vo. 2s. 6d.

CHURCH.—STORIES FROM THE BIBLE. By Rev. A. J. CHURCH, M.A. Illustrated. Cr. 8vo. 5s.

*CROSS.—BIBLE READINGS SELECTED FROM THE PENTATEUCH AND THE BOOK OF JOSHUA. By Rev. JOHN A. CROSS. 2d Ed., enlarged, with Notes. Gl. 8vo. 2s. 6d.

DRUMMOND.—INTRODUCTION TO THE STUDY OF THEOLOGY. By JAMES DRUMMOND, LL.D., Professor of Theology in Manchester New College, London. Cr. 8vo. 5s.

FARRAR.—Works by the Venerable Archdeacon F. W. FARRAR, D.D., F.R.S., Archdeacon and Canon of Westminster.
    THE HISTORY OF INTERPRETATION. Bampton Lectures, 1885. 8vo. 16s.
    THE MESSAGES OF THE BOOKS. Being Discourses and Notes on the Books of the New Testament. 8vo. 14s.

*GASKOIN.—THE CHILDREN'S TREASURY OF BIBLE STORIES. By Mrs. HERMAN GASKOIN. Edited with Preface by Rev. G. F. MACLEAR, D.D. 18mo. 1s. each. Part I.—OLD TESTAMENT HISTORY. Part II.—NEW TESTAMENT. Part III.—THE APOSTLES : ST. JAMES THE GREAT, ST. PAUL, AND ST. JOHN THE DIVINE.

GOLDEN TREASURY PSALTER.—Students' Edition. Being an Edition of "The Psalms chronologically arranged, by Four Friends," with briefer Notes. 18mo. 3s. 6d.

GREEK TESTAMENT.—Edited, with Introduction and Appendices, by Bishop WESTCOTT and Dr. F. J. A. HORT. Two Vols. Cr. 8vo. 10s. 6d. each. Vol. I. The Text. Vol. II. Introduction and Appendix.

SCHOOL EDITION OF TEXT. 12mo. Cloth, 4s. 6d. ; Roan, red edges, 5s. 6d. 18mo. Morocco, gilt edges, 6s. 6d.

*GREEK TESTAMENT, SCHOOL READINGS IN THE. Being the outline of the life of our Lord, as given by St. Mark, with additions from the Text of the other Evangelists. Arranged and Edited, with Notes and Vocabulary, by Rev. A. CALVERT, M.A. Fcap. 8vo. 2s. 6d.

*THE GOSPEL ACCORDING TO ST. MATTHEW. Being the Greek Text as revised by Bishop WESTCOTT and Dr. HORT. With Introduction and Notes by Rev. A. SLOMAN, M.A., Headmaster of Birkenhead School. Fcap. 8vo. 2s. 6d.

THE GOSPEL ACCORDING TO ST. MARK. Being the Greek Text as revised by Bishop WESTCOTT and Dr. HORT. With Introduction and Notes by Rev. J. O. F. MURRAY, M.A., Lecturer at Emmanuel College, Cambridge. Fcap. 8vo. [In preparation.

*THE GOSPEL ACCORDING TO ST. LUKE. Being the Greek Text as revised by Bishop WESTCOTT and Dr. HORT. With Introduction and Notes by Rev. JOHN BOND, M.A. Fcap. 8vo. 2s. 6d.

*THE ACTS OF THE APOSTLES. Being the Greek Text as revised by Bishop WESTCOTT and Dr. HORT. With Explanatory Notes by T. E. PAGE, M.A., Assistant Master at the Charterhouse. Fcap. 8vo. 3s. 6d.

GWATKIN.—CHURCH HISTORY TO THE BEGINNING OF THE MIDDLE AGES. By H. M. GWATKIN, M.A. 8vo. [In preparation.

HARDWICK.—Works by Archdeacon HARDWICK.

A HISTORY OF THE CHRISTIAN CHURCH. Middle Age. From Gregory the Great to the Excommunication of Luther. Edited by W. STUBBS, D.D., Bishop of Oxford. With 4 Maps. Cr. 8vo. 10s. 6d.

A HISTORY OF THE CHRISTIAN CHURCH DURING THE REFORMATION. 9th Ed. Edited by Bishop STUBBS. Cr. 8vo. 10s. 6d.

HOOLE.—THE CLASSICAL ELEMENT IN THE NEW TESTAMENT. Considered as a proof of its Genuineness, with an Appendix on the Oldest Authorities used in the Formation of the Canon. By CHARLES H. HOOLE, M.A., Student of Christ Church, Oxford. 8vo. 10s. 6d.

JENNINGS and LOWE.—THE PSALMS, WITH INTRODUCTIONS AND CRITICAL NOTES. By A. C. JENNINGS, M.A. ; assisted in parts by W. H. LOWE, M.A. In 2 vols. 2d Ed., revised. Cr. 8vo. 10s. 6d. each.

KIRKPATRICK.—THE MINOR PROPHETS. Warburtonian Lectures. By Rev. Prof. KIRKPATRICK. [In preparation.

THE DIVINE LIBRARY OF THE OLD TESTAMENT. By the same. [In prep.

KUENEN.—PENTATEUCH AND BOOK OF JOSHUA: An Historico-Critical Inquiry into the Origin and Composition of the Hexateuch. By A. KUENEN Translated by P. H. WICKSTEED, M.A. 8vo. 14s.

LIGHTFOOT.—Works by the Right Rev. J. B. LIGHTFOOT, D.D., late Bishop of Durham.

ST. PAUL'S EPISTLE TO THE GALATIANS. A Revised Text, with Introduction, Notes, and Dissertations. 10th Ed., revised. 8vo. 12s.

ST. PAUL'S EPISTLE TO THE PHILIPPIANS. A Revised Text, with Introduction, Notes, and Dissertations. 9th Ed., revised. 8vo. 12s.

ST. PAUL'S EPISTLES TO THE COLOSSIANS AND TO PHILEMON. A Revised Text, with Introductions, Notes, and Dissertations. 8th Ed., revised. 8vo. 12s.

THE APOSTOLIC FATHERS. Part I. ST. CLEMENT OF ROME. A Revised Text, with Introductions, Notes, Dissertations, and Translations. 2 vols. 8vo. 32s.

THE APOSTOLIC FATHERS. Part II. ST. IGNATIUS—ST. POLYCARP. Revised Texts, with Introductions, Notes, Dissertations, and Translations. 2d Ed. 3 vols. 8vo. 48s.

THE APOSTOLIC FATHERS. Abridged Edition. With short Introductions, Greek Text, and English Translation. 8vo. 16s.

ESSAYS ON THE WORK ENTITLED "SUPERNATURAL RELIGION." (Reprinted from the *Contemporary Review*.) 8vo. 10s. 6d.

MACLEAR.—Works by the Rev. G. F. MACLEAR, D.D., Warden of St. Augustine's College, Canterbury.

ELEMENTARY THEOLOGICAL CLASS-BOOKS.

*A SHILLING BOOK OF OLD TESTAMENT HISTORY. With Map. 18mo.

*A SHILLING BOOK OF NEW TESTAMENT HISTORY. With Map. 18mo. These works have been carefully abridged from the Author's large manuals.

*A CLASS-BOOK OF OLD TESTAMENT HISTORY. Maps. 18mo. 4s. 6d.

*A CLASS-BOOK OF NEW TESTAMENT HISTORY, including the Connection of the Old and New Testaments. With maps. 18mo. 5s. 6d.

AN INTRODUCTION TO THE THIRTY-NINE ARTICLES. [In the Press.

*AN INTRODUCTION TO THE CREEDS. 18mo. 2s. 6d.

*A CLASS-BOOK OF THE CATECHISM OF THE CHURCH OF ENGLAND. 18mo. 1s. 6d.

*A FIRST CLASS-BOOK OF THE CATECHISM OF THE CHURCH OF ENGLAND. With Scripture Proofs. 18mo. 6d.

*A MANUAL OF INSTRUCTION FOR CONFIRMATION AND FIRST COMMUNION. WITH PRAYERS AND DEVOTIONS. 32mo. 2s.

MAURICE.—THE LORD'S PRAYER, THE CREED, AND THE COMMANDMENTS. To which is added the Order of the Scriptures. By Rev. F. D. MAURICE, M.A. 18mo. 1s.

THE PENTATEUCH AND BOOK OF JOSHUA: An Historico-Critical Inquiry into the Origin and Composition of the Hexateuch. By A. KUENEN, Professor of Theology at Leiden. Translated by P. H. WICKSTEED, M.A. 8vo. 14s.

PROCTER.—A HISTORY OF THE BOOK OF COMMON PRAYER, with a Rationale of its Offices. By Rev. F. PROCTER. 18th Ed. Cr. 8vo. 10s. 6d.

*PROCTER and MACLEAR.—AN ELEMENTARY INTRODUCTION TO THE BOOK OF COMMON PRAYER. Rearranged and supplemented by an Explanation of the Morning and Evening Prayer and the Litany. By Rev. F. PROCTER and Rev. Dr. MACLEAR. New Edition, containing the Communion Service and the Confirmation and Baptismal Offices. 18mo. 2s. 6d.

THE PSALMS, CHRONOLOGICALLY ARRANGED. By Four Friends. New Ed. Cr. 8vo. 5s. net.

THE PSALMS, WITH INTRODUCTIONS AND CRITICAL NOTES. By A. C. JENNINGS, M.A., Jesus College, Cambridge; assisted in parts by W. H. LOWE, M.A., Hebrew Lecturer at Christ's College, Cambridge. In 2 vols. 2d Ed., revised. Cr. 8vo. 10s. 6d. each.

RYLE.—AN INTRODUCTION TO THE CANON OF THE OLD TESTAMENT. By Rev. H. E. RYLE, M.A., Hulsean Professor of Divinity in the University of Cambridge. Cr. 8vo. [In preparation.

SIMPSON.—AN EPITOME OF THE HISTORY OF THE CHRISTIAN CHURCH DURING THE FIRST THREE CENTURIES, AND OF THE REFORMATION IN ENGLAND. By Rev. WILLIAM SIMPSON, M.A. 7th Ed. Fcap. 8vo. 3s. 6d.

ST. JAMES' EPISTLE.—The Greek Text, with Introduction and Notes. By Rev. JOSEPH MAYOR, M.A., Professor of Moral Philosophy in King's College, London. 8vo. [In the Press.

ST. JOHN'S EPISTLES.—The Greek Text, with Notes and Essays. By Right Rev. B. F. WESTCOTT, D.D., Bishop of Durham. 2d Ed., revised. 8vo. 12s. 6d.

ST. PAUL'S EPISTLES.—THE EPISTLE TO THE ROMANS. Edited by the Very Rev. C. J. VAUGHAN, D.D., Dean of Llandaff. 5th Ed. Cr. 8vo. 7s. 6d.

THE TWO EPISTLES TO THE CORINTHIANS, A COMMENTARY ON. By the late Rev. W. KAY, D.D., Rector of Great Leghs, Essex. 8vo. 9s.

THE EPISTLE TO THE GALATIANS. Edited by the Right Rev. J. B. LIGHTFOOT, D.D. 10th Ed. 8vo. 12s.

THE EPISTLE TO THE PHILIPPIANS. By the Same Editor. 9th Ed. 8vo. 12s.

THE EPISTLE TO THE PHILIPPIANS, with Translation, Paraphrase, and Notes for English Readers. By the Very Rev. C. J. VAUGHAN, D.D. Cr. 8vo. 5s.

THE EPISTLE TO THE COLOSSIANS AND TO PHILEMON. By the Right Rev. J. B. LIGHTFOOT, D.D. 8th Ed. 8vo. 12s.

THE EPISTLES TO THE EPHESIANS, THE COLOSSIANS, AND PHILE-
MON; with Introductions and Notes, and an Essay on the Traces of Foreign
Elements in the Theology of these Epistles. By Rev. J. LLEWELYN DAVIES,
M.A. 8vo. 7s. 6d.

THE EPISTLE TO THE THESSALONIANS, COMMENTARY ON THE GREEK
TEXT. By JOHN EADIE, D.D. Edited by Rev. W. YOUNG, M.A., with Preface
by Prof. CAIRNS. 8vo. 12s.

THE EPISTLE TO THE HEBREWS.—In Greek and English. With Critical and
Explanatory Notes. Edited by Rev. F. RENDALL, M.A. Cr. 8vo. 6s.

THE ENGLISH TEXT, WITH COMMENTARY. By the same Editor. Cr.
8vo. 7s. 6d.

THE GREEK TEXT. With Notes by C. J. VAUGHAN, D.D., Dean of Llandaff.
Cr. 8vo. 7s. 6d.

THE GREEK TEXT. With Notes and Essays by the Right Rev. Bishop
WESTCOTT, D.D. 8vo. 14s.

VAUGHAN.—THE CHURCH OF THE FIRST DAYS. Comprising the Church
of Jerusalem, the Church of the Gentiles, the Church of the World. By C. J.
VAUGHAN, D.D., Dean of Llandaff. New Ed. Cr. 8vo. 10s. 6d.

WESTCOTT.—Works by the Right Rev. BROOKE FOSS WESTCOTT, D.D., Bishop of
Durham.

A GENERAL SURVEY OF THE HISTORY OF THE CANON OF THE NEW
TESTAMENT DURING THE FIRST FOUR CENTURIES. 6th Ed. With
Preface on "Supernatural Religion." Cr. 8vo. 10s. 6d.

INTRODUCTION TO THE STUDY OF THE FOUR GOSPELS. 7th Ed.
Cr. 8vo. 10s. 6d.

THE BIBLE IN THE CHURCH. A Popular Account of the Collection and
Reception of the Holy Scriptures in the Christian Churches. 18mo. 4s. 6d.

THE EPISTLES OF ST. JOHN. The Greek Text, with Notes and Essays.
2d Ed., revised. 8vo. 12s. 6d.

THE EPISTLE TO THE HEBREWS. The Greek Text, with Notes and Essays.
8vo. 14s.

SOME THOUGHTS FROM THE ORDINAL. Cr. 8vo. 1s. 6d.

WESTCOTT and HORT.—THE NEW TESTAMENT IN THE ORIGINAL
GREEK. The Text, revised by the Right Rev. Bishop WESTCOTT and Dr.
F. J. A. HORT. 2 vols. Cr. 8vo. 10s. 6d. each. Vol. I. Text. Vol. II.
Introduction and Appendix.

SCHOOL EDITION OF TEXT. 12mo. 4s. 6d.; Roan, red edges, 5s. 6d. Fcap.
8vo. Morocco, gilt edges, 6s. 6d.

WRIGHT.—THE COMPOSITION OF THE FOUR GOSPELS. A Critical En-
quiry. By Rev. ARTHUR WRIGHT, M A., Fellow and Tutor of Queen's College,
Cambridge. Cr. 8vo. 5s.

WRIGHT.—THE BIBLE WORD-BOOK: A Glossary of Archaic Words and
Phrases in the Authorised Version of the Bible and the Book of Common
Prayer. By W. ALDIS WRIGHT, M.A., Vice-Master of Trinity College, Cam-
bridge. 2d Ed., revised and enlarged. Cr. 8vo. 7s. 6d.

*YONGE.—SCRIPTURE READINGS FOR SCHOOLS AND FAMILIES. By
CHARLOTTE M. YONGE. In Five Vols. Ex. fcap. 8vo. 1s. 6d. each. With
Comments. 3s. 6d. each.

FIRST SERIES.—GENESIS TO DEUTERONOMY. SECOND SERIES.—FROM JOSHUA TO
SOLOMON. THIRD SERIES.—THE KINGS AND THE PROPHETS. FOURTH SERIES.
—THE GOSPEL TIMES. FIFTH SERIES.—APOSTOLIC TIMES.

ZECHARIAH—THE HEBREW STUDENT'S COMMENTARY ON ZECHARIAH,
HEBREW AND LXX. With Excursus on Syllable-dividing, Metheg, Initial
Dagesh, and Siman Rapheh. By W. H. LOWE, M.A., Hebrew Lecturer at
Christ's College, Cambridge. 8vo. 10s. 6d.

Printed by R. & R. CLARK, *Edinburgh.*

The English Illustrated Magazine.

Each Volume Complete in Itself.

Volume for 1884.

Containing 792 pages, with 428 Illustrations. Price 7s. 6d.

The Volume contains the following Complete Stories and Serials :—

The Armourer's 'Prentices. By C. M. YONGE. An Unsentimental Journey through Cornwall. By Mrs. CRAIK. Julia. By WALTER BESANT. How I became a War Correspondent. By ARCHIBALD FORBES. The Story of a Courtship. By STANLEY J. WEYMAN, etc.

Volume for 1885.

Containing 840 pages, with nearly 500 Illustrations. Price 8s.

The Volume contains the following Complete Stories and Serials :—

A Family Affair. By HUGH CONWAY. Girl at the Gate. By WILKIE COLLINS. The Path of Duty. By HENRY JAMES. Schwartz. By D. CHRISTIE MURRAY. A Ship of '49. By BRET HARTE. That Terrible Man. By W. E. NORRIS. Interviewed by an Emperor. By ARCHIBALD FORBES. In the Lion's Den. By the Author of "John Herring," etc.

Volume for 1886.

Containing 832 pages, with nearly 500 Illustrations. Price 8s.

The Volume contains the following Complete Stories and Serials :—

Kiss and be Friends. By the Author of "John Halifax, Gentleman." Aunt Rachel. By D. CHRISTIE MURRAY. A Garden of Memories. By MARGARET VELEY. My Friend Jim. By W. E. NORRIS. Harry's Inheritance. By GRANT ALLEN. Captain Lackland. By CLEMENTINA BLACK. Witnessed by Two. By Mrs. MOLESWORTH. The Poetry did It. By WILKIE COLLINS. Dr. Barrere. By Mrs. OLIPHANT. Mere Suzanne. By KATHARINE S. MACQUOID. Days with Sir Roger de Coverley, with pictures by HUGH THOMSON, etc.

Volume for 1887.

Containing 832 pages, with nearly 500 Illustrations. Price 8s.

The Volume contains the following Complete Stories and Serials :—

Marzio's Crucifix. By F. MARION CRAWFORD. A Secret Inheritance. By B. L. FARJEON. Jacquetta. By the Author of "John Herring." Gerald. By STANLEY J. WEYMAN. An Unknown Country. By the Author of "John Halifax, Gentleman." With Illustrations by F. NOEL PATON. A Siege Baby. By J. S. WINTER. Miss Falkland. By CLEMENTINA BLACK, etc.

Volume for 1888.

Containing 832 pages, with nearly 500 Illustrations. Price 8s.

Among the chief Contents of the Volume are the following Complete Stories and Serials :—

Coaching Days and Coaching Ways. By W. O. TRISTRAM. With Illustrations by H. RAILTON and HUGH THOMSON. **The Story of Jael.** By the Author of "Mehalah." **Lil : a Liverpool Child.** By AGNES C. MAITLAND. **The Patagonia.** By HENRY JAMES. **Family Portraits.** By S. J. WEYMAN. **The Mediation of Ralph Hardelot.** By Prof. W. MINTO. **That Girl in Black.** By Mrs. MOLESWORTH. **Glimpses of Old English Homes.** By ELIZABETH BALCH. **Pagodas, Aurioles, and Umbrellas.** By C. F. GORDON CUMMING. **The Magic Fan.** By JOHN STRANGE WINTER.

Volume for 1889.

Containing 900 pages, with nearly 500 Illustrations. Price 8s.

Among the chief Contents of the Volume are the following Complete Stories and Serials :—

Sant' Ilario. By F. MARION CRAWFORD. **The House of the Wolf.** By STANLEY J. WEYMAN. **Glimpses of Old English Homes.** By ELIZABETH BALCH. **One Night—The Better Man.** By ARTHUR PATERSON. **How the "Crayture" got on the Strength.** And other Sketches. By ARCHIBALD FORBES. **La Belle Americaine.** By W. E. NORRIS. **Success.** By KATHARINE S. MACQUOID. **Jenny Harlowe.** By W. CLARK RUSSELL.

Volume for 1890.

Containing 900 pages, with nearly 550 Illustrations. Price 8s.

Among the chief Contents of the Volume are the following Complete Stories and Serials :—

The Ring of Amasis. By the EARL OF LYTTON. **The Glittering Plain : or, the Land of Living Men.** By WILLIAM MORRIS. **The Old Brown Mare.** By W. E. NORRIS. **My Journey to Texas.** By ARTHUR PATERSON. **A Glimpse of Highclere Castle—A Glimpse of Osterley Park.** By ELIZABETH BALCH. **For the Cause.** By STANLEY J. WEYMAN. **Morised.** By the MARCHIONESS OF CARMARTHEN. **Overland from India.** By Sir DONALD MACKENZIE WALLACE, K.C.I.E. **The Doll's House and After.** By WALTER BESANT. **La Mulette, Anno 1814.** By W. CLARK RUSSELL.

Volume for 1891.

Containing 900 pages, and about 500 Illustrations. Price 8s.

Among the chief Contents of the Volume are the following Complete Stories and Serials :—

The Witch of Prague. By F. MARION CRAWFORD. **The Wisdom Tooth.** By D. CHRISTIE MURRAY and HENRY HERMAN. **Wooden Tony.** By Mrs. W. K. CLIFFORD. **Two Jealousies.** By ALAN ADAIR. **Gentleman Jim.** By MARY GAUNT. **Harrow School. Winchester College. Fawsley Park. Ham House. Westminster Abbey. Norwich. The New Trade-Union Movement: Russo-Jewish Immigrant. Queen's Private Garden at Osborne.**

MACMILLAN AND CO., LONDON.

VI.50.9.91.